LATIN

This book offers a complete course in Latin for beginners. Divided into three parts, it has been written to meet the needs of both those who are chiefly interested in learning to translate English into Latin and those who want to be able to read Latin as soon as possible. Part I introduces the main points of grammar and a basic vocabulary in a series of graded lessons, complete with exercises in translating Latin into English, easy extracts from Latin literature and Latin sayings. Part II comprises the English-into-Latin exercises, while Part III contains the Key to all the exercises, verb tables, a two-way vocabulary and a grammatical index.

D1375180

TEACH YOURSELF BOOKS

LATIN

Based on the work of
W. A. Edward

Completely revised and enlarged by
F. Kinchin Smith

TEACH YOURSELF BOOKS
Hodder and Stoughton

First printed in this form 1938
Fully revised edition 1948
Ninth impression 1980

This volume is published in the U.S.A. by David McKay Company Inc., 750 Third Avenue, New York, N.Y. 10017

ISBN 0 340 05801 3

Printed in Great Britain
for Hodder and Stoughton Paperbacks, a division of
Hodder and Stoughton Ltd, Mill Road, Dunton Green,
Sevenoaks, Kent (Editorial Office: 47 Bedford Square,
London WC1 3DP)
by Richard Clay (The Chaucer Press), Ltd, Bungay, Suffolk

INTRODUCTION

QUEEN ELIZABETH I at sixteen could talk Latin with her tutors readily and well : but few to-day will wish to emulate Queen Elizabeth. Writing Latin is good mental exercise, but our best reason for learning Latin is that we may read it. The civilisation of Europe has been built on the ruins of Rome : its literature and learning are the basis of much that is best in our own. Even to-day we cannot forget how far we are indebted : half the words we use in daily speech are derived from Latin. Latin is still the language of the Roman Church, and the language in which we write our mottoes, dedications and epitaphs. Rome is present in our daily life, whether we know it or not. We reckon time by Julius Cæsar's calendar, and take our holidays in the month that is named after the Emperor Augustus. When we write a.m., p.m., p.s., D.V., e.g. and scores of other abbreviations, we are writing Latin.

The Roman Empire included the greater part of Europe ; it stretched eastward to India, southward to the Sahara. Everywhere it has left its impress. The so-called Romance languages—Italian, French, Spanish, Portuguese, Rumanian—are in direct descent from Latin, so that you will find it easier to learn any one of them if you have learnt Latin first. The word *Romance* is itself another form of *Romanic*; change one letter in *Rumanian* and you have *Romanian*, the Roman language. After the barbarians had swept down upon Rome, and the great Empire had fallen

apart, Latin learning lingered in the monasteries, and
was the chief subject taught in the schools. The first
schools founded in England were Grammar Schools,
that is, schools founded for the teaching not of English
but of Latin grammar. The Revival of Learning in
the fifteenth century sprang from the re-discovery of
the Greek and Roman authors of classical times, and
they stimulated not only imitation but creative achievement. Shakespeare, though he knew "small Latin
and less Greek", is the crown of an age which, in
literature, owed much to the stimulus of Rome. In
the centuries that have followed, the influence of Latin
has been profound. It is felt not only in literature;
law, medicine and all exact sciences use a Latin phrase-
ology. In discovering Latin for ourselves we find a
key not only to the ancient world but to our own.

Roman power was founded upon armed force, yet
it is wrong to think of the Romans as primarily a
military people. True, they gained by the sword a
wide Empire, but they held it by their genius for
administration. They conquered, often ruthlessly, but
the races they conquered learned to value and admire
the civilisation they brought. They left a literature
whose qualities are untarnished by time; to read Virgil
or Tacitus in the original is to experience a pleasure
which outweighs all the labours of learning. It is
of little use to read them in translation, for English
and Latin are so different in character that their
essential qualities are lost in the process. Latin is
terse and accurate; it is content with one word where
we use three. Every sentence is a mosaic in which
the words are intricately fitted; alter one and the
pattern is destroyed. The structure of a Latin sentence
is quite different from that of an English one. An
English sentence tacks on one idea after another,
joining them loosely with "and's" and "but's", and

often tapering into a straggling finish. A Latin sentence is like a Roman column on the march, all neat and tidy, every part in due subordination to the whole, no straggling phrases, no unnecessary words, and all cleanly rounded off under the undisputed leadership of a main verb.

It is because of this fundamental difference between the Latin and the English language, that teachers for generations have insisted that the best way to learn Latin is to translate English into Latin. The original edition of this book adopted this method. There is much to be said for it. It is much easier to understand the complex structure of a Latin sentence when you try and construct such a sentence yourself. Translating English into Latin helps you to become familiar with the Latin accidence and syntax, and the order of Latin words will cease to seem unnatural. If you are learning Latin without a teacher, practice in writing Latin is almost essential. Moreover, the translation of English into Latin still occupies a considerable place in Latin examinations such as G.C.E.

But this approach to Latin has two disadvantages. It takes a long time, a longer time in fact than most students can spare, and the learning of Latin through the writing of " dog " Latin can easily degenerate into a mechanical application of over-simplified grammar-book rules. There has consequently been in recent years a growing revolt against this approach, and many teachers now believe that Latin should be learnt like a modern language from the study, both oral and written, of Latin itself, and that the first approach to grammar should be the discovery of its functioning in the live text, and the realisation of the need of it as the expression of the Roman mind.

The previous edition of this book was written on

the principle that (as stated in the original introduction) " in learning Latin you must begin by translating English into Latin ". English-into-Latin exercises consequently occupied a large portion of the
book, and the rules for writing Latin formed a basis
of most chapters. In the revising of this book a
compromise has been aimed at between the two
methods, and an attempt made to meet the needs
both of the students who want to translate English
into Latin, and of those who want to read Latin as
soon as possible. For the former the English-into-
Latin exercises have been retained, but transferred to
Part II. Their numbers, however, correspond to the
lessons in Part I; so that a student can do them, if
he wishes, after doing the Latin-into-English portions
of each lesson, and then check his efforts with the
key. Also for his sake, the rules for writing Latin
have been retained as the introduction to most chapters.
There is nothing, however, to prevent anyone who
wishes to discover a new rule or construction for
himself, from studying first the actual Latin, and
learning the grammar afterwards.

For the student who wishes a short cut to some
comprehension of Virgil and Cicero without the labour
of translating English into Latin, easy extracts from
Latin literature have been added throughout Part I.
The Romans did not write for children and the difficulty of finding actual Latin easy enough for beginners
is known to every Latin teacher. But proverbs,
pithy sayings, mottoes, the easier epigrams of Martial,
occasional lines from Horace and Virgil, and even a
short poem or two of Catullus, have been included in
the hope that even at the start they will not be too
difficult with the help of the notes, vocabulary, and
key. Another new element in the book is the addition
of Latin words and phrases that are now a part of the

English language. The translations in the key are
not intended to be good English but are intentionally
literal, almost word for word, in the belief that this is
what the beginner without a teacher needs.

In any case, whatever is your aim in learning Latin,
you should learn the grammar and vocabulary thoroughly from the first, or you will always feel lost and
uncertain in reading Latin. In using this book you
will be wiser to master each section before going on
to the next, and constantly to revise what you have
already learnt. This may seem dull at first, but it
will enable you to read Latin with greater ease and
rapidity when you are further advanced.

We wish to record our thanks to Miss E. Heath
of Wisbech High School for her assistance in finding
many of the Latin extracts for the revised edition.

The Value of Latin

(From a statement issued by the Council of the Classical
Association)

The Latin language has been the main vehicle of
Western culture. To a first-hand knowledge of the
creeds, codes, laws, literature, philosophy, and science
of Western Europe, considered in their historical
development, it remains an indispensable key. At
the present time, when great social changes are im-
pending, it is more than ever necessary that men and
women should have a clear understanding of the path
by which they have already come. This is impossible
without Latin. Latin culture is not an obstacle to
modern knowledge but a necessary element in it.
Our civilisation will lose in breadth and depth, in
stability and richness, if it is severed from its Latin
roots.

The linguistic training of Latin, emphasising as it

does constant processes of analysis and synthesis, teaches clarity and precision of thought, lucidity of expression in English, and in particular the ability to distinguish the thought and the form in which it is expressed. The position of Latin is unique in this respect because, more than any other language likely to be studied, it involves the translation not of single words but of ideas.

Not only is a knowledge of Latin indispensable as a scientific basis of European language studies, but we believe the training that it involves to be of unrivalled assistance towards the subsequent study of almost any new subject.

Method of Using this Book

Make certain resolutions before you begin :—

(i) Never to use the Key before you have attempted the exercise or translation for yourself.

(ii) Always to read the Latin through at least twice before beginning to translate. In this way you will accustom yourself to thinking in Latin.

The best way to use this book is to work right through it, exercise by exercise. Thus, write out Exercise 1 (*a*), then turn to Part II and correct your version before going further.

For thorough study constant revision is necessary. As soon as you have completed five lessons, then revise; as soon as you have finished the next five, revise again, and so on to the end of the book.

In the case of those students who are unaccustomed to grammatical form, and find the English–Latin exercises very difficult, the following plan may be recommended for a first reading. Read Lesson I, then work Exercise 1 (*a*). Turn to Part III (p. 242) and correct your version of 1 (*a*). Then, instead of turning back to Part I, keep at Part III, and turn 1 (*b*) (p. 268) into

English, afterwards correcting your version by comparing with 1 (*b*) (p. 199) in Part II. By doing this with all the Lessons you will get right through the book the first time without doing anything but Latin–English. You could then go through the book working in the ordinary way—using Part III as the Key throughout.

It is clear that the book may be used in various ways according to the needs of the student, the essential point about them all being that they can be followed without any other help than is given in the book itself.

N.B. The Latin exercises should always be attempted before the pieces of original Latin, as they are easier and give practice in the new grammar. For the first few chapters special vocabularies are provided, but these do not include the words in the original Latin selections. For these the student should consult the Vocabulary at the end of the book.

Since this book is often used by students who are working with an examination in mind, an index has been added to facilitate easy reference to rules, usages, and certain special words that a candidate needs to have continually in mind. The book will therefore continue to be useful when the student moves on to more advanced work.

CONTENTS

xiii

CONTENTS   xv

PART II

PART III

LATIN PASSAGES (excluding single lines)

PART I

PRELIMINARY CHAPTER

The Latin alphabet is the same as our own, except for three slight differences :

1. The Latin alphabet as *written* has no *w*.
2. *k* and *y* are rarely used.
3. *i* is very often written for *j*. The Latin word for " now " may be written *jam* or *iam*, and is pronounced *yam* in both cases.

Pronunciation

This is the pronunciation which it is believed was used by the Romans.

The vowels are pronounced as follows :

ă, that is short *a*, as in *fat*, e.g. *ămicus*, Latin for " friend ".

ā, that is long *a*, as in *father*, e.g. *irā*, in anger.

ĕ, that is short *e*, as in *net*, e.g. *ĕt*, and.

ē, that is long *e*, as in *they*, e.g. *mē*, Latin for " me ".

(Note that *e* is always sounded in Latin, e.g. *lĕgĕrĕ*, the Latin for " to gather ", has three syllables.)

ĭ, that is short *i*, as in *pin*, e.g. *ĭnsula*, island.

ī, that is long *i*, as in *police*, e.g. *servī*, slaves.

ŏ, that is short *o*, as in *not*, e.g. *bŏnus*, good.

ō, that is long *o*, as in *note*, e.g. *mōs*, custom.

ŭ, that is short *u*, as *oo* in *wood*, e.g. *domŭs*, a house.

ū, that is long *u*, as *oo* in *mood*, e.g. *domūs*, houses.

(Note that after *q*, and sometimes after *g* and *s*, *u* has the sound of *w*.)

Diphthongs

ae, au, oe in Latin are called Diphthongs—*i.e.* two vowels pronounced together to form one sound—and are pronounced as follows :

ae, as *ai* in *aisle*, e.g. *mensae*, table.

au, as *ow* in *cow*, e.g. *aureus*, golden.

oe, as *oi* in *oil*, e.g. *proelium*, battle.

ui, as Fr. *oui*, e.g. *huic*, to this (man).

eu, as in *news*, e.g. *heu*, alas !

Consonants

These are pronounced as in English for the most part, *but*—

c is always pronounced as in *cat*.

g is always pronounced as in *get*.

j (or *i* where it stands in place of *j*) is always pronounced as *y* in *yellow*.

s is always pronounced as in *son*.

t is always pronounced as in *top*, e.g. *ratio*, reason.

v is always pronounced as *w* in *wall*, e.g. *servi*, pronounced *serwee*.

th and *ch* are pronounced as *t* and *k*.

Double consonants are pronounced separately, as in Italian, or as in the English *book-keeper*.

Accent

Never accent a word on the last syllable.   If a word consists of two or more syllables, it is accented either on the second or third syllable from the end—on the second syllable from the end if it is long, on the third from the end if the second syllable is short, *e.g.* íră, poétă, ínsŭlă.

Where Latin examples of pronunciation are given, say them over to yourself several times for practice.

The Parts of Speech

Words are divided into various classes. We talk of Nouns, Adjectives, Pronouns, Verbs, Adverbs, Prepositions, Conjunctions, Interjections; and that we may always know exactly what we mean, we shall set down shortly what we understand by each of these terms.

1. *The Noun.*—Observe these words : *John, table, whiteness.* The first is the name of a person; the second is the name of a thing; the third is the name of a quality. These are all *Nouns*, and in Latin are sometimes called *Substantives*.

2. *The Adjective.*—The adjective names some quality possessed by the thing named by the noun. Thus, *table* names a certain article of furniture. It has a certain size, shape, etc. If we wish to name these we add an adjective to the noun, *e.g.* a *wooden* table, a *strong* table.

3. *The Pronoun.*—" John went into the house. *He* met his friend there." What does the word *he* do here ? It stands in place of the name *John.* A pronoun, then, is a word which stands in place of a noun.

4. *The Verb.*—" John ran along the road." " John chased a hare." " John now sleeps." In each of these sentences we talk of somebody doing something, or being in a certain state. The somebody is named by a noun (the Subject); the doing or state is described by a verb (the Predicate). Thus *ran, chased, sleeps* are verbs.

5. *The Adverb.*—" John ran quickly." " John chased

a hare eagerly." "John sleeps peacefully." In each case here we have a word (*quickly, eagerly, peacefully*) telling us something about the action or state marked by the verb. Such a word, used with a verb to describe its action, is called an adverb.

6. *The Preposition.*—"John ran quickly . . . his work." This is a broken sentence. *His work* is unconnected. Put in the word *to* before *his*. Now the sentence gives complete sense. This little word joins *work* to *ran quickly*, and shows the connection between them. Such a word we call a preposition (Latin *prae*, before, and *positus*, placed—a word placed before a noun). A preposition, then, is a word which connects words and shows the relation between them.

7. *The Conjunction.*—We have another class of words which connect—conjunctions. These, however, unlike prepositions, usually connect sentences. If I wish to make one big sentence out of the three sentences in paragraph 5, I write : "John ran quickly *and* chased a hare eagerly *and* sleeps peacefully." A conjunction, then, is a word which connects sentences. Occasionally conjunctions connect words, *e.g.* "John *and* James are sleeping." "*Either* John *or* James is a fool."

8. *The Interjection.*—"Hurrah ! John has caught the hare." In this sentence *Hurrah !* is just an exclamation, a shout. Such a word thrown into the sentence without connection is called an interjection.

No doubt you could go on to tell me a good deal more about these words and their uses, but this is all you must know before studying the following pages. Different people have different ideas on these words, but it is absolutely necessary that for the present you and I should agree to have the same.

The Inflections of Latin

" The king's brother now reigns."
" The brother of the king now reigns."

You see these two sentences express the same meaning in different ways. In the first sentence, to show the connection between *king* and *brother* we add an -'s, making a slight change in the end of the word. In the second case we connect the two by a preposition, at the same time altering the order. Latin in the great majority of cases uses the first method to show connection. Latin order is consequently almost always different from English.

The -'s in the first example we call an inflection—a change in the end of a word to show relationship to some other word or words. Such changes are made only in nouns, adjectives, pronouns, and verbs. The other parts of speech are never inflected. Latin of course uses prepositions too, but these only help the inflections, and are followed, according to certain rules, by changes in the end of the noun they go with. In English the prepositions have to do all the work, without any help from the endings of words.

The Inflections of Nouns in Latin

In English nouns may be made plural by the addition of such endings as -s, -es, -en : as, *dogs, witches, oxen*. Latin, in the same way, has certain endings to denote the plural, and other endings besides, which show the relationship of the noun to the other words in the sentence. The noun so changed is said to be in a certain *Case*. A list of all the cases of a noun is called the *Declension* of the noun. To decline a noun is to go through all its cases.

We have cases in English, as you know, but we do not always mark them by inflection. In fact we very seldom do so. We generally mark them by a preposition. The following are examples of the inflections found in English nouns and pronouns :—

" John's book is good."
" He struck him."

The first word, *John's*, we say is in the Possessive case. When the person is acting, you observe we use *He*, 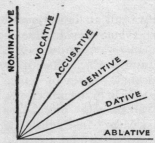 which is in the Nominative case, and called the Subject. The person who receives the action of the verb is named by *him*, which is in the Accusative case.

Case is a word which comes from the Latin word *casus*, which means *a falling*. It was applied to these forms of the noun because they were regarded as a falling away from the original form. Thus, if we regard the Nominative case as the upright straight line, as being really not a falling away at all, the other cases in Latin may be represented by sloping lines.

The Nominative case, then, is used when the noun is the Subject of the sentence.

The Vocative case is the case of the person addressed.

Thus in *Et tu, Brute* (which means *You also, Brutus*), *Brute* is in the Vocative case.

The Accusative case is usually dependent on a verb. It is used to express the Direct Object. The Object, therefore, in Latin can never be in the Nominative case, even when the Subject is concealed in the verb and there is no word in the Nominative case in the sentence. Thus, in *Nautam interfēcit* (which means *He killed a sailor*), *nautam* is in the Accusative case.

The Genitive case denotes possession. It is usually translated by *of* and the noun. Thus *insulae*, Genitive case, means *of the island*.

The Dative case is usually translated by *to* or *for* and the noun. Thus *insulae*, Dative case, means *to* or *for the island*.

The Ablative case is usually translated by *by, with, from, on* or *in* and the noun. Thus, *insulā*, Ablative case, means *from the island*; *gladiō*, Ablative case of *gladius*, means *by* or *with the sword*; *auctumnō*, Ablative case of *auctumnus*, means *in autumn*.

The following section is very important and should be studied carefully.

Order of Words in Latin

The order of words in a Latin sentence is usually different from English. The first word is emphatic, and is usually the subject of the sentence, and the last word, also emphatic, is usually the verb, *e.g.* in English we say " Brutus loves Lucia ", but Latin says " Brutus Lucia loves " (" *Brutus Luciam amat* "). " *Luciam Brutus amat* " would mean " it is *Lucia* that Brutus loves ". Adjectives in Latin come either before or after the nouns they qualify. Adverbs precede verbs, *e.g.* whereas in English we say " Caesar fights bravely ", Latin says " Caesar bravely fights " (*Caesar fortiter pugnat*). Other words or phrases, *e.g.* prepositions, and the words they qualify (*e.g.* " *in insula* "—" in the island "), relative clauses, and participles, are usually placed inside the sentence in the natural order of thought. Genitives frequently precede the word they qualify (*e.g.* " a good poet of Spain " would be " *bonus Hispaniae poeta* ", and " Brutus, a good inhabitant of Italy, often used to love Lucia with boldness " would be in Latin " *Brutus, bonus Italiae incola, Luciam ferocia saepe amabat* ".

N.B.—The Latin words will be found in Vocabularies 1 and 2.

LESSON I

FIRST DECLENSION

When a noun names one thing, we say it is singular; when more than one, plural.

In English a noun is said to be feminine when it is the name of a living thing of female sex; that is, gender in nouns corresponds to sex in living things; so a masculine noun is the name of a living thing of male sex. Thus *girl* is feminine, *boy* masculine. In Latin this rule holds good : *puella*, a girl, is feminine ; *puer*, a boy, is masculine. In English all other words are neuter : this is not so in Latin. This language gives gender to names of sexless things. *Insula*, an island, in Latin is feminine; *mūrus*, a wall, is masculine. Happily, fairly easy rules can be given for determining gender in each noun. These we shall give later.

A list of all the forms of a noun is called the *Declension* of the noun.   To go through this list is to *Decline* the noun.

There are five different sets of inflections in Latin. According as the noun takes the first, second, third, fourth, fifth set, we say it belongs to the First, Second, Third, Fourth, Fifth Declension.

Each declension is distinguished by the way in which the nouns belonging to it form the genitive singular. *Insul-a*, an island, makes genitive *insul-ae*.   *Mūr-us*, a wall, makes genitive *mūr-ī*.   *Insula* belongs to the First Declension; *mūrus* to the Second.   The other declensions will be explained later.

FIRST DECLENSION
Insul-a, f....an island

Singular

Nominative & Vocative	*Insul-a*	an (the) island
Accusative . .	*Insul-am*	an (the) island
Genitive . . .	*Insul-ae*	of an (the) island
Dative . . .	*Insul-ae*	to *or* for an (the) island
Ablative . . .	*Insul-ā*	by, with, from *or* in an (the) island

Plural

Nominative & Vocative	*Insul-ae*	(the) islands
Accusative . .	*Insul-ās*	(the) islands
Genitive . . .	*Insul-ārum*	of (the) islands
Dative . . .	*Insul-īs*	to *or* for (the) islands
Ablative . . .	*Insul-īs*	by, with, from *or* in (the) islands

Most nouns of the First Declension end in *-a* and are *feminine*, unless they are masculine through their own sex, e.g. *nauta*, a sailor, is masculine.

You notice in this that Latin has no word for *the* or *a*, the definite and indefinite article, as we call them. *Insula* means *an* island or *the* island, and the sense tells us which. Note that the ending -a in the Nominative is a short sound, but is a long sound in the Ablative.

The part in this noun, and in all nouns of any declension, left after removing the termination of the genitive singular we call the *stem*. A case, then, always consists of stem + inflection. Thus *insul-* is the stem, *-ae* the genitive inflection, *-am* the accusative inflection, and so on. To find the case of any noun, then, get the stem and add the inflection that marks that case.

Before going on to tackle an exercise with longer sentences it will be good to have a little practice in these inflections.

Exercise I (a)

Write down, then, the meanings of these Latin phrases :—

1. Amicitia incolarum Hispaniae. 2. Incolae Italiae. 3. Incolīs Italiae. 4. Ferocia nautae. 5. Irā nautarum. 6. Insulīs Italiae. 7. Insulas Hispaniae. (What case is *insulas*?) 8. Orae Hispaniae.

Vocabulary I

Amicitia, -ae, f....friendship	*Ira, -ae,* f....wrath
*Et...*and	*Italia, -ae,* f....Italy
Ferōcia, -ae, f....boldness	*Nauta, -ae,* m....sailor
Hispania, -ae, f....Spain	*Ora, -ae,* f....shore
Incŏla, -ae, m. or f....inhabitant	*Poēta, -ae,* m....poet
	Victōria, -ae, f....victory

Compare now what you have written with the Key in Part III, and so with each following exercise.

Many first declension Latin nouns have been taken over into the English language. They all end in *-a*.

Here are some of them : in some cases their meaning has changed.

villa	
via	(a road or route)
Magna Carta	(Charta was originally a leaf of papyrus, and so something written upon paper)
rota	(originally a "wheel", in English a duty list going round like a wheel)
paeninsula	(in English peninsula : *paene*, almost ; *insula*, an island)
inertia	
area	(in Latin an empty piece of ground, often a town square or playground)
persona grata	
arena	(originally "sand", with which the stadium was covered)

Also many girls' names, *e.g.* Clara, Stella, Viola, Victoria, and Vera. If you don't know their meanings, look them up in a dictionary.

Some Latin words taken over into English have kept the Latin plural, *e.g.* larva, larvae ; antenna, antennae.

Sometimes a genitive case has been taken over into English, *e.g.*

amor patriae . .	love of one's native land
lapsus linguae . .	slip of the tongue
aqua vitae . .	water of life

LESSON II

THE VERB.—PRESENT AND IMPERFECT ACTIVE

The verbs are divided into Conjugations as the nouns into declensions. The nouns were classed according to the termination of the genitive singular : the verbs are classed according to the termination of their Present Infinitive. To love, to advise, to rule, to hear are present infinitives in English. *Am-āre, mon-ēre, reg-ĕre, aud-īre* are the corresponding verbs in Latin. The termination is in each case *-āre, -ēre, -ĕre, -īre*; the other part may be called the *Present stem.*

Verbs with infinitives in *-āre* belong to the First Conjugation.

Verbs with infinitives in *-ēre* belong to the Second Conjugation.

Verbs with infinitives in *-ĕre* belong to the Third Conjugation.

Verbs with infinitives in *-īre* belong to the Fourth Conjugation.

In this lesson we shall take up the Present and Imperfect tense of *amo*. Watch carefully the English meaning of the tense.

PRESENT INDICATIVE

Sing. 1.	*Am-ō*	. . .	I love *or* am loving
2.	*Am-ās*	. .	Thou lovest *or* art loving
3.	*Am-at*	. .	He loves *or* is loving
Plur. 1.	*Am-āmus*	. .	We love *or* are loving
2.	*Am-ātis*	. .	Ye (you) love *or* are loving
3.	*Am-ant*	. .	They love *or* are loving

You will notice that the termination of each " person " has an " *a* " in it, except the first person singular, which is *am-o*. This is because it is a contraction for *ama-o*, and the "*a*" has dropped out, as you would expect if you say "*amao, amao, amao*" quickly many times.

For full conjugation of the present of *monēre* (to advise), i.e. *moneo* (Second Conjugation), of the present of *regere* (to rule), i.e. *rego* (Third Conjugation), and of the present of *audire* (to hear), i.e. *audio* (Fourth Conjugation), see Table of Verbs in Part III (p. 288).

PRESENT TENSE OF THE VERB "TO BE" (*Esse*)

Sum	. . .	I am
Es	. . .	thou art
Est	. . .	he, she, or it is
Sumus	. . .	we are
Estis	. . .	you (plural) are
Sunt	. . .	they are

I, thou, he, etc., are called the subjects of the verb and are said to be in the nominative case.

In the Latin, you notice, they are represented by the inflection or termination only. It is as if *amo* meant *love I* and *-o* stood for *I*, and so forth. As a rule do not translate the English pronoun into Latin when it is the subject of the verb.

Further, this inflection shows whether it is the person speaking who is acting (first person), or the person spoken to (second person), or the person spoken about (third person).

This is true both of the first three forms, and also of the last three. The difference in the last three is that the persons are now plural—we are speaking of more than one.

When we say the verb is singular and use the singular forms in Latin, we mean there is one person acting.

When we say the verb is plural and use the plural forms in Latin, we mean there is more than one person acting. The first person denotes that the person speaking is acting; the second person denotes that the person spoken to is acting; and the third person denotes that the person spoken about is acting.

We have used the term Indicative above. The Indicative mood of the verb makes a plain straightforward statement, for example : *amo*, I love. The Present terminations also show that the action described by the verb is going on just now—at present. This form of the verb we call the Present tense.

Another termination tells you what person *was* acting and when the action *was* taking place. This tense denotes an action *going on in the past and not completed*; hence its name—*Imperfect*.

e.g. When I *was eating* plums, I swallowed a stone. " Was eating " is important. You will notice again that the " *a* " of the stem is kept throughout—*a*bam, *a*bas, *a*bat, etc.

IMPERFECT INDICATIVE

1. *Am-ābam* .	. .	I was loving *or* used to love
2. *Am-ābās* .	. .	Thou wast loving *or* used to love
3. *Am-ābat* .	. .	He was loving *or* used to love
1. *Am-ābāmus*	. .	We were loving *or* used to love
2. *Am-ābātis*	. .	Ye (you) were loving *or* used to love
3. *Am-ābant* .	. .	They were loving *or* used to love

Similarly imperfect tense of *monēre* is *monēbam*, etc.
    ,,   ,,   ,,   *regere* is *regēbam*, etc.
    ,,   ,,   ,,   *audire* is *audiēbam*, etc.
For full conjugation *v.* Table of Verbs in Part III. Imperfect tense of *esse* is *eram* (I was, etc.).

Note.—The following and all future exercises you

should write referring to the vocabulary; then, after finishing, learn the vocabulary off by heart. It is easy to remember the meaning of many Latin words by the English words derived from them,

> e.g. *flagro* (blaze) gives the English *flagrant*.
> *concilio* (win friendship), conciliate.
> *pugno* (fight), pugnacious.

In Part III you will find a correct translation of the exercises by means of which to correct your own. Watch carefully any notes that are given there, and carefully attend all through the book to differences in the order of the words in Latin and in English. You will see the order is seldom the same in the two languages.

Exercise 2 (*a*)

Turn into English :—

1. Incolas Hispaniae Barca concitat. 2. Primo incolarum amicitiam rogabat. 3. Saepe incolas hujus terrae superabatis. 4. Italiam nunc non amas, neque amabas. 5. Cum incolis insulae pugnas, atque ferocia et ira flagras. 6. In insula Sicilia pugnabamus, sed incolae amicitiam negabant. 7. Amicitiam rogatis et impetratis. 8. Victoriam nunc speramus.

Notice the order of words. In Latin the verb is usually at the end of a sentence.

In insula Sicilia. The Latin says " in the island Sicily ", but English says " in the island *of* Sicily ". The Latin is really more exact, because the island is Sicily, and does not belong to Sicily. The genitive in Latin denotes possession, e.g. *nautae victoria*—" the victory of (*i.e.* belonging to) the sailor ", or " the sailor's victory ". Thus *insula Siciliae* would mean " Sicily's island ", like *poetae insula*, which would mean " the poet's island ". Therefore " the island which is Sicily " is not *insula Siciliae*, but *insula Sicilia*. This construction is called *apposition* because the two words are placed next to each other.

Vocabulary 2

Armō, āre...to arm
Atque...and
Autem...however
Barca, -ae, m....Barca
Conciliō, -āre...to win (friendship, etc.). Imperfect Indicative will express trying-to-win
Concītō, -āre...to stir up
Cum (and ablative)...along with
Flagrō, -āre...to blaze
Hōc [1]...this (accusative)
Hujus [2]...of this (genitive)
Impetrō, -āre...to obtain by request
In (and ablative)...in
In (and accusative)...against
Neque...nor
Negō, -āre...to say . . . not, to deny, to refuse
Nōn...not
Nunc...now
Prīmō...at first
Pugnō, āre...to fight
Renōvō, āre...to renew
Rogō, -āre...to ask, to ask for
Saepe...many times, often
Sed...but
Sicilia, -ae, f....Sicily
Sperō, -āre...to hope, to hope for
Supero, -are...to conquer
Terra, -ae, f....land
Tibi...to you (dative)
Tum...then

Note.—The vocabularies include only new words. If you forget any word given already, you must turn to the Vocabulary at the end of the book.

Latin in English

What do the following words mean literally?

ignoramus   veto
concordat   terra firma
habitat

If necessary, consult vocabulary.

[1] Nom. or acc. neut. sing. of *hīc, haec, hōc*.
[2] Gen. sing. of *hīc, haec, hōc*.

Some Roman Sayings

1. Vita non est vivere, sed valere.
2. (On a sundial.)   Horas non numero, nisi[1] serenas.
3. Bis dat, qui cito dat.
4. Dum spiro (breathe), spero.
5. Laborare est orare.

LESSON III

SECOND DECLENSION.—PREPOSITIONS

Learn these two nouns off by heart, paying particular attention to the terminations or inflections :—

	Murus, m....a wall.		*Bellum*, n....war.	
	Singular.	Plural.	Singular.	Plural.
Nom.	Mūr-us	-ī	Bell-um	-a
Voc.	Mūr-e	-ī	Bell-um	-a
Acc.	Mūr-um	-ōs	Bell-um	-a
Gen.	Mūr-ī	-ōrum	Bell-ī	-ōrum
Dat.	Mūr-ō	-īs	Bell-ō	-īs
Abl.	Mūr-ō	-īs	Bell-ō	-īs

Decline like this all nouns ending in *-us* and *-um* with genitive in *-i*.

We shall not print the meanings of the cases any more.   You must refer to Lesson I if you forget them.

Some nouns of this declension end in *-er*, and are then declined like the two following.

Note.—Nouns in *-us* and *-er* are masculine ; nouns in *-um* neuter.

	Puer, m....a boy.		*Ager*, m....a field.	
	Singular.	Plural.	Singular.	Plural.
N. &. V.	Puer	-ī	Ager	Agr-ī
Acc.	Puer-um	-ōs	Agr-um	-ōs
Gen.	Puer-ī	-ōrum	Agr-ī	-ōrum
Dat.	Puer-ō	-īs	Agr-ō	-īs
Abl.	Puer-ō	-īs	Agr-ō	-īs

---

[1] *nisi*—"if not" or "unless".

Notice *ager* forms all its other cases from *agr-*, dropping the *e*. The *e* is inserted in the nominative. This generally happens when the *e* has a consonant before it.

Exercise 3 (a)

Turn into English :—

1. Puer caprum amabat. 2. Magistri Philippi filios amabant. 3. Philippi equos concitabatis. 4. Animos filiorum Philippus concitabat. 5. Equi Philippi in agris sunt. 6. Filii Philippo dona dant. 7. Dona filiis Philippi damus. 8. Ubi sunt filii Philippi cum equis?

Vocabulary 3

Animus, -ī, m...,mind
Caper, -rī, m....goat
Do, -are...to give
Dōnum, -ī, n....gift
Equus, -ī, m....horse
*Est...*is

Fīlius, -iī, m....son
Magister, -rī, m....master
Philippus, -ī, m....Philip
Sunt...(they) are,
    belong to (with gen.)
*Ubi ?...*where ? (adverb)

Latin and English

Many Latin second declension nouns in *-us* have come into English, *e.g.*

circus	circle
focus	hearth, centre of family life.
stimulus	goad
chorus	
discus	
genius	(in Latin the " life spirit " of a person, a kind of guardian angel)

Some still keep the Latin plural, *e.g.*

terminus	"boundary"	plural	termini
radius	"ray"	plural	radii
narcissus		plural	narcissi
fungus	"mushroom"	plural	fungi

Latin second declension nouns ending in *-er* in English include

cancer . . . (lit. crab)
arbiter . . . minister

There are also many neuter nouns, *e.g.*

studium
album . . . lit. "a white thing", then a tablet on which notices were written
forum
aquarium . . . what does *aqua* mean?
medium . . . what is the plural?
maximum
minimum
vacuum
spectrum . . . *i.e.* an image
curriculum . . . orig. a little chariot, then a race-course
momentum
rostrum

Prepositions

In this lesson a few hints on the prepositions will be given. These in Latin help the inflections. The inflections in Latin show the relation between the noun and other words in the sentence, but often require prepositions to help them in doing this, and to indicate special relations. Latin, then, has two ways of showing the relation between nouns and other words, Prepositions and Inflections. We have practically only one—Prepositions.

The following prepositions take the *Ablative* :—

It will help you if you learn by heart the following rhyme :—

> Put the ablative with de,
> cum and coram, ab and e,
> Sine, tenus, pro and prae.

Meanings

De	.	.	concerning, or down from.
Cum	.	.	with
Coram	.	.	in the presence of
Ab *or* a	.	.	by or from (*ab* is used before a vowel)
Ex *or* e	.	.	out of (*ex* before a vowel)
Sine	.	.	without
Tenus	.	.	as far as
Pro	.	.	before, or on behalf of
Prae	.	.	because of.

All other prepositions take the Accusative except *in* and *sub*, which can take either Accusative or Ablative, but have a different meaning according to the case. When "*motion towards*" is meant, they take the Accusative. *Super* and *subter*, *over* and *under*, can take both, but are rarer.

e.g. in villam	.	.	into the house.
sub muros	.	.	up to the walls.

When "*place where*" is meant, they take the ablative, *e.g.*

in villa	. .	in the house
sub muris	. .	underneath the walls.

An Epigram from Martial

Tongilianus habet nasum, scio, non nego. Sed jam
Nil praeter nasum Tongilianus habet.

Martial, who lived in the second half of the first century A.D., wrote twelve books of short poems (called "Epigrams"), mostly satirising the diverse characters and life of contemporary Rome. Tongilianus was a critic who, the epigram implies, was so fastidious that he turned up his nose at everything. He is all nose, *i.e.* a critic and nothing else.

Latin Phrases and Sayings in English

1. Facta non verba.
2. Per ardua [1] ad astra (R.A.F. motto).
3. per annum.
4. ad infinitum.
5. e.g. is abbreviated from *exempli gratia*, "for the sake of an example".
6. pro bono publico.
7. In vino veritas, "In wine truth".
8. Post hoc, propter hoc, "after this, therefore because of this".
9. v. sup., abbrev. for *vide supra*, "see above".
10. v. infr., abbrev. for *vide infra*, "see below".
11. pro tempore, "for a time".

[1] *Ardua* is a neuter plural adjective, *lit.* "high things".

12. ad hoc, " with reference to this ".

13. reductio ad absurdum.

14. in memoriam.

15. inter alia, " among other things ".

16. P.S., abbrev. for *post scriptum*, " after the thing written ".

17. pares cum paribus, *lit.*, " equals with equals ". Proverb—" birds of a feather flock together ".

LESSON IV

THE VERB.—FUTURE AND PERFECT INDICATIVE ACTIVE.

We shall now take two more tenses of the verb of the First Conjugation :—

FUTURE INDICATIVE

1. *Am-ābŏ* .	. .	I shall love *or* shall be loving
2. *Am-ābis*	. .	Thou wilt love *or* wilt be loving
3. *Am-ābit*	. .	He will love *or* will be loving
1. *Am-ābimus*	. .	We shall love *or* shall be loving
2. *Am-ābitis*	. .	Ye (you) will love *or* will be loving
3. *Am-ābunt*	. .	They will love *or* will be loving

Futures of monēre	regere	audire	esse	are :—
(*warn*)	(*rule*)	(*hear*)	(*be*)	
monēbo	regam	audiam	ero	
monēbis	reges	audiēs	eris	
monēbit	reget	audiet	erit	
monēbimus	regēmus	audiēmus	erimus	
monēbitis	regētis	audiētis	eritis	
monēbunt	regent	audient	erunt	

For full conjugations see Table of Verbs in Part III.

PERFECT INDICATIVE

1. *Amāv-ĭ* .	. .	I have loved *or* I loved
2. *Amāv-istī*	. .	Thou hast loved *or* thou lovedst
3. *Amāv-it*	. .	He has loved *or* he loved
1. *Amāv-imus*	. .	We have loved *or* we loved
2. *Amāv-istis*	. .	Ye (you) have loved *or* ye (you) loved
3. *Amāv-ērunt* or *-ēre* .	.	They have loved *or* they loved

PERFECT TENSES OF OTHER CONJUGATIONS

monui	rexi	audivi	fui
monuisti	rexisti	audivisti	fuisti
monuit	rexit	audivit	fuit
monuimus	reximus	audivimus	fuimus
monuistis	rexistis	audivistis	fuistis
monuērunt	rexērunt	audivērunt	fuērunt
(or monuēre, rexēre, etc.)			

Learn these two tenses off by heart, paying particular attention to the terminations.

It is plain from the above that the *Future* tense states some event as going to happen, and that the *Perfect* tense states some completed act. You may translate the latter also by *I did love*, etc.

As soon as we come to the Perfect tense we require a new stem. In the First Conjugation we take the Present stem (*am-ā*) and add *v*; then to this we add the inflections given above.

Question.—What is the Perfect stem of *concito, supero, bello, flagro, armo, pugno*?

Translate the following exercise now into English.

Exercise 4 (a)

1. Cum Poenis ter, O Romani, pugnavistis. 2. Primo in Italia cum Romanis pugnavimus. 3. Auxilio ventorum Romanos superabis. 4. Tandem adversarios superavere. 5. O Poeni, non jam victoriam sperabitis et bellum renovare recusabitis. 6. Amicitiam adversariorum rogabimus atque impetrabimus. 7. Itaque postea Poeni amicitiam Romanorum conciliaverunt. 8. Romanus cum Gallo pugnavit.

Vocabulary 4

Adversarius, -iī, m....opponent, enemy
Apud (and accusative)...near
Auxilium, -iī, n....aid
Erant...were
Gallus, -ī, m....a Gaul
Itaque...accordingly
Non jam...no longer

Poenus, -ī, m....Carthaginian
Postea...afterwards
Recūso, -āre...to refuse
Romānus, -ī, m....Roman
Tandem...at last
Ter...thrice
Ventus, -ī, m....wind

LESSON V

ADJECTIVES, CLASS I.—TIME WHEN, TIME HOW LONG

In English the terminations of adjectives do not tell us much. In fact inflection has almost disappeared from the English adjective. In *this boy, these boys, this* is singular, *these* plural. In Latin such changes are the rule, and not the exception, as in English. If we use an adjective with a singular masculine noun it has one form, with a feminine noun another, with a neuter noun another. In fact, we may say adjectives take inflections to show differences in number and gender and case; and they always agree in these respects with the noun with which they go. Thus *pueri* is masc. sing. gen. of *puer*. *Boni* is masc. sing. gen. of *bonus*. Of a good boy, then, is in Latin *boni pueri*. Similarly, of a good girl is *bonae puellae*.

There are two great classes of adjectives in Latin. The masculine in the first class ends in *-us* or *-er*, and is declined like *murus* or *ager* or *puer*. The feminine is declined like a noun of the First Declension, and the nominative of course ends in *-a*. The neuter is declined like a neuter noun of the Second Declension, and of course the nominative ends in *-um*. Take the masculine form, then, in the nominative case of any adjective of this class, and to find the feminine treat it as a noun of the Second Declension and find what we have called the stem. To this add *-a, -um*, for feminine and neuter respectively, and decline by the above rules.

1. Thus *malus* (bad) gives stem *mal-*. The feminine, then, is *mala*, and the neuter *malum*.

2. Thus *asper* (rough) gives stem *asper*. The feminine, then, is *aspera*, and the neuter *asperum*.

3. So *ater* (black) gives stem *atr-* (like *ager*). The feminine, then, is *atra*, and the neuter *atrum*.

To distinguish between 2 and 3 you will require always to know and keep in mind what the *stem* of the adjective is. We now give an example declined in full for reference.

Bŏnus, -a, -um...good (like *murus*).

	Singular.			Plural.		
	Masc.	Fem.	Neut.	Masc.	Fem.	Neut.
Nom.	Bon-us	-a	-um	Bŏn-ī	-ae	-a
Voc.	Bŏn-e	-a	-um	Bŏn-ī	-ae	-a
Acc.	Bŏn-um	-am	-um	Bŏn-ōs	-ās	-a
Gen.	Bŏn-ī	-ae	-ī	Bŏn-ōrum	-ārum	-ōrum
Dat.	Bŏn-ō	-ae	-ō	Bŏn-īs	-īs	-īs
Abl.	Bŏn-ō	-ā	-ō	Bŏn-īs	-īs	-īs

Asper, -a, -um...rough (like *puer*).

	Singular.			Plural.		
	Masc.	Fem.	Neut.	Masc.	Fem.	Neut.
N. & V.	Asper	-a	-um	Asperī	-ae	-a
Acc.	Asper-um	-am	-um	Asper-ōs	-ās	-a
Gen.	Asper-ī	-ae	-ī	Asper-ōrum	-ārum	-ōrum
Dat.	Asper-ō	-ae	-ō	Asper-īs	-īs	-īs
Abl.	Asper-ō	-ā	-ō	Asper-īs	-īs	-īs

Ater, atra, atrum...black (like *ager*).

	Singular.			Plural.		
	Masc.	Fem.	Neut.	Masc.	Fem.	Neut.
N. & V.	Ater	atr-a	atr-um	Atr-ī	-ae	-a
Acc.	Atr-um	-am	-um	Atr-ōs	-ās	-a
Gen.	Atr-ī	-ae	-ī	Atr-ōrum	-ārum	-ōrum
Dat.	Atr-ō	-ae	-ō	Atr-īs	-īs	-īs
Abl.	Atr-ō	-ā	-ō	Atr-īs	-īs	-īs

Like *asper* are declined *liber* (free), *miser* (wretched), *tener* (tender), and a few uncommon adjectives. All other adjectives in -*er* are declined like *ater*.

Time When, Time How Long

1. *Auctumno fŏlia sunt rubra.* In autumn the leaves are red.

Auctumno answers to the question, At what time? When? *Auctumno* here is the *Ablative* case. This is how Latin expresses *point of time* as opposed to *duration of time*, which is put in the *Accusative*.

2. *Vīgintī annōs Poenī cum Romānīs bellābant.* During twenty years the Carthaginians waged war with the Romans.

But if the word itself does not denote time (if it is not a word like winter, summer, spring, daybreak, etc.) you would require to insert the preposition *in* in the first case, keeping the *Ablative case*, as :—

3. *In bellō irā flagramus.* In time of war we blaze with anger.

In the second example, in which we denote length or duration of time, we might use, for emphasis, *per*, a preposition which means *during*. Thus :—

Per viginti annos cum Romanis Poeni bellabant. During twenty years, etc. (just a little more emphatic than in 2).

Exercise 5 (a)

1. Folia et rami atrae cupressi in horto meo mihi sunt cara. 2. Cupressus est umbrosa. 3. Equus filii Philippi erat semper pulcherrimus. 4. Sicilia est insula magna et pulchra. 5. Cupressi Siciliae sunt

atrae et asperae.   6. Poeni miseri erant ubi hoc specta-
bant.   7. Magna maestitia videtur esse in animis.
8. Per multos annos cum Romanis pugnavi atque
semper pugnabo.

Vocabulary 5

Annus, -i, m....year
Carus, -a, -um...dear
Cupressus, -i, f....cypress [1]
Enim...for
Erat...was (imp. indic. of *Esse*
= to be)
Esse...to be
Folium, -ii, n....leaf
Hortus, -i, m....garden
Maestitia, -ae, f....sadness
Magnus, -a, -um...large, tall
Meus, -a, -um [2]...my
Mihi...to me (dative)

Miser, -a, -um...wretched
Multus, -a, -um...many
Pulcher,   -ra,   -rum...beautiful,
lovely
Pulcherrimus, -a, -um...loveliest
Ramus, -i, m....bough
Semper...always
Spectro, -are...to look at, to behold
Ubi...when (conjunction)
Umbrosus, -a, -um...full of shade
Vetustus, -a, -um...old
Videtur...it seems

Revision of Vocabulary:

Out of the Latin words you have already learnt, write
down those to which the following English words are
related—

(Example : pugnacious—*pugno.*)
irate, nautical, insuperable, negative, equine,
auxiliary, ventilate, foliage, spectator.
(Check your answer from the Key.)

Uses of the Adjective

The Latin adjective is often used like an English
noun. Thus *boni* might mean " good men "; *bonae*
might mean " good women "; *bona* might mean " good
things ", and *bonum* " a good thing ".   And if we are

---

[1] Names of trees are always feminine in Latin.

[2] *Meus, -a, -um,* and adjectives like it, are usually placed after the
noun. thus : *In horto meo,* in my garden.

translating such phrases into Latin we need not put a word for " man ", " woman ", or " thing "; the case-endings *-us, -a, -um* are sufficient :—

Sapientes virtutem amant. Wise men (or the wise) love virtue.

Omnia mea mecum porto. I am carrying all my property (things) with me (*mecum = me + cum, cum* being here a preposition).

Then note such phrases as :—

Multa et magna sperabat. His hopes were great and many; *literally*, He was hoping for many and great things.

Multa cogitaverat. He had had many thoughts : *literally*, He had thought many things.

Latin Phrases

1. Caeca est invidia.
2. Littera scripta (written) manet.
3. Humanum est errare.

Dyed Hair

Cana est barba tibi; nigra est coma; tingere barbam
Non potes [1]—haec [2] causa est—et potes, Ole, comam.
—*Martial.*

LESSON VI

PLUPERFECT AND FUTURE PERFECT INDICATIVE.—*SI*, *UBI*, *POSTQUAM* WITH FUTURE PERFECT INDICATIVE

You remember we formed the Perfect stem by adding *-v* to the Present stem. Two other tenses are formed

---

[1] Second person singular of *possum, v.* Lesson XXVI.
[2] Feminine of *hic, v.* Lesson XV.

from the resulting Perfect stem *amav-*, namely, the Pluperfect and the Future Perfect. Thus, where in English we say *I had loved*, in Latin we say *amāveram*. This tense denotes an action which was completed some time ago (Pluperfect = Past Perfect). Again, where in English we say *I shall have loved*, in Latin we say *amāverō*. This tense is called Future Perfect, because it denotes an action as completed in the future.

Watch carefully, as usual, the terminations in learning the following :—

PLUPERFECT INDICATIVE

1. *Amāv-eram*	I had loved	*Amāv-erāmus*	We had loved
2. *Amāv-erās*	Thou hadst loved	*Amāv-erātis*	Ye (you) had loved
3. *Amāv-erat*	He had loved	*Amāv-erant*	They had loved

FUTURE PERFECT INDICATIVE

1. *Amāv-erō* . . .	I shall have loved
2. *Amāv-eris* . . .	Thou wilt have loved
3. *Amāv-erit* . . .	He will have loved
1. *Amāv-erimus* . .	We shall have loved
2. *Amāv-eritis* . .	Ye (you) will have loved
3. *Amāv-erint* . .	They will have loved

Similarly *Pluperfects* of other conjugations :—
Monueram, rexeram, audieram (or audiveram), etc.
For full conjugations see Table of Verbs in Part III.

Pluperfect of esse is fueram . . " I had been ", etc.
                    fuerās
                    fuerat
                    fuerāmus
                    fuerātis
                    fuerant

Similarly *Future Perfects* of other conjugations :—
Monuero, rexero, audiero (or audivero).

Future Perfect of esse is fuero
                              fueris
                              fuerit
                              fuerimus
                              fueritis
                              fuerint.

Si, Ubi, Postquam with Future Perfect Indicative

1. If we arm
2. When we arm } the inhabitants, we shall conquer the Romans.
3. After we arm

Here the verb *arm* in the three sentences is Present
Indicative in English; but observe, we must *have*
armed the inhabitants before we can conquer the
Romans.   The action must be future and completed in
each case.   What we ought to say in English is : " If
(When, After) we shall have armed the inhabitants we
shall conquer the Romans "; and this is what we do
say in Latin.   The Latin tense is thus more strictly
accurate and reasonable than the English one.   In all
such sentences as this, then, where in English the
Present really denotes an action future and completed,
you must use a *Future Perfect Indicative*.

1. *Si*
2. *Ubi* } *incolas armaverimus, Romanos superabimus.*
3. *Postquam*

" After " in Latin

" After " in English can be a preposition, an adverb,
or a conjunction.   Think carefully which it is when you
translate " after " into Latin.

" After " when a **preposition is**   e.g. *post mortem, post*
            post   *scriptum* (P.S.)

"After" when an **adverb** is
postea

e.g. *postea negavit;*
"afterwards he
refused"

„ when a **conjunction** is
postquam

e.g. *postquam femi-
nam spectaverat,
negavit*, "he re-
fused, after he had
seen the woman"

Exercise 6 (a)

1. Magnus adulescentulorum numerus hunc locum oppugnaverat. 2. Si adulescentuli hunc locum oppug-naverint Romani bellum renovabunt. 3. Ubi Africam a Poenis abalienaverimus, Hispaniam oppugnabimus. 4. Postquam imperium propagaveritis, magna pertinacia conservabitis. 5. Romanos, ubi magno in periculo erant, conservaveramus. 6. Consilium Poenorum com-probare dubitaveratis. 7. Postquam Gallos supera-verint, imperium ad Hispanos propagabunt. 8. Recusaverant Romanos oppugnare quod amicitiam conciliaverant. 9. Si incolas hujus insulae armavero, pugnabunt. 10. In hoc loco Poeni cum Romanis multos annos pugnaverant.

Vocabulary 6

Abaliēno, -āre...to estrange
Adulescentulus, -i, m....young man
Africa, -ae, f....Africa
Comprobo, -āre...to approve
Conservo, -āre...to preserve
Consilium, -ii, n....plan
Dubito, -āre...to hesitate
Hispānus, -i, m....Spaniard
Hunc [1]...this (accusative)

Impĕrium, -ii, n....command,
power, hence empire
Lŏcus, -i, m....place
Numerus, -i, m....number
Oppugno, -āre...to attack
Periculum, -i, n....danger
Pertinacia, -ae, f....stubbornness
Propăgo, -āre...to extend
Quod...because (conjunction)
Vir, -i, m....man

---

[1] Acc. masc. sing. of *hic, haec, hoc.*

LESSON VII

THIRD DECLENSION.—DESCRIPTIVE GENITIVE.—*EST* AND GENITIVE

In this declension there are nouns of all genders. In masculine and feminine nouns the terminations are usually as follows :—

	Singular.	Plural.
N. & V.	(various)	-ēs
Acc.	-em	-ēs
Gen.	-is	-um
Dat.	-ī	-ibus
Abl.	-e	-ibus

Most Third Declension nouns have genitive plurals in *-um*, but the following two kinds have genitive plurals in *-ium*.

1. Parasyllabics (*i.e.* with same number of syllables in nominative and genitive singular), *e.g.* nubes, nubis, nūbium.

except

	Gen. Sing.	Gen. Plural.	
pater	patris	patrum	**father**
mater	matris	matrum	**mother**
frater	fratris	fratrum	**brother**
juvenis	juvenis	juvenum	**young man**
senex	senis	senum	**old man**
canis	canis	canum	**dog**

2. Monosyllabic nouns ending in two consonants—
    e.g. urbs, urbis, urbium, city
    mens, mentis, mentium, mind.

To decline any noun (masc. or fem.) in this declension find the genitive singular (which must be learned by heart), drop the termination (*-is*), and add the endings given above. You must learn the nominative form in the case of each noun.

Learn the fully declined nouns off by heart and practise those in the lists given after.

Rex, m....a king.

	Singular.	Plural.
N. & V.	Rex (g + s = x)	Rēg-ēs
Acc.	Rēg-em	Rēg-ēs
Gen.	Rēg-is	Rēg-um
Dat.	Rēg-ī	Rēg-ibus
Abl.	Rēg-e	Rēg-ibus

Mos, m....a custom.

	Singular.	Plural.
N. & V.	Mōs	Mōr-ēs
Acc.	Mōr-em	Mōr-ēs
Gen.	Mōr-is	Mōr-um
Dat.	Mōr-ī	Mōr-ibus
Abl.	Mōr-e	Mōr-ibus

Labor, m....labour.

	Singular.	Plural.
N. & V.	Labor	Labōr-ēs
Acc.	Labōr-em	Labōr-ēs
Gen.	Labōr-is	Labōr-um
Dat.	Labōr-ī	Labōr-ibus
Abl.	Labōr-e	Labōr-ibus

Urbs, f....a city.

	Singular.	Plural.
N. & V.	Urbs	Urb-ēs
Acc.	Urb-em	Urb-ēs
Gen.	Urb-is	Urb-ium
Dat.	Urb-ī	Urb-ibus
Abl.	Urb-e	Urb-ibus

Civis, m., f....a citizen.

	Singular.	Plural.
N. & V.	Cīvis	Cīv-ēs
Acc.	Cīv-em	Cīv-ēs
Gen.	Cīv-is	Cīv-ium
Dat.	Cīv-ī	Cīv-ibus
Abl.	Cīv-e	Cīv-ibus

Nubes, f....a cloud.

	Singular.	Plural.
N. & V.	Nūbēs	Nūbēs
Acc.	Nūb-em	Nūb-ēs
Gen.	Nūb-is	Nūb-ium
Dat.	Nūb-ī	Nūb-ibus
Abl.	Nūb-e	Nūb-ibus

Practise the following :—

Genitive plural in *-um.—Dux, ducis*, m., leader; *consul, consulis*, m., consul; *princeps, principis*, m., chief; *terror, terrōris*, m., terror; *imperātor, -tōris*, m., commander-in-chief; *error, errōris*, m., error.

Genitive plural in *-ium.—Hostis, -is*, m., f., enemy; *classis, -is*, f., fleet; *navis, -is*, f., ship; *fīnis, -is*, m., end; *gens, gentis*, f., race (remember *gens* is for *gen(t)s* : a similar thing happens with nouns having *d* before the *s*).

Descriptive Genitive (or Ablative)

We talk in English of *a man of great wisdom*. In Latin " of great wisdom " may be expressed by either the genitive or the ablative. This is called the Descriptive Ablative or Genitive. Note the order of the words carefully : *Magnā vir sapientiā* or (sometimes) *magnae vir sapientiae*.

Note.—There must be an adjective with the noun; thus, *a man of wisdom* is not *vir sapientiae*, but *vir sapiens*, a wise man.

Est and Genitive

Where in English we say it is the part of, the duty of, the mark of, somebody to do something, in Latin we use *est* and the *genitive* merely.

It is the part of a general to overcome the enemy.
Est   ducis   superare   hostēs.

Two Gender Rhymes

1. Here is a *rhyme* to help you to remember the gender of words ending in *-is* of the third declension. The following are masculine, all others (and there are many) are feminine, or (as with *civis* and *hostis*) either masculine or feminine

Certain nouns in *is* we find
to the *Masculine* assigned :
amnis, axis, crinis, collis,
ignis, orbis, fascis, follis,
panis, piscis, lapis, mensis,
pulvis, sanguis, unguis, ensis,
finis, manes end the rhyme,
ghosts are always masculine.

Meaning.
river, axle, hair, hill,
fire, sphere, bundle, bellows,
bread, fish, stone, month,
dust, blood, nail, sword,
end, ghosts.

2. Third declension nouns ending in *-ns* are feminine, except :—

Masculine are fons and mons,
Dens and cliens, torrens, pons,

fountain, mountain,
tooth, client, torrent, bridge.

Exercise 7 (a)

1. Est Romanorum fines imperii propagare. 2. Hamilcar, summa vir ferocia, belli cupiditate flagrabat.

3. Mente agitabamus bellum renovare. 4. Equis, armis, viris, pecunia totam locupletabimus Africam. 5. Hieme in coelo sunt atrae nubes. 6. Classem Poenorum apud insulas superaverunt Romani. 7. Populus Romanus ceteras gentes virtute superat. 8. Est principis populum gubernare. 9. Rex Britannorum, magna vir sapientia, cum Romanis saepe pugnabat. 10. Si pacem conciliaverint naves conservabunt.

Vocabulary 7

Arma, -orum, n. pl....arms
Britanni, -orum, m. pl....Britons
*Ceteri, -ae, -a...*all other (plural)
Coelum, -i, n....the sky
*Conciliare pacem...*to make peace
Cupiditas, -tatis, f....desire
*Guberno, -are...*to govern
Hamilcar, -is,[1] m....Hamilcar
Hannibal, -is,[2] m....Hannibal
Hiems, -ēmis, f....winter

*Locuplēto, -are...*to enrich
*Mente agitare...*to ponder in mind, to meditate
Pax, pācis, f....peace
Pecūnia, -ae, f....money
Populus, -i, m....a people
*Summus, -a, -um...*very great
*Tōtus, -a, -um...*whole
Virtūs, -tūtis, f....virtue, valour

Some Third Declension Latin Nouns Used in English

Look up the verbs in the vocabulary for their meaning.

1. *Ending in -or.*

(a) *From First Conjugation roots.*

	Verb.
creator	*creo*
curator	*curo*
liberator	*libero*
agitator	*agito*
spectator	*specto*
violator	*violo*
educator	*educo* (I nourish)

[1] Pronounce the genitive Ha-milc'-ăris.
[2] „   „   „   Ha-nib'-ălis.

(b) *From Second Conjugation roots.*

motor	. . .	*moveo*
doctor	. . .	*doceo*
monitor	. . .	*moneo*

(c) *From Third Conjugation roots.*

creditor	. . .	*credo*
captor	. . .	*capio*
victor	. . .	*vinco*
rector	. . .	*rego*
pastor	. . .	*pasco* (I feed)

2. *Ending in other terminations.*

sanitas
crux
index (a pointer)
omen
animal
apex
axis (axle)

Latin Phrases

1. ars gratia artis (*motto of Metro-Goldwyn Films*).
2. ars est celare artem.
3. honoris causa.
4. in loco parentis.
5. homo sum, et nihil humanum alienum est mihi.—
   Terence (adapted).
6. quot homines, tot sententiae.—*Proverb.*

Live Today!

Non est, crede mihi, sapientis dicere " Vivam ".
Sera nimis vita est crastina : vive hodie.

—Martial.

Crede and *vive* are imperatives; *crede mihi*—" believe
me ", *vive*—" live ! " (*v.* Lesson XXV).

LESSON VIII

THIRD DECLENSION: NEUTER NOUNS.—MOTION TO AND FROM A PLACE

All *neuter* nouns of the third declension have the accusative singular and plural the same as the nominative and vocative singular and plural respectively.

The nominative plural usually ends in *-a* and the genitive plural in *-um*; but if the nominative singular is stem + *e*, the ablative singular has *-i*, the nominative plural has *-ia*, and the genitive plural *-ium*.

Thus, *tempus, temporis*, n., time, *nōmen, nōminis*, n., name, have *-a* and *-um*; but *mare, maris*, n., sea, has *marī, maria, marium*.

Learn the fully declined nouns off by heart and practise those in the list given after :—

	Nomen, n....a name.		*Tempus*, n....time.	
	Singular.	Plural.	Singular.	Plural.
N., V. & Acc.	Nōmen	Nōmin-a	Tempus	Tempor-a
Gen.	Nōmin-is	Nōmin-um	Tempor-is	Tempor-um
Dat.	Nōmin-ī	Nōmin-ibus	Tempor-ī	Tempor-ibus
Abl.	Nōmin-e	Nōmin-ibus	Tempor-e	Tempor-ibus

	Mare, n....a sea.		*Vectigal*, n....a tax.	
	Singular.	Plural.	Singular.	Plural.
N., V. & Acc.	Mar-e	Mar-ia	Vectigal	Vectigāl-ia
Gen.	Mar-is	Mar-ium	Vectigāl-is	Vectigāl-ium
Dat. & Abl.	Mar-ī	Mar-ibus	Vectigāl-ī	Vectigāl-ibus

The stems of nouns like *mare* usually end in *-al*, *-il*, *-ar*, and in a few like *vectīgal* the *e* of the nominative singular has been lost. Do not confuse these with masculine nouns in *-al*, *-il*, *-ar*, as *sal*, m., salt, *lar*, m., household god.

Practise the following : *Cognōmen, -inis*, n., surname; *munus, -eris*, n., gift; *foedus, -eris*, n., treaty; *genus, -eris*, n., class, kind; *lītus, -oris*, n., shore; *hastīle, -is*, n., spear shaft; *sedīle, -is*, n., seat; *animal, animālis*, n., animal.

Motion To and From a Place

1. *Hannibal pecuniam Roma ad Africam portavit.* Hannibal brought the money from Rome to Africa.

2. *Romam ab Africa navigāvimus.* To Rome from Africa we sailed.

Rule.—Express motion to a place in Latin by a preposition with the accusative, but use the accusative with no preposition in the case of a town or small island.

Express motion from a place with a preposition and the ablative, except in the case of a town or small island, when you omit the preposition.

Exercise 8 (*a*)

1. Hamilcar, cognomine Barca, magna [1] cum classe in Italiam navigavit. 2. Et mari et terra Poenos Romani superaverunt. 3. Non enim suae est virtutis [2] pacem rogare. 4. Societatem foedere confirmabant.

---

[1] "With a large fleet." Latin prefers this order of words.
[2] Latin says "it is of my valour" (*est* with genitive). English says "it is in keeping with my valour."

5. Foedera Karthaginienses violaverunt. 6. Romam ad Caesarem[1] munera magna portant. 7. Melita Romam magna difficultate navigavimus. 8. Animal providum est homo. 9. Cunctorum animalium providentissimum est homo. 10. Ferrum ex hastili in corpore erat.

Vocabulary 8

Caesar, ăris, m....Caesar
Confirmo, -are...to ratify, to make strong
Copia, -ae, f....amount, supply
Copiae, -arum, f....forces
Corpus, corpŏris, n....body
Cunctus, -a, -um...all
Difficultas, -tātis, f....difficulty
Ferrum, -i, n....iron, steel
Hŏmō, -inis, m....man
Karthaginiensis, -is, m....Carthaginian
Londinium, -ii, n....London
Longus, -a, -um...long

Mari et terrā...by land and sea
Melita, -ae, f....Malta
Navigatiō, -ŏnis, f....voyage
Navigo, -are...to sail, to voyage
Providentissimus, -a, -um...most prudent
Providus, -a, -um...prudent, foreseeing
Societas, -tatis, f....alliance
Supero, -are...to surpass
Terra marique[2]...by land and sea
Violo, -are...to violate, to break

Latin Phrases

1. a verbis ad verbera.
2. O tempora, O mores.—*Cicero.*
3. ex tempore.
4. mens sana in corpore sano.—*Juvenal.*

An Anonymous Epitaph

5. Balnea, vina, Venus corrumpunt corpora nostra,
   Sed vitam faciunt balnea, vina, Venus.

                                           —*Martial.*

---

[1] *Romam ad Caesarem.* "To Caesar at Rome." The Romans say "To Rome to Caesar", putting (logically) the place first.
[2] There are a number of little words in Latin which are put at the end of other words and cannot stand alone. These are called *enclitics.* Thus *que* = and; hence *marique* = and by sea.

LESSON IX

A FEW HINTS ON THE THIRD DECLENSION.—PLACE WHERE

You will find this the hardest declension in Latin, because of its variety and the consequent difficulty in giving good general rules. Below are given a few examples of well-marked classes of nouns in this declension. In future try when you come across a noun to think which noun it is like among those you know, and so get the nouns into groups in your mind. The declension will become quite easy by practice. If you try to learn it all at once you will only become confused. See that the case-endings are thoroughly mastered and leave the rest to time and experience.

Practise yourself in these nouns and remember the type of formation.

	stem				
Natiō, f., nation	*nation*	Acc.	Gen.	Dat.	Abl.
Ratiō, f., reason, method	*ration*	*-em,*	*-is,*	*-i,*	*-e,* etc.
Mentiō, f., mention	*mention*				

There are many nouns like these in the declension.

	stem				
Civitas, ., State	*civitāt*	Acc.	Gen.	Dat.	Abl.
Cupiditas, f., greed, desire	*cupiditāt*	*-em,*	*-is,*	*-i,*	*-e,* etc.
Calamitas, f., disaster	*calamitāt*				

You may perhaps have noticed by this time that a *d* or *t* in the stem is dropped before *s* in the nominative singular.

	stem				
Fortitūdō, f., bravery	*fortitudin*	Acc.	Gen.	Dat.	Abl.
Multitūdō, f., multitude	*multitudin*	*-em,*	*-is,*	*-i,*	*-e,* etc.
Consuetūdō, f., custom	*consuetudin*				
Imago, f., image	*imagin*				

So commonly with nouns in *do* and *go*.

Gender in the Third Declension

The gender in this declension in the case of sexless things is rather perplexing. The following three rules will help you, but there are numerous exceptions :—

1. If the nominative of the noun ends in *-o*, *-or*, *-os*, *-er*, or in *-es* with more syllables in the genitive than in the nominative, it is generally *masculine*.

2. If the nominative ends in *-as*, *-aus*, *-is*, *-do*, *-go*, *-io*, *-x*, *-s* following a consonant, or in *-es* without more syllables in the genitive than in the nominative, it is generally *feminine*.

3. Nouns ending in *-l*, *-a*, *-n*, *-c*, *-e*, *-t*, *-ar*, *-ur*, *-en*, *-us* are usually *neuter*. Remember the word *lancet* and it will help you.

Place Where. Locative Case

Caesar Romae habitat, Caius Athēnis.   Caesar lives at Rome, Caius at Athens.

Caesar in Africa nunc habitat.   Caesar is now living in Africa.

These sentences give examples of how to translate *place where* in Latin. The Rule is—Generally use *in* and the *ablative* : but with the name of a town or a small island (*i.e.* an island consisting only of a town with the same name) which is a singular noun of the First or Second Declension use the *genitive*, with all others the *ablative*, *i.e.* with plural nouns of First and Second Declension and all nouns of Third, Fourth and Fifth.

Exercise 9 (a)

1. Zamae autem Hannibalem Scipio superavit. 2. Syracusis quidem Cicero annum unum habitavit. 3. Magnam hostium multitudinem Caesar oppugnavit. 4. Karthagine bellum mente agitabamus. 5. Caesar fortitudine cunctos superabat. 6. In Africa multae et magnae ferae sunt. 7. Athenis, Atheniensium urbe, multa et pulchra templa sunt. 8. Hac ratione Hannibal magnae civitatis amicitiam conciliavit. 9. Pecuniae cupiditate multi homines flagrant. 10. Non est meae consuetudinis diu Cumis habitare.

Vocabulary 9

Amor, -ōris, m....love
Athēnae, -arum, f....Athens
Atheniensis, -is, m....Athenian
Bellicōsus, -a, -um...warlike
Carthāgo, -inis, f....Carthage
Cumae, -arum, f....Cumae
Fama, -ae, f....glory
Fera, -ae, f....wild beast
Habito, -are...to live, to dwell
Hāc...abl. fem. of *Hic* = this
Lux, lucis, f...light
Natio, -nis, f....tribe, nation

Pompeius, -i, m....Pompeius (a famous Roman)
Prima luce...at break of day (abl. of time)
Quidem...indeed (adverb)
Statua, -ae, f....statue
Syracusae, -arum, f....Syracuse (in Sicily)
Templum, -i, n....temple
Unus, -a, -um...one
Zama, -ae, f....Zama (town near Carthage)

Latin Sayings

1. infra dignitatem.
2. Solitudinem faciunt, pacem appellant.—*Tacitus*, " Agricola " (said by the British chieftain about the Romans).

3. Beneficium accipere libertatem est vendere.
4. Magna est veritas et praevalebit (prevail).

False Teeth

5. Thais habet nigros, niveos Laecania dentes.
   Quae ratio est? emptos haec habet, illa suos.
   —Martial.

haec, lit. " this (woman) here ", " the latter ".
illa „ " that „ there ", " the former ".

LESSON X

ADJECTIVES, CLASS II.—*AMANS.*—GENITIVE OF PRICE

The remaining adjectives in Latin should not give
any trouble. You remember the adjectives we have
had already ended in the nominative in *-us, -a, -um,*
and were declined like nouns of the First and Second
Declensions. The other adjectives are declined like
nouns of the Third Declension, or are indeclinable (that
is, they have one form for all cases). The former are
easily declined, because, with the exception of the
Present Participle and the *comparative form* (to be
explained later), they have all *-i* for the ablative
singular, *-ium* for the genitive plural, and *-ia* for the
nominative neuter plural respectively. Here is an
example of each kind :—

	Masc.	Fem.	Neut.	
1.	Omnis	omnis	omne	all
2.	Acer	ācris	ācre	keen, spirited
3.	Ingens	ingens	ingens	huge

From this you infer that in the nominative they may be of one, two or three terminations; but they all form the remaining cases in a similar manner. Below, each is declined in full. Note the similarity between the case-endings and those of the nouns of the Third Declension.

	Singular.		Plural.	
	Masc. & Fem.	Neut.	Masc. & Fem.	Neut.
Nom. & Voc.	Omnis	omne	Omnēs	omnia
Acc.	Omnem	omne	Omnēs	omnia
Gen.	Omnis		Omnium	
Dat. & Abl.	Omnī		Omnibus	

	Singular.			Plural.	
	Masc.	Fem.	Neut.	Masc. & Fem.	Neut.
Nom. & Voc.	Ācer	ācris	ācre	Ācrēs	ācria
Acc.	Ācrem		ācre	Acrēs	ācria
Gen.	Ācris			Ācrium	
Dat. & Abl.	Acrī			Acribus	

	Singular.		Plural.	
	Masc. Fem. & Neut.		Masc. & Fem.	Neut.
Nom. & Voc.	Ingens		Ingentēs	ingentia
	Masc. & Fem.	Neut.		
Acc.	Ingentem	ingens	Ingentēs	ingentia
Gen.	Ingentis		Ingentium	
Dat. & Abl.	Ingentī		Ingentibus	

Note that in all three the masculine, feminine and neuter are the same in the genitive singular and plural, and in the dative and ablative singular and plural, and that *the ablative sing. ends in -i.*

Amans

You remember we got the Present stem of *am-o* by dropping the personal ending *-o*. If we add to this

-*ans* we get *am-ans*, which means *lov-ing*. This part of the verb, because it is *partly* a verb and *partly* an adjective, we call the *Participle*; and since it refers to present time we call it the *Present Participle*. It is declined exactly like *ingens*, but has -*e* in the ablative singular (*amante*), when it functions as a participle, but -*i* when it is used as an adjective.

Examples of the Ablative Singular

Similarly, Present Participle, monēre — monens, monentis, etc.

„   „   „   regere — regens, regentis, etc.

„   „   „   audire — audiens, audientis, etc.

Ab amanti filia, "by a loving daughter", but *Ab amante puerum filia*, " by a daughter loving (*i.e.* who loves) a boy ".

Genitive of Price

Hoc donum maximi aestimo. I value this gift at a very great price.

In cases like this the price is sometimes put as the *genitive* of an *adjective*. This is called the *genitive of price.*

Similarly *magni*, " at a great price ".

Exercise 10 (*a*)

1. Hostes quidem sese armantes fugavimus. 2. Jam enim omnes inimicos superaverat. 3. Tum postridie ingens hostium multitudo Caesarem oppugnabat.

4. Namque prudentem maximi semper aestimamus.
5. Scipio quoque uxorem suam amore acri amabat.
6. Mox acribus equis Carthaginienses oppugnabitis et
fugabitis. 7. Catonem magni, pluris Caesarem Romani
aestimabant. 8. Hamilcar enim non solum hostes a
muris Carthaginis fugavit, sed etiam ingentem pecuniae
copiam comparavit. 9. Tum consilia ducis omnia
milites maximi aestimabant. 10. Fortibus militibus
praemia ingentia Caesar dabat.

Vocabulary 10

Acer, acris, ācre...passionate, fiery
Aestimo, -are...count, reckon
Cato, ōnis, m....Cato (a famous Roman)
Comparo, -are...to prepare
Do, dare...to give
Dux, -cis, m....general
Etiam...still (conj.)
Explōro, -are...to explore
Fortis, -e...brave, strong
Fugo, -are...to put to flight
Mīles, -itis, m....soldier
Mox...soon

Nam or *namque*, conj....for
Non sōlum . . . sed etiam...not only . . . but also
Parvus, -a, -um...little
Parvi...at a low value
Plus, pluris...more
Postrīdiē...on the next day
Praemium, -ii, n....reward
Quoque...also
Sēsē...himself, themselves, etc. (acc.) another form of *se*
Suus, -a, -um...his own, her own, its own

Revision of Vocabulary:

Out of the Latin words you have already learnt,
write down those to which the following English words
are related—

conservative, imperial, propagate, virile, cupidity,
popular, corporal, amorous, defamatory, plural, bus.

Latin Phrases

1. Fortuna favet fortibus.
2. Annus mirabilis.

Latin Extracts

3. Omnia vincit amor.—*Virgil.*
4. Sed fugit interea, fugit irreparabile tempus.—

Virgil.

5. Amantium irae amoris integratio est.—*Terence.*
6. Ars longa, vita brevis.

7.　　　　*To an Unpopular Poet* (Nimis poeta es)

Et stanti legis et legis sedenti,
currenti legis et legis jacenti.
In *thermas* [1] fugio : sonas ad aurem.
Piscinam [2] peto : non *licet* [3] natare.
Ad cenam propero : tenes *euntem.* [4]
Ad cenam venio : fugas edentem.
Lassus dormio : suscitas jacentem.
Vir justus, probus, innocens *timeris.* [5]

—*Martial.*

LESSON XI

FOURTH DECLENSION.—PRESENT AND IMPERFECT SUBJUNCTIVE.—FINAL CLAUSES

	Exercitus, m....army.		*Cornu*, n....horn.	
	Singular.	Plural.	Singular.	Plural.
N. & V.	Exercit-us	-ūs	Corn-ū	-ua
Acc.	Exercit-um	-ūs	Corn-ū	-ua
Gen.	Exercit-ūs	-uum	Corn-ūs	-uum
Dat.	Exercit-uī	-ibus	Corn-uī	-ibus
Abl.	Exercit-ū	-ibus	Corn-u	-ibus

You will find this declension very easy. The
nominative always ends in -*us* in masculine and feminine
nouns, and in -*u* in neuter nouns. The genitive always

[1] Baths.　　[2] Swimming-pool.　　[3] It is allowed.
[4] (Me) going, *i.e.* as I go.　　[5] You are feared.

ends in *-ūs* (pronounced like *oo* in *mood*). The nouns are declined like the two above.

Here is an irregular noun which is so common that it should be learned off by heart. In some cases, it will be observed, it takes Second Declension forms.

Domus, f....house.

	Singular.	Plural.
N. & V.	Dom-us	Dom-ūs
Acc.	Dom-um	Dom-ōs
Gen.	Dom-ūs	Dom-uum *or* -ōrum
Dat.	Dom-uī	Dom-ibus
Abl.	Dom-ō	Dom-ibus

Domī means "at home"; *domō*, "from home"; *domum*, "homewards". N.B.—*Domi* is an old "place-where" or locative case.

Present and Imperfect Subjunctive

Hitherto in our lessons on the verb we have talked only of the *Indicative Mood*, but there is another mood, called the *Subjunctive Mood*. In this mood there are four tenses—the *Present, Imperfect, Perfect* and *Pluperfect*. The meaning of the mood is best learned by practice.

The Present Subjunctive is formed from the present stem *am-*.

	Singular	Plural.
1.	Am-em	Am-ēmus
2.	Am-ēs	Am-ētis
3.	Am-ēt	Am-ent

You may notice that each person, save the first, is got by changing *a* of the *Present Indicative* into *e*, and so with all verbs of the First Conjugation.

The present subjunctive of *monere* is *moneam, moneas,*
etc.

   „   „   „   *regere* is *regam, regas,* etc.

   „   „   „   *audire* is *audiam, audias,*
etc.

   „   „   „   *esse* is *sim*

                                 sis

                                 sit

                                 simus

                                 sitis

                                 sint.

The Present Infinitive of *amō* is *am-āre,* to love.   To
get the Imperfect Subjunctive add *-m* to this, and conjugate as follows :—

Singular.	Plural.
1. Amāre-m	Amarĕ-mus
2. Amāre-s	Amarĕ-tis
3. Amāre-t	Amāre-nt

The imperfect subjunctive of *monēre* is *monērem,* etc.

   „   „   „   *regere* is *regerem,* etc.

   „   „   „   *audīre* is *audīrem,* etc.

   „   „   „   *esse* is *essem,* etc.

You will observe that every tense, Indicative or
Subjunctive, which you have had so far ends in all
its persons in *-m* (or *-o*), *-s, -t, -mus, -tis, -nt.*   These
are the letters you add to the Present Infinitive to
make the Imperfect Subjunctive.   This is so in almost
every verb in Latin.   If you know the Present Infinitive,
then, of any verb, you can always form the Imperfect
Subjunctive.

Purpose or Final Clauses, expressed by Ut and Ne

He is arming his soldiers *to attack* the enemy.

He has armed his soldiers *in order to attack* the enemy.

He will arm his soldiers *for the purpose of attacking* (*that he may attack*, etc., etc.) the enemy.

On consideration of these sentences, it will be found that the three versions after "soldiers" all express the same purpose, although they use different words. In Latin the translation for each and all is commonly the same :—

Milites armat (armavit, armabit) ut hostes oppugnet.

Literally, His soldiers he is arming (etc.) that the enemy he may attack.

Sequence of Tenses

The Present Subjunctive is used in such clauses expressing a purpose after a Present, Perfect (with " have ") or Future tense in the main clause.

Note.—The Perfect must mean " has *or* have armed ", etc., not simply " armed ".

But the *Imperfect Subjunctive* is used in such clauses *after an Imperfect, Perfect* (without " have ") *or Pluperfect* in the main clause.

E.g. he was arming (armed, had armed) his soldiers to attack (that he might attack, etc., etc.) the enemy. *Milites armabat (armavit, armaverat) ut hostes oppugnaret.*

After this we shall call the Present, Perfect (with " have ") and Future *primary tenses*; the Imperfect, Perfect and Pluperfect we shall call *historic tenses*.

Note that " that not " is *ne*. For example : *Milites armabat ne hostes urbem oppugnarent.* He was arming his soldiers *that* the enemy might *not* attack the city.

Exercise 11 (a)

1. Itaque Carthaginienses magno cum exercitu in Italiam navigaverunt ut Romanos oppugnarent. 2. Prima luce equitatus magnam Poenorum manum fugavit. 3. Cives postea tres exercitus comparabunt ne urbem hostes oppugnent. 4. Interim Gallos concitabat ut saltum noctu occuparent. 5. Cum omnibus gentibus Romani pugnaverunt. 6. Cornua caprorum sunt maxima et dura. 7. Hannibal et legati postridie domi cenaverunt. 8. Tertio mense igitur Romam domo navigabimus. 9. Itaque sese armavit ut domum conservet. 10. Namque hoc consilium comprobaveratis ut casum vitaretis.

Vocabulary 11

Casus, -ūs, m....disaster
Ceno, -are...to dine
Domi...at home (called the locative case of *Domus*)
Durus, -a, -um...hard
Equitatus, -ūs, m....cavalry
Exercitus, -ūs, m....army
Igitur...therefore (never first in the sentence)
Interim...meanwhile
Legātus, -i, m....officer

Magistrātus, -ūs, m....magistrate
Manus, -ūs, f....(1) hand, (2) band
Mensis, -is, m....month
Noctū...by night (adv.)
Occupo, -are...to seize
Saltus, -ūs, m....defile
Tertius, -a, -um...third
Tres, tria, n....three
Vito, -are...to avoid

Fourth Declension Latin Words in English

hiatus...yawning, gap
prospectus...forward looking
apparatus...(look up *apparo* in vocab.)
consensus...(look up *consentio*)

impromptu...(*in promptu* dicere " to have something *in readiness* to say ")
in situ...in position
in statu quo (*status, -ūs*...position)
pari passu...with equal step

Outside a Roman Theatre in Spain

(An inscription on a stone discovered in Spain and now in the British Museum.)

CIRCUS PLENUS
IANUAE CLAUSAE [1]
CLAMOR INGENS

One Author to Another

Cur non mitto meos tibi,[2] Pontiliane, libellos? [3]
Ne mihi [4] tu mittas, Pontiliane, tuos.—*Martial.*

The Motto of the S.C.M.

Ut omnes unum sint.

LESSON XII

FIFTH DECLENSION.—PERFECT AND PLUPERFECT SUBJUNCTIVE.—*CUM* AND SUBJUNCTIVE

Of the nouns there is only one declension left—the *Fifth*. This again is a small and easy one. The nouns are all declined like the one given below. Their genitive ends in -*ēi*, the nominative in -*es*; there are only two nouns in the declension in which the plural is found complete—*dies*, *diēi*, m. or f., a day; *res*, *rei*, f., a thing.

[1] *Ianuae*, "doors". *Clausae*, " shut "—past participle passive of *claudo* (I shut).
[2] *tibi*, " to you ".
[3] " little books." Diminutive of *liber*, " book".
[4] *mihi*, " to me ".

	Dies, m., f.[1]...a day.		*Res*, f....a thing.	
	Singular.	Plural.	Singular.	Plural.
N. & V.	Di-ēs	di-ēs	R-ēs	r-ēs
Acc.	Di-em	di-ēs	R-em	r-ēs
Gen.	Di-ēī	di-ērum	R-eī	r-ērum
Dat.	Di-ēī	di-ēbus	R-eī	r-ēbus
Abl.	Di-ē	di-ēbus	R-ē	r-ēbus

We called *am-āre* the Present Infinitive, and added *-m* to form the Imperfect Subjunctive. To form the Perfect Subjunctive and Pluperfect Subjunctive we go to a different stem—the *Perfect stem*, which in the First Conjugation is formed by adding *-v* to the present stem, e.g. *amavi*. This stem is, in this verb, *amāv-*. To this add the terminations given below and you get the Perfect and Pluperfect Subjunctive.

The Infinitive which means *to have loved* is called the *Perfect Infinitive*, because it denotes a completed action. This is always formed by adding *-isse* to the *Perfect stem*, e.g. *amavisse*, and it is worth noting that the Pluperfect Subjunctive is formed from it by adding *-m*, *-s*, *-t*, *-mus*, *-tis*, *-nt* (compare the formation of the Imperfect Subjunctive). The meanings of these two tenses will also be best learned by practice.

PERFECT SUBJUNCTIVE.		PLUPERFECT SUBJUNCTIVE.	
Singular.	Plural.	Singular.	Plural.
1. Amāv-erim	amāv-erimus	Amāv-issem	amāv-issēmus
2. Amāv-eris	amāv-eritis	Amāv-issēs	amāv-issētis
3. Amāv-erit	amāv-erint	Amāv-isset	amāv-issent

Similarly, the Perfect Subjunctive of *monēre* is *monuerim*, etc.

    "   "   "   " *regere* is *rexerim*, etc.

---

[1] In the plural this noun is masculine only.

Similarly, the Perfect Subjunctive of *audīre* is *audierim*, etc., or *audiverim*, etc.

   „   „   „   „   *esse* is *fuerim*

Similarly, the Pluperfect Subjunctive of *monēre* is *monuissem*, etc.

   „   „   „   „   *regere* is *rexissem*, etc.

   „   „   „   „   *audīre* is *audissem*, etc., or *audivissem*, etc.

   „   „   „   „   *esse* is *fuissem*

For full conjugations see Tables of Verbs in Part III.

Cum and Subjunctive

1. *Cum Hannibal Hispanos concitaret, bellum in mente agitabant Romani.*
2. *Cum Hannibal Hispanos concitavisset, bellum renovaverunt Romani.*

1. Since (When) Hannibal was stirring up the Spaniards, the Romans began to think of war.
2. When (Since) Hannibal had stirred up the Spaniards, the Romans renewed the war.

Since or *when*, with a past tense in English, is translated by *cum* (sometimes written *quum*) with Imperfect or Pluperfect Subjunctive in Latin.

When the English tense denotes a *continuous action* (like *was stirring*) use the *Imperfect Subjunctive*.

When the English tense denotes a *completed action* (like *had stirred*) use the *Pluperfect Subjunctive*.

Exercise 12 (a)

1. Tum magna sperabatis, cogitabatis maesta. 2. Boni et bonae virtutem, sapientiam, fidem amant.

3. Itaque cum primam aciem superavissem, secundam oppugnavi. 4. Hodie haud dubie aciem hostium fugabunt. 5. Cum igitur in acie Romani starent, pugnare dubitavimus. 6. Cum Galli legiones Romanas superavissent, urbs Roma erat in magno periculo. 7. Summa enim spe Romam navigavimus. 8. Cum *deos multa* [1] oravisset, viros armavit. 9. Hannibal contra summa fide pacem conservabat.

Vocabulary 12

Acies, -ēī, f....line of battle, battle array
Considero, -are...to consider, to think
Contra...on the other hand (adv.)
Deus, dei, m....god
E contrario...on the contrary (adv. phrase)
Fides, -ēi, f....good faith
Haud...not
Haud dubiē...without doubt (literally : not doubtfully) (adv.)

His...abl. plur. of *Hic* = this
Hodie...to-day (adv.)
Legio, legionis, f....legion
Maestus, -a, -um...sad
Oro, -are...to pray, ask for...
Primus, -a, -um...first
Respublica,[2] *rei publicae*, f.... commonwealth
Sapientia, -ae, f....wisdom
Secundus, -a, -um...second
Spes, spei, f....hope
Sto, stare [3]...to stand

Fifth Declension Words in English

1. series (look up *sero*, " I join ").

2. species (originally " appearance ", later " sort ", " kind ").

3. a.m. stands for *ante meridiem*.

   p.m. stands for *post meridiem*.

What do these words mean ?   See vocabulary.

4. sine die.

5. prima facie.

[1] *Note.*—*Oro* can take two accusatives, one, the person asked, and the other, the thing asked for.   "Ask many things of the gods."
[2] *Note.*—This word is a compound of *res* and the feminine of *publicus* = public.   Decline it like any noun and adjective—*respublica rem publicam, rei publicae*, etc.
[3] *Note.*—The perfect, *stĕti*, is irregular.

Two Famous Lines

1. Moribus antiquis res [1] stat Romana virisque.—
Ennius.

2. Sunt lacrimae rerum [2]; mentem mortalia tangunt.
—*Virgil.*

Phrases

1. In medias res.
2. Mox nox, in rem.
3. Salus reipublicae suprema lex.

LESSON XIII

SUPINE, FUTURE PARTICIPLE ACTIVE AND PAST
PARTICIPLE PASSIVE.—SUPINE AFTER A VERB
OF MOTION.—NOUN AND PARTICIPLE FOR
ENGLISH ABSTRACT NOUN.—PRONOUNS

Omitting the *Gerund* and *Gerundive*, and the *Imperative*, which we shall treat of farther on, we have now
had all the *Active Voice* of the First Conjugation except
one or two parts which come from a stem we have not
mentioned yet. In *amo* this stem is *amat-*, which
you get by dropping the termination *-um* in a part of
the verb called the *Supine—amatum*. This form has
the same translation in English as the *Present Infinitive*
(*to love*, for example), but is used in one special case.
We say in Latin :—

> *Ad Hispaniam navigavit hostes oppugnatum.*
> He sailed to Spain to attack the enemy.

---

[1] *res Romana, i.e.* the Roman state; cf. *respublica.*
[2] *rerum*—does this mean "of things" or "for things"? A
famous, beautiful and untranslateable line.

In Latin the Present Infinitive *oppugnare* would be quite wrong. You could have used, however, *ut* and the *Imperfect Subjunctive* (Lesson XI). The *Supine*, then, may be used to denote *purpose* after a *verb of motion*.

From this stem *amat-* you can form three other parts of the verb. (No matter what the verb is, the principle is the same.)

1. Supine stem + *-u* gives the *Second Supine* : thus *amat* + *-u* = *amatu*, meaning *in loving*. This is not often used except in poetry. It follows adjectives only and corresponds to the English adjective and infinitive.

e.g. *mirabile dictu*—wonderful to tell.

2. Supine stem + *-urus, -a, -um*, gives the *Future Participle Active* : thus *amat-urus, -a, -um*, meaning *about to love, likely to love*, or *intending to love*.

3. Supine stem + *-us, -a, -um*, gives the Past Participle Passive : thus *amatus, -a, -um*, meaning *having been loved*. These two participles are just like adjectives; when they go with nouns or pronouns, they must agree with them in gender, number and case as adjectives do. They are declined like adjectives of Class I. (Look back to Lesson V as a reminder.)

For practice, look up the Supine stem of *moneo, rego, audio*, and then write down the Future Participle Active and Past Participle Passive of each verb, as we have already done with *amo*. (*V*. p. 291 ff., and Key, p. 254.)

English derivatives are usually taken from the Supine, e.g., *monitor, rector, auditor*, etc.

Note on the Past Participle Passive

The Latin Past Participle Passive denotes an action which is past in time and passive in sense. Thus *amatus* means *having been loved*, and nothing else. English in many cases uses its participles loosely. We say, " Mounting his horse he rode away ", " Drawing his sword he slew the man ", " Charging at full speed they routed the enemy ", where in each case we mean, strictly speaking, " having mounted ", " having drawn ", " having charged ", etc. We must never use our Participles in this loose way in Latin. The verb must denote a completed action before the Past Participle Passive can be used. There is no Past Participle Active in Latin.

Abstract Nouns in English and Latin

As a rule Latin does not like abstract nouns (such nouns as conquest, rout, etc.), and has a very neat expression with the Past Participle Passive to get rid of them. Thus " before the preparation of the feast " becomes " before the feast prepared ", *ante convivium paratum*; " before the rout of the Romans " becomes *ante Romanos fugatos*; " after the end of the supper " becomes *post cenam dimissam*. *Post* and *ante* are prepositions governing *convivium* and *cenam* in the accusative, and the Participles are in agreement with the nouns.

The Four Parts of a Verb

As a general rule, then, in Latin you must know four parts before you can conjugate the verb :—

The *Present Indicative*.
The *Perfect Indicative*.

The *Supine*.

The *Present Infinitive*.

This last part tells the Conjugation—First, Second, Third or Fourth. The above four parts in the First Conjugation end as a rule in -ō, -āvi, -ātum, -āre, and it will be sufficient to note merely the irregular formations. Any verb, then, when given in the Present Indicative will easily be turned into the other stems by dropping of -o and the addition of these terminations -āv-, -āt-. There are only a few verbs which do not form their stems thus. Two common ones are—

> Dŏ, dĕdi, dătum, dăre, to give (note short ă).
> Stŏ, stĕti, stătum, stāre, to stand.

Pronouns. *Ego* and *tu*

Latin has pronouns to translate our English " I " and "you", but remember as nominatives they are employed only when very emphatic. *Ego*, I, is declined thus :—

	Singular.		Plural.	
Nom.	Ego	I	Nos	we
Acc.	Me	me	Nos	us
Gen.	Mei	of me	Nostrum or Nostri [1]	of us
Dat.	Mihi	to me	Nobis	to us
Abl.	Me	from me	Nobis	from us

The Pronoun *Tu*, thou or you (singular) is declined thus :—

	Singular.		Plural.	
Nom.	Tu	thou (you)	Vos	you
Acc.	Te	thee (you)	Vos	you
Gen.	Tui	of thee (you)	Vestrum or Vestri [1]	of you
Dat.	Tibi	to thee (you)	Vobis	to you
Abl.	Te	from thee (you)	Vobis	from you

---

[1] *Nostrum* and *vestrum* are partitive genitives, e.g. *Unus nostrum,* " one of us ". *Nostri* and *vestri* are objective genitives, e.g. *Memor vestri,* " mindful of you ".

Note there is the same form for the masculine and feminine. Be careful to notice when the English " you " is singular and when plural, and to use the singular or plural accordingly in Latin.

Is, ea, Id

The Latin word for *that, those*, is declined as follows :—

	Singular.			Plural.		
	Masc.	Fem.	Neut.	Masc.	Fem.	Neut.
Nom.	Is	ea	id	Ei (ii)	eae	ea
Acc.	Eum	eam	id	Eōs	eas	ea
Gen.	Eius (all genders)			Eōrum	eārum	eōrum
Dat.	Ei (all genders)			Eis (iis) (all genders)		
Abl.	Eō	eā	eō	Eis (iis) (all genders)		

The forms given in brackets are less common.

When used alone as a *pronoun* this means *he, she, it,* etc., as *Puer eam amat,* the boy loves *her* ; but, *Puer eam puellam amat,* the boy loves *that* girl.

Exercise 13 (a)

1. Cum autem Hannibal eam urbem occupaverit, manus dabimus. 2. Jovi optimo maximo hostiam immolatum Romam navigaverat. 3. Post occupatam urbem fines explorabitis. 4. Id factum initio risum spectantibus concitabat. 5. Deinde exercitum in litore collocatum oppugnabunt. 6. Eas hostium manus oppugnaturus magnas copias comparavit. 7. Hostes castra clam oppugnaturos Romani subito fugaverant. 8. Oppida abalienata ut recuperaremus ad Africam navigaveramus. 9. Eum exercitum superatum spectaturi sunt. 10. Quot e magnis eis exercitibus patriam rursus spectaturi erant ?

Vocabulary 13

Castra, -orum, n....camp (Latin always plural)
Clam...secretly (adv.)
Colloco, -āre...to station
Deinde...next (adv.)
E, ex...out of (*Ex* before vowel or *h*)
Factum, -i, n....deed, action
Hostia, -ae, f....victim
Immolo, -are...to sacrifice
Initio...in the beginning
Initium, -ii, n....beginning

Jupiter optimus maximus...Jove most high and holy (acc. *Jovem*, gen. *Jovis*, dat. *Jovi*, abl. *Jove*)
Manūs dāre...to surrender (*literally*, to give hands)
Quot ?...how many ? (indeclinable pronoun)
Recupero, -are...to recover
Risus, -ūs, m....laughter
Rursus...again (adv.)
Subito...suddenly (adv.)

Latin Phrases

1. i.e. stands for id est.
2. Pax vobiscum.
3. moriturus te saluto (see *morior*).
4. Non mihi, non tibi, sed nobis (motto of a Public Library).
5. Dictum (*lit.* " a thing said "). Obiter dictum, " a remark by the way ".
6. Data (*lit.* " things given ").
7. Erratum (*lit.* " a thing erred "), *i.e.* a mistake.

Latin Extracts

1. Graecia capta [1] ferum victorem cepit.[2]—*Horace.*
2. Difficilis, facilis, jucundus, acerbus es idem :
   Nec tecum possum vivere nec sine te.—*Martial.*

[1] Past participle of *capio.*
[2] Perfect of *capio.*

LESSON XIV

ABLATIVE ABSOLUTE.—*SE, SESE*

Before doing the following exercises, you should revise the tenses of *all four conjugations*, as given in the Tables of Verbs in Part III. In fact it will help you to learn by heart at any rate the Present, Imperfect, and Future Indicative of each conjugation, noting carefully where the endings are different. Practice going through the tenses in other verbs besides *moneo, rego*, etc.

Ablative Absolute

In Latin there is a common construction called the *Ablative Absolute*. Look at these examples :—

Hac pugna pugnata urbem occupavit. This battle having been fought, he seized the city.
Urbibus abaliēnatis Carthaginem oppugnaverunt. The cities having been estranged, they attacked Carthage.

Hac pugna pugnata and *urbibus abalienatis* have no grammatical connection with the rest of the sentence, and they are therefore put into the ablative case. We are less fond of using past participles in English, and would probably say instead : *After the battle*, and *When the cities had been estranged*. The Latin construction is briefer and neater.

The Ablative Absolute must never be used if it is possible to make the participle agree with the subject or object of the sentence; e.g. *The soldiers burnt the city which they had captured* must be translated *Milites captam urbem incenderunt*, not *Urbe capta, milites eam incenderunt*.

Participles

The use of Participles in Latin can be seen from examples, *e.g.*

1. *Magister deceptus celeriter fugit.*
   " When the master was tricked, he quickly fled."
2. *Magistrum deceptum pueri riserunt.*
   " When the master was tricked, the boys laughed at him."
3. *Magistro decepto, pueri gaudebant.*
   " When the master was tricked, the boys rejoiced."

N.B.—The Present Participle (*v.* Lesson XV) can similarly be used, *e.g.*

1. *Magistro errante, pueri gaudebant.*
   " As the master was making a mistake, the boys rejoiced."
2. *Magistrum errantem pueri riserunt.*
   " The boys laughed at the erring master."

Se, Sese

Learn this pronoun off by heart.

Acc. *Se* or *sese*   These forms are both singular and plural, masculine
Gen. *Sui*   and feminine. They mean respectively—them-
Dat. *Sibi*   selves, himself, herself, itself; of themselves, of
Abl. *Se* or *sese*   himself, etc., etc.

This is called the *Reflexive Pronoun*, because it is used only when the *subject* of the verb is denoted as acting on itself, that is, the action of the verb is bent back (*re* = back, *flecto* = I bend) on its subject.

Hostes sese interficiunt.   The enemy are slaying themselves.
Mortem sibi adsciscit.   He commits suicide (adjudges death to himself).

Suus

Connected with the reflexive pronoun in Latin is the possessive adjective *suus, sua, suum*, " his, her, its ", which is used only when we are referring to the subject of the sentence. Otherwise *his* would be *ejus*. In fact, however, unless there is some stress on the adjective or pronoun, or unless some ambiguity would arise if it were omitted, Latin does not use possessive adjectives or pronouns at all. Compare Sentences 5 and 8 of Exercise 14 (*a*) for the use of these words, and also the following :—

Patrem suum interfecit. He killed his own father.
Patrem ejus interfecit. He killed his (somebody else's) father.

Exercise 14 (*a*)

1. Magnam pecuniae copiam habemus et semper habebimus. 2. Nunc omnes gentes vincunt et semper vincent. 3. In Hispaniam magnum exercitum ducam. 4. Romanos tertio die videbunt et vincent. 5. Ante ejus adventum et mari et terra male res gerebant. 6. Hamilcar ubi bellum gerit nunquam hostes vincit. 7. Sed extremo prope ad desperationem perveniunt. 8. Oppida Africae valentissima imperio suo tenet. 9. At Hamilcar magnas res secunda fortuna gerit. 10. Hamilcaris perpetuum odium erga Romanos secundum bellum Punicum concitabit.

Vocabulary 14

Adventus, -ūs, m....arrival
Ante...before (prep. governing acc.)
At...but (conj.)
Desperatio, -nis, f....despair (act of despairing)
Duco, duxi, ductum, ducěre...to lead

Erga...towards, for (prep. governing acc.)
Extrēmō...at last (adv.)
Fortūna, -ae, f....fortune
Gero, gessi, gestum, gerěre...to wage, to carry out
Habeo, habui, habitum habēre...to have

Malĕ...badly (adv.)
Odium, ŏdii, n....hatred
Oppĭdum, -i, n....town
Perpetuus, -a, -um...undying
Pervenio, -vēni, -ventum, -venire ...to arrive
Prŏpe...almost (adv.)
Punĭcus, -a, -um...Punic, Carthaginian

Secundus, -a, -um...favourable or second
Teneo, tenui, tentum[1], *tenēre*...to hold
Valentissimus, -a, -um...very strong, strongest
Video, vīdi, vīsum, vidēre...to see
Vinco, vīci, victum, vincĕre...to conquer

Latin Phrases

1. D.V. (stands for *Deo volente*).
2. vice versa (*i.e.* a change having been made).
3. Fortis qui se vincit.
4. Homo doctus in se semper divitias habet.

LESSON XV

INFINITIVE AND PARTICIPLES.—ACCUSATIVE AND INFINITIVE.—*HIC, HAEC, HOC*

In the First Conjugation, if we add *-ans* to the present stem, we get the *Present Participle*—

Am-ans.

Similarly, adding *-ens* to the other three, but inserting *i* before it in the Fourth Conjugation, we get—

Mon-ens, reg-ens, aud-iens
(Genitive) Mon-entis, reg-entis, aud-ientis.

Remember the terminations of the Present Infinitives— *-āre, -ēre, -ĕre, -īre*.

The Perfect Stem

When the verb is regular, to get this stem add to the present stem in the—

First Conjugation	*av*	. .	*amāv-*
Second Conjugation	*u*	. .	*monu-*
Third Conjugation	*s*	. .	*rex-* (for *regs*)
Fourth Conjugation	*iv*	. .	*audīv-*

[1] Tentum is never used with the simple verb, only in compounded forms.

If the verb is irregular consult the Dictionary or Vocabulary, or the table of irregular verbs, and learn the Perfect by heart.

Note in *reg-o* that *g + s* gives *x*.

In each case if to this stem we add *-isse* we get the *Perfect Infinitive* :—

Amāv-isse	.	.	to have loved
Monu-isse	.	.	to have warned, advised
Rex-isse	.	.	to have ruled
Audīv-isse	.	.	to have heard

The Supine Stem

The *Supine* must be learned from the Table of Verbs at the end of the volume, and then the stem is got by dropping *-um*; by adding *-u* to this you get the *Second Supine*; by adding *-ūrus* you get the *Future Participle* (which is declined like an adjective) :—

SUPINE.		SECOND SUPINE.		FUTURE PARTICIPLE.
Amāt-um	gives	amāt-ū	and	amat-ūrus (-a, -um, etc.)
Monit-um	„	monit-ū	„	monit-ūrus (-a, -um, etc.)
Rect-um	„	rect-ū	„	rect-ūrus (-a, -um, etc.)
Audīt-um	„	audīt-ū	„	audīt-ūrus (-a, -um, etc.)

Join to the Future Participle the Present Infinitive of the verb *esse* (to be), and you get the *Future Infinitive* :—

Amaturus esse	.	.	to-be about-to-love
Moniturus esse	.	.	to-be about-to-advise
Recturus esse	.	.	to-be about-to-rule
Auditurus esse	.	.	to-be about-to-hear

Accusative and Infinitive

Scio eum stultum esse means either " I know him to be a fool ", or " I know that he is a fool ". Latin has only one way, *i.e.* the first, of expressing *Indirect Statement*.

After a verb of *saying* or *thinking*, English usually has a " that " clause, which we call a noun clause; but

in Latin a peculiar construction is used, called the
accusative and infinitive. Thus the subject of each of
the above " that " clauses, nominative in English,
becomes accusative in Latin; and the verb becomes,
though Indicative in English, Infinitive in Latin, while
" that " is dropped. The tense used is the tense of
the actual words of the speaker.

Thus, *Dīcit Rōmānōs arma adversariīs* $\begin{cases} \textit{tradere} \\ \textit{tradidisse} \\ \textit{traditūrōs esse} \end{cases}$ means

He says that the Romans $\begin{cases} \text{are surrendering} \\ \text{have surrendered} \\ \text{will surrender} \end{cases}$ their arms to the enemy.

The words used in each case by the speaker were :—

1. " The Romans are surrendering ". Therefore use here the
Present Infinitive.
2. " The Romans have surrendered ". Therefore use here the
Perfect Infinitive.
3. " The Romans will surrender ". Therefore use here the Future
Infinitive.

If we had had " he " for " the Romans " and the
sentences had been " He says that he is surrendering,
has surrendered," etc., the pronoun " he " might have
given some trouble. If you had translated it by *eum*,
you would have meant " He says that somebody else ";
if by *se*, " He says that he himself ", etc. *Se* and *suus*
in the accusative and infinitive clause usually refer to
the subject of the main sentence. E.g. *Dixit se suam
magis quam ejus patriam amāre*, " He said that he
loved his own more than that man's country ". The
English does not show clearly what were the man's
actual words; the Latin does.

N.B. " I say that...not ". Latin does not say *dico...non*, but **nego**
(I deny), e.g. *Nego hoc verum esse* = " I say that this is not true ".

Remember the Future Participle agrees with its subject in gender, number and case. Thus :—

He says that that $\left\{ \begin{matrix} \text{man} \\ \text{woman} \end{matrix} \right\}$ will surrender $\left\{ \begin{matrix} \text{his} \\ \text{her} \end{matrix} \right\}$ arms.

Dicit $\left\{ \begin{matrix} eum \\ eam \end{matrix} \right\}$ *arma* $\left\{ \begin{matrix} traditurum\ esse. \\ tradituram\ esse. \end{matrix} \right.$

Hic, haec, hoc...this (pronoun and adjective)

	Singular.			Plural.		
	Masc.	Fem.	Neut.	Masc.	Fem.	Neut.
Nom.	Hic	haec	hōc	Hī	hae	haec
Acc.	Hunc	hanc	hōc	Hōs	has	haec
Gen.	Hūius (all genders)			Hōrum	hārum	hōrum
Dat.	Huic (all genders)			His (all genders)		
Abl.	Hōc	hāc	hōc			

This pronoun may be used as an adjective with **a** noun. Thus :—

(Pronoun) *Hi totam abaliēnavērunt Africam.* These estranged **all** Africa.
(Adjective) *Hi montes ardui sunt.* These mountains are steep.

Exercise 15 (*a*)

1. Hamilcar se putat hujus belli finem facturum esse.
2. Hic eum putat horum bellorum finem facere. 3. Haec eum putat hoc fecisse. 4. Si hic negaverit se hoc bellum compositurum esse, ex Sicilia decedemus. 5. In Africam veniemus hunc interfectum et Carthaginem deletum. 6. Vettones eum in proelio pugnantem interfecerunt. 7. Adstantes dicent hunc esse fortem virum. 8. Ex Sicilia prima luce se decessuros esse dicunt. 9. Ex Sicilia decessuri cum hoc rege pacem conciliatis. 10. Cras Romam advenient.

Vocabulary 15

Adstantes...bystanders (nom. mas. plur. partic.)

Adsto, adstiti, adstare...to stand by (no Supine)

Advenio, -vēni, -ventum, -venire...to arrive

Compōno, -posui, -positum, -ponēre...to settle, to end

Crās...to-morrow (adv.)

Deleo, delēvi, delētum, delēre...to destroy

Decēdo, decessi, decessum, decēdēre...to depart, to leave (with the abl.)

Dico, dixi, dictum, dīcēre...to say

Facio, fēci, factum, facēre [1]...to make or do

Interficio, -fēci, -fectum, -ficēre, [1] ...to slay

Puto, -are...to think

Venio, vēni, ventum, venīre...to come

Revision of Vocabulary :

Out of the Latin words you have already learnt, write down those to which the following English words are related—

manuscript, initial, Lancaster, fact, recuperate, belligerent, invincible, delete, malefactor.

I do not love you, Dr. Fell

Non amo te, Sabidi [2]; nec possum dicere quare;
 Hoc tantum possum dicere, " non amo te ".

—*Martial.*

The Primrose Way

Facilis descensus Averno ; [3]
Noctes atque dies patet atri janua Ditis : [4]
Sed revocare gradum superasque [5] evadere ad auras,
Hoc opus, hic labor est.

—*Virgil, Aen.* VI.

[1] Verbs in -*io* with infinitive in -*ēre* belong to the Third Conjugation, but are conjugated in the parts from the Present stem like verbs of the Fourth. The Present Imperative usually ends in *e*. *Dico, duco, facio* have, however, Present Imperative *Dic, duc, fac*.
[2] The vocative of masculine nouns ending in -*ius* ends in -*i*. E.g. *Corneli,* " O Cornelius ". [3] The Lower World.
[4] Dis is another name for Pluto.
[5] -*que* joined to the end of a word = *et*.

LESSON XVI

ACCUSATIVE AND INFINITIVE.—*QUI, QUAE, QUOD.*—
ADJECTIVES WITH -*ĪUS* IN THE GENITIVE AND -*Ī*
IN THE DATIVE.—*IPSE, -A, -UM*

Before doing the following exercises, revise the
Perfect, Pluperfect and Future Perfect tenses (*v.* Tables
of Verbs at end of book) of all four conjugations.

Some More Hints on the Accusative and Infinitive

1. *Dixit se arma trādere* or *tradidisse.*
2. *Dixit se arma tradidisse.*
3. *Dixit se arma traditurum esse.*

1. He said that he surrendered.
2. He said that he had surrendered.
3. He said that he would surrender.

In the previous Chapter we made the verb of *saying*
Present tense in each case; when this verb is *Past* the
difficulty is greater.

In each sentence you must find the actual words of
the speaker in order to get the tense of the *Infinitive* to
use. You must try to find out the exact words which
the speaker said.

Thus, in sentence 1 the speaker said,

either (a) I surrender, *or* I am surrendering
or (b) I surrendered (*e.g.* when I was captured).

If (a) gives the actual words used, use the *Present
Infinitive.*

If (b) gives the actual words used, use the *Perfect
Infinitive.* The English is not clear: you can tell
which was used only by the sense. As far as the
English goes, either meaning may be implied.

So, when translating from Latin, after a Past tense of a verb of *saying* the Present and Perfect Infinitive are both translated by the form used in sentence 1.

In sentence 2 the actual words were *I have surrendered* : therefore translate this by the *Perfect Infinitive*.

In sentence 3 the actual words were *I shall surrender* : therefore translate this by the *Future Infinitive*.

Qui, quae, quod

The Relative Pronoun, *who, which*, is declined as follows in Latin. You will observe all these pronouns we have given are irregular in declension, yet have similarities worth remarking.

	Singular.			Plural.		
	Masc.	Fem.	Neut.	Masc.	Fem.	Neut.
Nom.	Quī	quae	quod	Quī	quae	quae
Acc.	Quem	quam	quod	Quōs	quas	quae
Gen.	Cūjus	cūjus	cūjus	Quōrum	quārum	quōrum
Dat.	Cuī	cuī	cuī	Quibus	quibus	quibus
Abl.	Quō	quā	quō	Quibus	quibus	quibus

Construction of the Relative

The Relative pronoun takes :—

(1) its *number* (singular or plural), *gender* and *person* from the word in the main clause to which it refers (sometimes called the *antecedent*, " the thing that goes before "), but

(2) its case from its own clause, *i.e.* depending on whether it is the subject or object, etc., of the verb.

The following examples will illustrate this important rule. Learn them carefully.

(1) *Imperator urbes delevit* quas *superavit.*
> The general destroyed the cities which he conquered.

(2) *Delevit urbes* quae *erant valentissimae.*
> He destroyed the cities which were the strongest.

(3) *Delevit urbes* quarum *incolae erant inimici.*
> He destroyed the cities whose inhabitants were hostile.

N.B.—In English the Relative pronoun is often omitted. In Latin it never is.

e.g. Sentence 1 might be translated in English :—
> " The general destroyed the cities he conquered."

Adjectives with -*ius* in the Genitive and -*ī* in the Dative

This is a class of adjectives which, from the terminations of the nominative singular, you would expect to belong to Class I, and which really do belong in declension to this class *except in the genitive and dative singular.* These cases, instead of ending in *-i, -ae, -i* and *-o, -ae, -o*, have *-ius* and *-ī.* Thus *solus, -a, -um,* adj. = *alone,* is declined as follows :—

	Singular.		
	Masc.	Fem.	Neut.
Nom.	Sol-us	-a	-um
Acc.	Sol-um	-am	-um
Gen.	Sol-ius (all genders)		
Dat.	Sol-i (all genders)		
Abl.	Sol-ō	-ā	-ō

The plural is quite regular, like *bonus.*

Similarly are declined *unus,* one ; *totus,* whole ; *ullus,* any; *nullus*, not any, no one; *alter*, one of two; *uter ?* which of two? *neuter*, neither of two.

(*Uter* and *neuter* are like *ater* in the nominative—*uter*, *utra*, *utrum*. *Alter* is like *asper* in the nominative—*alter*, *altera*, *alterum*.)

Ipse, ipsa, ipsum

Ipse, a pronoun meaning " -self ", also used like an adjective, is declined exactly like *solus*, but has *-e* instead of *-us* in the nominative masculine singular. Thus, *ipse*, *ipsa*, *ipsum*, etc.

> *Puer ipse cantat.*   The boy himself sings.
> *Ipsi cantamus.*   We ourselves are singing.

It simply emphasises the noun or pronoun to which it refers. In the first sentence it is an adjective and emphasises *puer*; in the second it is a pronoun and emphasises the subject (*we*) of *cantamus*, to which it refers.

Exercise 16 (a)

1. Ipsi negavimus eos belli finem facturos esse.   2. Hannibal ipse dixerat se solum hoc bellum composuisse. 3. Si dixeritis eos belli finem facturos, Carthaginem prima luce navigabunt.   4. Ipsi putavistis hos magno cum dedecore domum rediisse.   5. Qui Corinthum veniunt, statuas inspiciunt.   6. Ii ipsi dixerunt se solos a muris Carthaginis hostes removisse.   7. Neuter dixerat se captivos occidere.   8. Alter putavit eos haec dicere; alter negavit.   9. Videratis eum quem Catulus apud Aegates insulas superavit.   10. Uter dixit Caesarem eis solis provincias dedisse?

Vocabulary 16

Aedificium, -ii, n....building
*Alter . . . alter...*the one . . . the other
Captivus, -i, m....captive
Dēdecus, -oris, n....disgrace
*Inspicio, inspexi, inspectum, inspicĕre...*to look at, to examine (see footnote 1 to Vocabulary 15)
*Ita (ĭta)...*so (adv.)

Occīdo, occīdi, occīsum, occīdĕre ...to kill
Patria, -ae, f....country (in the sense of fatherland)
Provincia, -ae, f....province
Redire, rediisse [1]...to return, to have returned
Removeo, -mōvi, -mōtum, -movēre ...to remove
*Rēstĭtŭo, -stitui, -stitūtum, -stituĕre...*to restore

Note.—As in the ninth sentence of Exercise 16 (*a*),
" the man who " is always rendered in Latin by *is . . .
qui,* he . . . who.

Latin Phrases

1. Nulli secundus.
2. ipso facto.
3. A famous line of Horace :—
   Coelum, non animum mutant, qui trans mare currunt.

4. " *Writ on wind and water.*"

Nulli se dicit mulier mea nubere [2] malle [3]
　　Quam [4] mihi, non si se Juppiter ipse petat.
Dicit : sed mulier cupido quod dicit amanti,
　　In vento et rapida scribere oportet [5] aqua.

—*Catullus.*

[1] Neglect the other parts for the present. The verb is irregular.
[2] " To be married to " (of a woman).
[3] Present infinitive of *malo.*
[4] " rather than ".
[5] Here—" she ought " (*lit.* it is necessary).

LESSON XVII
CONSECUTIVE CLAUSES.—*ILLE, ISTE*

For this lesson revise the Present and Imperfect Subjunctive of the verbs of each conjugation. Learn these by heart from the table at end of book.

Consecutive or Result Clauses with *ut*

1. *Tam ferox est ut Catulum oppugnet.*
   He is so bold that he is attacking Catulus.
2. *Adeo ferox erat ut Catulum oppugnaret.*
   He was so bold that he was attacking Catulus.
3. *Adeo ferox erat ut Catulum oppugnaverit.*
   He was so bold that he attacked Catulus.

In each sentence here the " that " clause expresses a result or consequence. In Latin such a clause is introduced by *ut* = that, and always has its verb in the Subjunctive. The next point to decide is which tense of the *Subjunctive* to use. You remember in *final clauses* you could only use the Present or Imperfect Subjunctive : here any tense is possible according to the sense. Thus, in the first sentence the result is an action in the present : therefore the tense of the *Subjunctive* is *Present*. In the second the result was a continuous action in the past : therefore the *Imperfect Subjunctive* is the tense. In the third the result was an *act* in the past : therefore use the *Perfect Subjunctive*. You need not consider the tense of the verb in the first or principal clause at all : all you need look to is the actual meaning of the verb. The rule given by Dean Bradley is : *Use the tense you would use if the verb were, as in English, in the Indicative Mood.*

Do not confuse these clauses with *Final Clauses.*

In *Final Clauses* " that " means " in order that ". In *consecutive* clauses it means " in such a way that ", or " to such an extent that ", and has almost always an adverb like *ita*, *adeo* or *sic* (all meaning *so*) in the main clause to prepare you for it, or *tam* followed by an adjective, an adverb, or a correlative such as *tantus* (so great), *talis* (such), etc. If the consecutive clause were negative (that is, had a " not " in it) you would use *ut non*, never *ne*. (See also Note at end of Vocabulary 17.)

Ille, Iste

Turn back now and make sure of the declension of the adjectives with *-ius* and *-i* in the Genitive and Dative. Then learn these two pronouns :—

	Singular.				Singular.		
	Masc.	Fem.	Neut.		Masc.	Fem.	Neut.
Nom.	Ille	illa	illud	Nom.	Iste	ista	istud
Acc.	Illum	illam	illud	Acc.	Istum	istam	istud
Gen.	Illīus (all genders)			Gen.	Istīus (all genders)		
Dat.	Illī (all genders)			Dat.	Istī (all genders)		
Abl.	Illō	illā	illō	Abl.	Istō	istā	istō

In the plural both are declined like *boni, bonae, bona,* etc.

Ille means " that yonder " near *him*; *Iste* means " that near *you* ". They can both be used with nouns as *adjectives*, or alone as pronouns meaning *he, him,* etc.

Illum librum legi. I have read that book yonder.
Istum librum legi. I have read that book of yours.
Ille istum librum legit. Yon man (*he*) has read that book of yours.

Note.—*Ille* is often used to imply respect, and *iste* contempt. E.g. *ille dux*—" that famous leader "; *iste homo*—" that man again ! "

Exercise 17 (a)

1. Romam tanta ferocia oppugnamus ut nullam salutis spem habeatis. 2. Ille tam ferociter Erycem defenderat ut Marcellus negaret se eum unquam capturum esse. 3. Istam urbem sic defenditis ut nullam victoriae spem habeamus. 4. Adeo feroces erant ut negarent se urbem tradituros esse. 5. Ita male Poeni bellum gerunt ut oppida totius Africae amittant. 6. Istius fortitudo gentis tanta erat ut semper adversarios superarent. 7. Adeo sapiens erat ille ut intellegeret haec esse falsa. 8. Tantum in Africa intestinum bellum exarsit ut, O Poeni, nunc omnia oppida amittatis. 9. Neuter adeo ferox est ut cum illo pugnet. 10. Diximus nunc tandem eos imperium totius Africae amisisse.

Vocabulary 17

Amitto, amīsi, amissum, amittĕre ...to lose

Capio, cēpi, captum, capĕre [1]...to take, to capture

Defendo, defendi, defensum, defendĕre...to defend

Eryx—Erycis, m....a mountain in Sicily.

Exardesco, exarsi, exarsum, exardescĕre...to blaze up, to break out

Falsus, -a, -um...false

Ferōciter...boldly, with bravery (adv.)

Ferox, ferōcis...bold (one termination)

Fortitūdo, -inis, f....bravery

Intellego, intellexi, intellectum, intellegĕre...to perceive, to see

Intestīnus, -a, -um...internal

Marcellus, -i, m....Marcellus

Nunc tandem...now at length (adv.)

Salus, salūtis, f....safety

Sapiens, sapientis...wise (adj.)

Tantus, -a, -um...so great

Trado, tradidi, traditum, tradĕre ...to surrender, to hand over

Tuus, -a, -um...your (when " you " is singular)

Vester, -ra, -rum...your (when " you " is plural)

Note.—It may be as well here to say something of the Negative and Negative sentences. If there is a

[1] See footnote to Vocabulary 15.

" not " in a sentence, or a " no ", or a word compounded of either, such as " none ", " no one ", " nor ", " neither ", we say these sentences are negative; and " not " we call the Negative, the others being negative words. Note carefully that in Final sentences " that not " is *nē*, in Consecutive sentences *ut nōn*.

Here is a beautiful picture from Virgil of Aeneas and the Sibyl entering the Lower World at night :—

Night

Ibant [1] obscuri sola sub nocte per umbram
perque domos Ditis vacuas et inania regna :
quale [2] per incertam lunam sub luce maligna
est iter in silvis, ubi caelum condidit umbra
Juppiter, et rebus nox abstulit [3] atra colorem.
—*Aeneid*, VI, 269.

LESSON XVIII

ALIUS.—THE GERUND

Revise the Perfect and Pluperfect Subjunctive of all four conjugations, and re-read now the previous chapter, on Consecutive clauses, and the lesson (XII) on *Cum* with the Subjunctive when it translates " when " with a past tense in English.

Alius, alia, aliud

The Latin word for " other " is *alius, alia, aliud*. Compare this with *ille, illa, illud* and *iste, ista, istud*. Note carefully the genitive and dative singular.

[1] " They went." Imperfect of *eo*, " I go ".
[2] " just as " agreeing with *iter* : introduces a simile.
[3] " has taken away from the world " (*lit*. " from things ").

| | Singular. | | | Plural. | | |
	Masc.	Fem.	Neut.	Masc.	Fem.	Neut.
Nom.	Alius	alia	aliud	Aliī	aliae	alia
Acc.	Alium	aliam	aliud	Aliōs	aliās	alia
Gen.	Alīus	alīus	alīus	Aliōrum	aliārum	aliōrum
Dat.	Aliī	aliī	aliī	Aliīs	aliīs	aliīs
Abl.	Aliō	aliā	aliō	Aliīs	aliīs	aliīs

Note.—Alii...alii = some...others.

The Gerund

Am-andum   Mon-endum   Reg-endum   Aud-iendum

Each is declined like a neuter noun of the Second Declension—*amandum, -i, -o, -o,* etc., *but has no nominative.*

The Gerund is always formed from the Present stem :—

> In the First Conjugation by adding *-andum.*
>   " Second   "   "   *-endum.*
>   " Third   "   "   *-endum.*
>   " Fourth   "   "   *-iendum.*

It is a *verbal noun, i.e.* it is declined like a noun, but acts in certain ways like a verb. For instance, it is modified by adverbs and can govern a case. It is translated by the corresponding English noun in " -ing "—loving, advising, ruling, hearing.

> *Haec sunt utilia ad scribendum.*
> These things are useful for writing.
> *Nullum locum nocendi eis dedit.*
> He gave them no opportunity (place) of injuring.

In the following sentence it has an adverb with it :—

> *Haec sunt utilia ad bene vivendum.*
> These things are useful for living well (for a good life).

In this one it governs a case :—

> *Parcendo hostibus vincēmus.*
> By sparing the enemy we shall conquer.

Here *parcendo* (from the verb *parcĕre,* to spare)

governs a *dative*, because *parcere* governs a *dative*, as it is really an intransitive verb meaning " to be merciful ".

Exercise 18 (*a*)

1. Illo tempore tam magnopere timebamus ut auxilia ab Romanis petiverimus atque impetraverimus. 2. Cum Poeni in Sicilia omnia amisissent pacem conciliaverunt. 3. Erycem tanta fortitudine defendebant ut Romani de victoria desperarent. 4. Cum, O Romani, belli finem facere statuissetis, rem Regulo permisistis. 5. Adeo cupiditate bellandi flagrabat ut recusaverit ex Sicilia decedere. 6. Alii studio pugnandi flagrabant, alii decedendi. 7. Cum haec inutilia ad bene vivendum cognovissent abjecerunt. 8. Tot mercenarii milites desciverunt ut Poeni desperent. 9. Aliis studium bellandi permittitis. 10. Parcendo vitae aliorum amorem et amicitiam conciliabitis.

Vocabulary 18

Abicio, abiēci, abiectum, abicěre [1] ...to cast away

Bello, -are...make war

Benĕ...well (adv.)

Bona, -orum, n....property (plural of *bonus*)

Cognosco, cognŏvi, cognĭtum, cognoscere...to discover, to know

Descisco, descīvi, descītum, desciscěre...to revolt

Despēro, despēravi, despēratum, despērare...to despair

Etiam...even (adv.)

Inutilis, -e...useless

Magnopere...greatly (adv.)

Mercenarius, -a, -um...mercenary

Perdo, perdidi, perdĭtum, perděre ...to destroy

Permitto, -mīsi, -missum, -mittěre ...to entrust, impart, allow

Peto, petīvi (or *petii*), *petĭtum, petěre*...to seek

Regulus, -i, m....Regulus (a famous Roman)

Statuo, statui, statūtum, statuěre ...to resolve

Studium, -ii n....desire

Timeo, timui, timēre...to be afraid

Tot...so many (indeclinable pron.)

Vita, -ae, f....life

Vivo, vixi, victum, vivěre...to live

[1] See footnote to Vocabulary 15.

Latin in English

1. referendum.
2. modus operandi (" of working ").
3. modus vivendi.
4. innuendo (*lit.* " by nodding ").
5. solvitur ambulando.

A Line of Ennius

Unus homo nobis cunctando [1] restituit rem.

The man was Quintus Fabius, the Roman general, who saved the Roman State by his delaying tactics in the Second Punic War and was called " Cunctator " in consequence.

A Proverb

Nihil agendo homines male agere discunt.

The Death of a Pet Sparrow

These charming and sympathetic lines are from a poem written by *Catullus* to his lady-love on the death of her pet bird. Read them aloud before you try to translate them. The metre is called Hendecasyllables (eleven syllables). Tennyson copied it in a poem beginning " O you chorus of indolent reviewers ". It scans as follows :—

" Look I	cóme to the	tést a	tíny	póem,
All com	posed in a	metre	of Cat	ullus ", etc.
Pásser	mórtuus	ést me-	aé pu-	éllae.

[1] " by delaying."

Lines from Catullus

Passer mortuus est meae puellae,
Passer deliciae meae puellae,
Quem plus illa oculis suis [1] amabat,
Nam mellitus erat suamque norat [2]
Ipsam [3] tam bene quam puella matrem.
Nec sese a gremis illius movebat,
Sed circumsiliens modo huc modo illuc
Ad solam dominam usque pipilabat.
Qui nunc it [4] per iter tenebricosum
Illuc, unde negant redire quemquam.[5]
O factum male, vae miselle [6] passer !
Tua nunc opera meae puellae
Flendo turgiduli [6] rubent ocelli.[6]

A most successful translation of this poem has been
made into the dialect of Burns by G. S. Davies :—

Weep, weep, ye Loves and Cupids all,
And ilka Man o' decent feelin' :
My lassie's lost her wee, wee bird,
And that's a loss, ye'll ken, past healin'.

The lassie lo'ed him like her een :
The darling wee thing lo'ed the ither,
And knew and nestled to her breast,
As ony bairnie to her mither.

[1] Ablative of comparison, " than her eyes ".
[2] *norat*, contraction for *noverat*.
[3] Servants called their " mistress " *ipsa*.
[4] *it*, " goes ", from *eo*, " I go ".
[5] *quemquam:* acc. of *quisquam*, " anyone " (usually in negative
sentences).
[6] Diminutives of *miser, turgidus, oculus*, expressing affection or
pity. " Poor little . . ."

Her bosom was his dear, dear haunt—
So dear, he cared na lang to leave it;
He'd nae but gang his ain sma' jaunt,
And flutter piping back bereavit.

The wee thing's gane the shadowy road
That's never travelled back by ony:
Out on ye, Shades! ye're greedy aye
To grab at aught that's brave and bonny.

Puir, foolish, fondling, bonnie bird,
Ye little ken what wark ye're leavin':
Ye've gar'd my lassie's een grow red,
Those bonnie een grow red wi' grievin'.

LESSON XIX

PERFECT TENSES OF THE PASSIVE AND *SUM*, ETC.— A AND ABLATIVE

We cannot take the verb in the passive until we know the conjugation of the verb *esse*, " to be ". This is an irregular verb, so called because it does not form its tenses and persons according to the rules laid down for the four conjugations previously given. Turn to the Table of Verbs (p. 288), and learn the tenses that come from the Present stem, both *Indicative* and *Subjunctive*. Note the following points :—

1. The *Present Indicative* is very irregular.

2. The *Imperfect Indicative* has just the terminations and nothing more of the Pluperfect Active of the regular verb, *eram*, *eras*, *erat*, etc.

3. The *Future Indicative* has just the Future Perfect terminations of the regular verb, but instead of *erint* we have *erunt*.

4. The *Imperfect Subjunctive* has the Pluperfect Subjunctive endings of the regular verb, with *e* for *i*.

These hints should aid your memory considerably. If now we take the *Supine stem* in each Conjugation—

| Amatum | Monitum | Rectum | Auditum |

and change the final *m* into *s*, we get the *Past Participle Passive*—

Amātus, -a, -um	. .	Having been loved
Monitus, -a, -um	. .	Having been warned (or advised)
Rectus, -a, -um	. .	Having been ruled
Audītus, -a, -um	. .	Having been heard

declined in each case like an adjective of the first class. If you combine this with the Present Indicative of *sum* you get the *Perfect Indicative Passive*—

Amātus (-a, -um) sum	I have been loved *or* I was loved
Amātus (-a, -um) es	Thou hast been loved *or* thou wast loved
Amātus (-a, -um) est	He has been loved *or* he was loved
Amāti (-ae, -a) sumus	We have been loved *or* we were loved
Amāti (-ae, -a) estis	You have been loved *or* you were loved
Amāti (-ae, -a) sunt	They have been loved *or* they were loved

If you combine it with the Imperfect Indicative of *sum* you get the *Pluperfect Indicative Passive*—

Amātus (-a, -um) eram	. .	I had been loved
Amātus (-a, -um) eras	. .	Thou hadst been loved
Amātus (-a, -um) erat	. .	He had been loved
Amāti (-ae, -a) eramus	. .	We had been loved
Amāti (-ae, -a) eratis	. .	You had been loved
Amāti (-ae, -a) erant	. .	They had been loved

If you combine it with the Future of *sum* you get the *Future Perfect Indicative Passive*—

Amatus (-a, -um) erō	. .	I shall have been loved
Amatus (-a, -um) eris	. .	Thou wilt have been loved
Amatus (-a, -um) erit	. .	He will have been loved
Amati (-ae, -a) erimus	. .	We shall have been loved
Amati (-ae, -a) eritis	. .	You will have been loved
Amati (-ae, -a) erunt	. .	They will have been loved

In a similar way you may form the corresponding Passive tenses in the other four Conjugations (see the Table of Verbs). You observe that the subject of the verb is in all these cases being acted on. The forms of the verb which show that the subject is being acted on are called the *Passive* voice of the verb (Latin *patior*, to suffer). Remember you must make *amatus*, or whatever Perfect Participle you are using, agree with the subject of the verb in gender, number and case (always nominative, of course).

Ablative of Agent and Instrument

1. *Caesar a Bruto interfectus est.*
   Caesar was killed by Brutus.
2. *Caesar pugione interfectus est.*
   Caesar was killed with a dagger.

In the first sentence, the action is performed by a living person, Brutus. We call him the *agent*. In the second, the action is performed by an inanimate thing— a dagger. We call this the *instrument*.

The agent is always put into the ablative case with the preposition *a* or *ab*. (*Ab* is always used when the following word begins with a vowel or with *h*; before other words *a* is generally used.) The instrument is always put into the ablative, but without a preposition. We may combine both in one sentence—

Caesar a Bruto pugione interfectus est.

Exercise 19 (a)

1. Cum in Sicilia essemus ab urbe discessit. 2. Spectandi causa statuas diu Athenis illi erant. 3. Caesar ubi Romae erit (see Note at end of Vocabulary

19) leges conservabit.   4. Tunc festinabant ut Romae illo die essent.   5. Ille pugnans a Gallo ingenti corpore occisus est.   6. Illi captivi post pugnam Cannensem ab Hannibale occisi erant.   7. Tunc quidem ex Graecia decedemus ubi ab Romanis victi erimus.   8. Si hoc proelio victi erunt Carthaginienses, in magno periculo erunt.   9. Post subactas bellicosissimas gentes a servo in itinere interfectus est.   10. Femina a servo, cui multa dona dederat, prodita est.

Vocabulary 19

Bellicōsissimus, -a, -um...very warlike, most warlike
Cannensis, -e...at Cannae (literally : belonging to Cannae, a town in Italy) (adj.)
Capitōlium, -ii, n....the Capitol
Causa, (prep.) with gen....for the purpose of
Discēdo, -cessi, -cessum, -cēdĕre... to depart
Diu...long, for a long time (adv.)
Femīna, -ae, f....woman
Festīno, -avi, -atum, -are...to hasten
Graecia, -ae, f....Greece

Ingens, ingentis...huge
Iter, itinĕris, n....journey
Lex, lēgis, f....law
Nunc quidem...just now
Prōdo, -didi, ditum, -dĕre...to betray
Profecto...certainly (adv.)
Pugiō, pugiōnis, m....dagger
Pugna, -ae, f....battle
Servus, -i, m....slave
Subigo, subēgi, subactum, subigĕre...to subdue
Tunc or *tum*...then (adv.)
Tunc quidem...just then, then indeed (adv.)

Note.—In the third sentence of Exercise 19 (*a*), and in the third and fourth of Exercise 19 (*b*), note that the meaning is : " When Caesar shall be ", not " shall have been "; " If I shall be " and " When you shall be ", not " If I shall have been " and " When you shall have been ".

LESSON XX

PERFECT TENSES OF *SUM*.—THIRD PERSON SINGULAR PASSIVE OF VERBS.—COMPOUNDS OF *SUM*

The tenses of the verb *esse* (to be) which come from the Perfect stem (which is *fu-*) are formed quite regularly. You merely add the terminations you have learned already for these tenses to this stem *fu-*. Turn now to the table of the verb *esse* and learn these before going farther.

Note that there is no Supine in the verb *to be* : but there is a Future Participle, *futūrus, -a, -um,* " about to be ". Add *esse* (to be) to this and you form the Future Infinitive, *futurus esse,* " to be about to be ".

General Hint on the Passive Voice

One general hint about the Passive Voice of the regular verbs may be given here. If to the third person singular and plural of the tenses formed from the Present stem you add *-ur* you get the corresponding Passive form in each case. Thus, *amat* means " he loves ", *amatur* " he is loved "; so *amant, amantur.* And again *amābat* means " he was loving ", *amābatur* " he was being loved "; so *amābant, amābantur.* And so you may form this person in all the tenses (Indicative and Subjunctive) formed from the *Present stem* in each Conjugation. (Consult the tables for illustrations.) So, for example, if you wish to form the third person singular Imperfect Subjunctive Passive of *audio,* find the Active and add *-ur*; thus *audiret, audiretur.* *Observe* this holds good only in the third person singular and in the third person plural.

Compounds of Sum

Once you have mastered *sum* you can conjugate a good many verbs without any difficulty, as *sum* forms many compounds. These compounds, it is worth remembering, usually take a *dative* after them. Two common ones are *prōsum*, " I benefit, I do good to ", and *praesum*, " I am at the head of ". These are simply *sum* with the prefixes *pro* and *prae*. However, in *prosum* (and in *prosum* only), if the *o* of *pro* is followed by an *e* you insert a *d* between the two. Thus, *prodes*, *prodest*; but *profui*, *prosunt*, and so on.

Exercitui praefuit or *praeerat.* He was at the head of the army.
Rei publicae proderat. He used to do good to the State.

Exercise 20 (*a*)

1. Erycem sic defendimus ut bellum eo loco gestum esse non videretur. 2. Tanta bella tum exarserunt ut hae urbes paene delerentur. 3. Cum centum milia facta essent militum mercenariorum, a muris Karthaginis eos removit. 4. Illa urbs maximo barbarorum numero obsidebatur. 5. Tam ferociter pugnaverunt ut hostes expellerentur. 6. Locorum angustiis clausae feminae fame ac morbo interficiebantur. 7. Romae Hannibal fuit, non Romani Carthagine. 8. Ante urbem ab Hispanis obsessam magnus Poenorum numerus interfectus est. 9. Fuerant sapientes, fortes, bellicosi, omnibus in rebus satis periti. 10. Eis malis adeo sunt mulieres perterritae ut auxilium petiverint.

PERFECT TENSES OF *SUM*   105
Vocabulary 20

Angustiae, -arum, f....narrowness (narrow places, straits)
Barbărus, -i, m....barbarian
Centum...a hundred (numeral adj., not declined)
Claudo, clausi, clausum, claudĕre...to shut in
Expello, -puli, -pulsum, -pellĕre...to drive out
Fames, famis, f....famine, hunger
Loca, -orum, n. pl....places, position
Mala, orum, n. pl....ills
Malus, -a, -um...bad

Milia, -ium, n. pl....thousands (noun)
Morbus, -i, m....disease
Mulier, -eris, f....woman
Obsideo, -sēdi, -sessum, -sidēre...to besiege
Paene...almost (adv.)
Peritus, -a, -um...skilled
Perterreo, -terrui, -territum, -terrēre...to terrify
Plures, plura...more (adj.)
Satis...enough, sufficiently (adv.)
Similis, -e...like (adj.)
Vexo, -avi, -atum, āre...to harass

Revision of Vocabulary:

Out of the Latin words you have already learnt, write down those to which the following English words are related—

inspection, patriotic, provincial, ferocious, intellectual, abject, perdition, itinerary, expulsion, vexatious.

A Night Scene from Virgil

Nox erat, et placidum carpebant fessa soporem [1]
Corpora per terras, silvaeque et saeva quierant [2]
Aequora, cum medio volvuntur sidera lapsu,[3]
Cum tacet omnis ager, pecudes pictaeque [4] volucres,
Quaeque lacus late liquidos quaeque aspera dumis [5]
Rura tenent, somno positae [6] sub nocte silenti
Lenibant [7] curas et corda oblita [8] laborum.

[1] *sopor*, " sleep ".
[2] *quierant* is contracted for *quieverant*, pluperfect of *quiesco*, " I rest ".
[3] *medio . . . lapsu*, *lit.* " the stars are rolled round in the middle movement ", *i.e.* midway in their gliding path.
[4] *pictae*, " painted ", *i.e.* of various colours.
[5] *dumus*, " a thicket ".   [6] *positae: v. pono*.
[7] *lenibant*, contraction for *leniebant*, " smoothed ".
[8] *oblita laborum*, " forgetful of labours ".

HINTS FOR LATIN TRANSLATION

We are now ready to read two short passages taken from *Cornelius Nepos*, one of the lesser Roman historians. He lived in the time of Cicero and Julius Caesar, in the first century before the birth of Christ. Most of his works are lost, but from what remains he is not among the great Roman writers. However, the plainness of his style and his usually short sentences and limited vocabulary are an advantage to beginners. He wrote some short biographies of famous men, and of these we have chosen for reading the lives of Hamilcar and Hannibal, father and son. They were in turn military leaders of Carthage, a flourishing merchant city on the north coast of Africa, which for a long time struggled with Rome for supremacy in the Mediterranean. In the first war Hamilcar was the Carthaginian leader; in the second, his more famous son, Hannibal, who carried the war even to the gates of Rome. He crossed the Alps with an army and with elephants, made a lightning march southward, and came very near to destroying the Roman power in the ancient world.

Read the whole piece through slowly in Latin, first to yourself and then aloud, trying to see the natural thought-groups into which the sentences fall. From this you will begin to see something of the general meaning of the passage, and you have now to consider it in detail.

Look first for a verb in the Indicative Mood; this is usually found at or near the end of the sentence. See whether this is singular or plural, and then look for the subject, which of course will be a noun or pronoun in the Nominative Case, and singular or plural according as the verb is singular or plural. The subject is usually near the beginning of the sentence. From the meaning of the verb (which you will find, if you do not know it already, in the general Vocabulary at the end of the book) you will be able to tell if it requires an object. If it does, look for this next. The object will be a noun or pronoun in the Accusative Case. You will notice, as a general rule in Latin, at the beginning of each clause a word, usually a conjunction or relative pronoun, joining the sentence to the preceding one. With the nouns in the nominative or accusative there may be adjectives in agreement. Besides these four things, connective, nominative or subject (with adjectives), accusative or object (with adjectives), and verb, some words or phrases may be left. These are frequently nouns and adjectives in the ablative, dative or genitive. The first two are nearly always connected with the verb; the genitive is more commonly connected with some noun. Thus the ablative, from what you know already, may tell the time at which the action of the verb took place, the place where it occurred, or the means by which it was performed. The genitive often describes some quality of the thing or person named by the noun—*vir summi ingenii*, a man of the greatest ability. The dative is usually closely connected with some verb. Though it is helpful at first to analyse a Latin sentence in this way, noticing particularly the terminations rather than the beginnings of words, you should try also to comprehend the meaning in the Latin order. In a long and involved sentence this is often difficult, but it is well worth acquiring the habit, as the Latin order is the order of the Latin thought and no small clue to its meaning.

Now let us tackle, with these hints, the first sentence in the passage No. 1 given on p. 111 :—

You have to look to the second last word for the verb—*coepit*. *Praeesse* is of course a verb, but you will at once see it is not Indicative Mood. *Coepit* is third person singular (ending in -*it*). Looking up the Vocabulary you find it is Perfect tense and means " began ". *Coepit*, then, is third person singular Perfect Indicative. A glance at the beginning presents *Hamilcar* as the first nominative; but in quick succession you get *pater*, *Barca*, *Karthaginiensis*, all evidently Nominative Case. Here, then, are four nominatives, four subjects to the verb ! Not so : the three later nominatives must be in apposition, else the verb would be plural, for two or more singular nominatives, as in English, require a verb in the plural. You now translate *Hamilcar coepit*, " Hamilcar began ", and you feel you require an object, to tell you what he began ; but on looking you find no noun in the Accusative Case. The word *praeesse* gets us out of the difficulty. Very often a verb which you feel requires an object in the Accusative Case takes an Infinitive to fill out its meaning. Translating *praeesse* now you get, " Hamilcar began to be in command ". The remainder of the sentence consists of three phrases, *primo Poenico bello*, *temporibus extremis*, *in Sicilia*; with an adverb *admodum*, a nominative *adulescentulus*, an ablative *cognomine*, and a dative *exercitui*. *Adulescentulus* must go with the subject, and must be a nominative in apposition. The first two phrases may be ablative or dative : you will find they cannot be translated as datives. Try them with " to " or " for " after the verb *coepit* : " He began to the last times ", " to the first Punic war ". This makes no sense. They must, then, be ablatives. Try them as Ablatives of Time : " Hamilcar, in the first Punic war, but in the last times, began to be in command ". This gives some sense, so we go on. *In Sicilia* offers no difficulty : it means " in Sicily ", *in*, the preposition, taking the Ablative Case. *Cognomine* is the ablative singular of *cognomen*, " a surname ", by, with, or from a surname, that is, " Barca by name ". The Vocabulary tells you *admodum* is an adverb, meaning " very ", " quite ". It goes, then, with a *verb, adjective* or *adverb*. Adverbs usually precede the words they go with. It must, then, go with *adulescentulus*, which is practically an adjective : " quite a young man " gives good sense. If it went with the verbs *praeesse* or *coepit*, it would be placed nearer them. *Exercitui* alone remains, and you remember *praeesse* governs a dative (being a compound of *sum*). This, then, will naturally be dative after *praeesse*. Your sentence now runs :—

" Hamilcar, father of Hannibal, by surname Barca, a Carthaginian, in the first Punic War, but in the last times (*or* days), quite a young man, began in Sicily to be in command of the army."

Now, all the passages—and all Latin sentences, in fact—must be treated carefully after this manner. The process is slow at first ; but, if faithfully followed out, it soon makes the work very easy, and is the only way to ensure accuracy. Pay particular attention to the endings of the words : they are the most important parts of words in Latin. Without them you could do nothing : a sentence deprived of them would at once become nonsense. Never pass a noun without being able to tell what case it is in and why it is in that case. Never pass a verb without telling its mood, number and tense. Above all, never be in a hurry : always take plenty of time to the sentence you are at. Do not worry about it. If you find a sentence beats you, pass on to the next one, and return to the difficulty when the light of the remainder of the passage has been thrown on it. *Never write nonsense as a translation*, or anything which you do not understand *yourself*. The passages *all* have a meaning. After you have done your best and think your version is fairly correct, turn to the Key at the end of the book and compare your translation with it. If you use this Key to *solve* the difficulties, you will never go far in Latin. You will remain in the state of the man who never tries to swim without the swimming-belt. Two translations will be given at first—one very close to the Latin, not proper English at all; the other rather freer and more like what an Englishman would write. If you have not exactly the same translation as the Key, you are not necessarily wrong. See if the *meaning* is the same in your copy and in the Key. There is always a variety of translations for any passage in any language.

No special vocabularies will be given now. You must make your own vocabulary. This is the plan you ought to adopt in all your future reading. When a word occurs which you do not know, or a phrase which you think worth remembering, jot it down in a special

note-book.   This consultation of the general Vocabulary
at the end will prepare you for the use of a dictionary
after you have finished this book and started to read
for yourself.

N.B.—The key to the following passages—*Life of
Hamilcar, Life of Hannibal*, etc.—is given in Part III.

Passage No. I

LIFE OF HAMILCAR, FATHER OF HANNIBAL

Hamilcar, Hannibalis pater, cognomine Barca, Karthaginiensis, primo Poenico bello, sed temporibus
extremis admodum adulescentulus in Sicilia praeesse
coepit exercitui. *cum* ante eius adventum et mari et
terra male res *gererentur* Karthaginiensium, ipse, ubi
adfuit, numquam *hosti* cessit neque locum nocendi
dedit, saepeque e contrario *occasione data* lacessivit
semperque *superior* discessit. *quo facto*, cum paene
omnia in Sicilia Poeni amisissent, ille Erycem sic
defendit, *ut* bellum eo loco gestum non *videretur*.
interim Karthaginienses classe apud insulas Aegates a
C. Lutatio, consule Romanorum, superati,[1] statuerunt [2]
belli facere finem eamque rem arbitrio permiserunt
Hamilcaris.

Notes on the Words in Italics

Extremis : this is a superlative with no positive. Its comparative is *exterior*, and means " outer ". It is therefore irregular. It
means " outmost " or " last ".

Cum : We have said this with a Past tense takes the Subjunctive
and means *when* or *since*; it may also mean *although*. This is the
meaning here.

Gererentur : find what *gererent* is, and this is the Passive of it.

---

[1] *Superati classe,* " defeated by a fleet ".
[2] *Statuo* takes the Infinitive after it.

Hosti : is dative after *cessit* (from *cedo*). If you have any difficulty in finding the Present of the verb in the Vocabulary owing to the change (as, for example, *cedo, cessi*) from Present to Perfect, or for any other reason, consult the Table of Irregular Verbs given at the end of the book.

Occasione data : you can be pretty sure when an ablative has a Participle with it that it is Ablative Absolute, as here.

Superior : the positive of this adjective is *superus*, upper, applied to a thing which is above another; comparative is *superior* as here, higher, superior; superlative is *supremus* or *summus*, highest.

Quo facto : note the relative connecting this sentence to the one before, where we would say " on this being done ". *Quo facto* is, of course, Ablative Absolute.

Ut . . . videretur : this is consecutive *ut*, " so that ". *Esse* should be understood after *gestum*.

LESSON XXI
PRESENT, IMPERFECT AND FUTURE INDICATIVE PASSIVE.—GERUNDIVE

These are tenses formed from the Present Stem. They are each formed from the Active in the same way.

To the first person singular ending in a vowel add *r*. Thus *amo*, Active; *amor*, Passive. When ending in *m* change *m* into *r*—*amābam, amābar*.

For the second person singular change *s* into *ris* or *re*—*amās, amāris* or *amāre*.

For the third person singular (as explained in Lesson XX) add *ur*—*amat, amātur*.

For the first person plural change *s* into *r*—*amāmus, amāmur*.

For the second person plural change *tis* into *mini*—*amātis, amāminī*.

For the third person plural (as explained in Lesson XX) add *ur*—*amant, amantur*.

Thus also—

Moneō *gives* moneor;	mones *gives* monēris *or* monēre, etc.
Regō *gives* regor;	regis *gives* regēris *or* regēre, etc.
Audiō *gives* audior;	audis *gives* audīris *or* audīre, etc.

In the second person singular Present Indicative of the Third Conjugation you find *regĕris* where you might expect *regĭris*, and in the second person singular Future Indicative of the First and Second Conjugations *amāberis* where you might expect *amabiris*, and *monēbĕris* where you might expect *monebiris*.

In the first and second persons plural by these rules

Monēmus *gives* monēmur;	monētis *gives* monēminī, etc.
Regimus *gives* regimur;	regitis *gives* regimini, etc.
Audīmus *gives* audīmur;	audītis *gives* audīminī, etc.

and similarly you form the other two tenses.

The Gerund and Gerundive

The *Gerundive is an adjective* got by changing the *m* of the Gerund into *s*. Thus *amandum, amandus*. It is declined like an adjective of the first class (*-us, -a, -um*), and means " to-be-loved, advised ", etc.

If we wish to translate a sentence like the following into Latin, we must use the nominative of the Gerund :—

> We must pay regard to peace.
> *Paci a nobis serviendum est.*
> (There is a need-to-pay-regard to peace by us.)

But if *servio* had been a transitive verb (taking the accusative case), we must have used the *Gerundive*. Thus *servare* (to preserve) is a transitive verb, and therefore takes an accusative case. The sentence " We must preserve peace " is in Latin therefore *Pax nobis servanda est* (not *Pacem nobis servandum est*), " Peace is to-be-preserved by us ". With the Gerund and Gerundive in this sense, the agent is put in the dative, not in the ablative with *a* or *ab*—unless, as in the first sentence above, there is a dative with the verb already, when the ablative is used to prevent ambiguity.

Rule.—With an intransitive verb use the nominative of the Gerund to express necessity and the dative of the agent (the person on whom the necessity rests), or the ablative with *a* or *ab* if there would be confusion with another dative. With a transitive verb the verbal adjective, *i.e.* the Gerundive, in the nominative case, in agreement with the noun.

Examples

1. They must spare the enemy.
   Hostibus ab eis parcendum est.
   (There is a necessity-to-be-merciful to the enemy by them.)

Parcěre, " to spare ", is intransitive, taking a dative after it.

2. The Romans must attack the city.
   Urbs Romanis oppugnanda est.
   (The city is necessary-to-be-attacked by the Romans.)

Oppugnare is a transitive verb taking the accusative.

Compare these remarks now with those in Lesson XVIII on the Gerund.

3. *Urbem sacerdotibus defendendam tradunt.*
   They hand over the city to be defended by the priests.

The Gerundive Construction

In Lesson XVIII you were taught how to translate a sentence like :—

> *Vincemus hostibus parcendo.*
> We shall conquer by sparing the enemy.

But this is not always a possible construction if the Gerund has the accusative after it. Thus we might say,

Hi pacem conciliandi causa venerunt.
These men have come for-the-sake-of-making peace (to make peace).

where we have used the genitive of the Gerund followed
by an accusative. But the Romans preferred to say,

Hi pacis conciliandae causa venerunt.
These men have come for-the-sake-of peace necessary-to-be-made.
N.B.—*causa* usually follows the Gerundive.

In the second construction we have used the
Gerundive in agreement with the noun, the whole
phrase being in the *case* the Gerund would have been in.
This Gerundive construction *must* always be used when
the Gerund would be in the accusative or dative. In
the ablative and genitive either Gerund or Gerundive
may be used. *Hi ad pacem conciliandum venerunt* must
never be used, but *Hi ad pacem conciliandam venerunt.*
So *Decemviros legibus scribendis creaverunt*: They
appointed Decemvirs for laws necessary-to-be-drawn-
up, *that is*, for the drawing up of laws *or* to draw up
laws; not *leges scribendo* (dative of Gerund). But you
may have either, *Colendo agros divites erimus* or
Colendis agris divites erimus: We shall be rich by
cultivating the fields; and *pacis conciliandae causa* or
pacem conciliandi causa : For the sake of making peace.
But the Gerundive is more usual.

When the noun in the genitive is plural and is of the
first or second declension, and the genitive if used would
cause two consecutive words to end in *-orum* or *-arum*,
the Gerundive is never employed. Thus *Romanorum
videndorum causa* would never be used for *Romanos
videndi causa* : For the sake of seeing the Romans.

Summary of Gerund and Gerundive Constructions

1. The Gerund is a Verbal Noun, is *active* and is
declined in the singular.

2. The Gerundive is a Verbal Adjective, is *passive* and is declined in both singular and plural.

3. *The Gerund* of an Intransitive verb in the *nominative* case involves the idea of " must ".

e.g. *Mihi est eundum* = I must go.

4. In all other cases there is no idea of " must ".

e.g. *Studiosus erat canendi* = He was keen on singing.

Exercise 21 (*a*)

If you are still uncertain of the conjugation of the passive voice, this short exercise will give you practice. Turn the following sentences from active to passive, or from passive to active (for Key see p. 262):

1. Milites urbem obsident. 2. Femina servis rosas dedit.[1] 3. Cleopatra Antonium maxime amabat. 4. Castra aggeribus contra hostes muniet. 5. Puellae a barbaris captae sunt. 6. Omnia in Hispania ab isto imperatore iam amissa sunt.

Passage No. 2

LIFE OF HAMILCAR (*continued*)

In this piece there are one or two rather difficult things. It will help you if you consult the fuller notes in the Key.

Compositurum : supply *esse* after this word.
Nisi ille . . . decederent : " unless he and his friends should depart " (*ille cum suis* takes a plural verb).
Periturum : supply *esse* after this word.
Quam rediret : " than (he would) return home ".
Ut succumbente patria : this is the consecutive clause after *tanta fuit ferocia*.
Suae esse virtutis : " to be the (quality) of his valour ", so " to be consistent with his valour ".

---

[1] For principal parts of *do* see Vocabulary.

Ille, etsi flagrabat bellandi cupiditate, tamen paci serviendum putavit, quod patriam exhaustam sumptibus, diutius calamitates belli ferre [1] non posse [2] intellegebat, hoc consilio pacem conciliavit, in quo tanta fuit ferocia, cum Catulus negaret bellum *compositurum, nisi ille* cum suis, qui Erycem tenuerant, armis relictis Sicilia *decederent, ut succumbente patria* ipse periturum se potius dixerit, *quam* cum tanto flagitio domum *rediret*: non enim *suae esse virtutis* arma a patria accepta adversus hostes adversariis tradere. huius pertinaciae cessit Catulus.

Latin Gerundives in English

1. Amanda (*i.e.* lovable).
   Miranda (*i.e.* admirable).
2. agenda.
3. propaganda.
4. memoranda.
5. addenda.
6. corrigenda.
7. mutatis mutandis (*lit.*, "the things to be changed having been changed"—Ablative Absolute).

Latin Phrases and Thoughts

1. De gustibus non disputandum.
2. Q.E.D.—quod erat demonstrandum.
3. Q.E.F.—quod erat faciendum.
4. Delenda est Carthago.—*Cato*.
5. Nil desperandum.—*Horace*.

---

[1] *Ferre :* Present Infinitive = to bear, to endure. An irregular verb : see Lesson XXVIII.

[2] *Posse :* Present Infinitive = to be able. An irregular verb : see Lesson XXVI.

6. Nunc est bibendum, nunc pede libero
   pulsanda tellus (understand " est ").—*Horace.*
7. Quidquid erit, superanda omnis fortuna ferendo est.
   —*Virgil.*

LESSON XXII

COMPARISON OF ADJECTIVES.—ABLATIVE OF COMPARISON.—GENITIVE AFTER SUPERLATIVES.—IRREGULAR COMPARISONS

The Comparison of Adjectives

In English we can talk of one thing being *hard*, of another being *harder*, and of a third being *hardest* of all. These three forms express different degrees, as they are called, of the quality named by the adjective. The first is called the Positive Degree, the second the Comparative Degree, the third the Superlative Degree. In English the two latter are usually formed by adding *-er* and *-est* to the Positive form. In Latin we add *-ior* and *-issimus* to the stem of the adjective (got by dropping the genitive termination). Thus Positive *durus*, Genitive *duri*, hard, gives Comparative *durior*, harder, Superlative, *durissimus*, hardest. Similarly Positive *ingens*, Genitive *ingentis*, Comparative *ingentior*, Superlative *ingentissimus*.

Adjectives like *asper* and *niger*, however, in the superlative double the *r* and add *-imus*. Thus :—

Positive.	Genitive.	Comparative.	Superlative.
Asper	asperi	asperior	asperrimus
Niger	nigri	nigrior	nigerrimus

Adjectives of the Third Declension like *acer, acris, acre*, also come under this rule. Thus :—

Acer	acris	acrior	acerrimus

You notice in these, from the presence of *e*, that the superlative is not formed from the genitive, but from the nominative.

Exceptions

Facilis, -e, easy   *Humilis, -e*, low   *Similis, -e*, like
Difficilis, -e, difficult   *Gracilis, -e*, slender   *Dissimilis, -e*, unlike

These adjectives form the superlative in a similar manner by doubling the *l* and adding *-imus* :—

Facilis   facilior   facillimus

The Superlative forms are declined like adjectives of the First Class, *asperrimus, -a, -um*, etc.

The Comparatives are declined thus :—

	Singular.			Plural.	
	Masc. & Fem.	Neut.		Masc. & Fem.	Neut.
Nom.	Durior	durius		Duriōrēs	duriōra
Acc.	Duriorem	durius		Duriōrēs	duriōra
Gen.	Duriōris			Duriōrum	
Dat.	Duriōri			Duriōribus	
Abl.	Duriōre			Duriōribus	

Sometimes the comparative, instead of expressing a higher degree, expresses too high a degree of the quality named by the adjective. Thus :—

Hoc est durius.   This is too hard.

Similarly the superlative may express a very high degree :—

Hoc est durissimum.   This is very hard.

When two things are compared, after the comparative you may use *quam* (than) and put the two things in the same case, or omit the *quam* when the second thing is put in the ablative case :—

Illud est durius quam hoc (nom. sing. neut.).   That is harder than this.
Illud est hoc (abl. sing. neut. *durius*.   That is harder than this.

The superlative usually has a genitive after it :—

Hoc est omnium durissimum.   This is the hardest of all things.

Irregular Comparisons :

Some adjectives are very common and yet do not form their comparatives and superlatives regularly. One or two of them you may have noticed already. Thus :—

Bonus, good,	gives *melior*, better,		*optimus*, best.
Malus, bad,	„	*pejor*, worse,	*pessimus*, worst.
Magnus, great,	„	*major*, greater,	*maximus*, greatest.
Parvus, small,	„	*minor*, smaller,	*minimus*, smallest.
Multus, many (in plur.)	„	*plus* (n.), more (gen. *pluris*),	*plurimus*, most.

The following four are irregular in the superlative; you have seen most of them already :—

(*Exterus*, outer),	*exterior*, outer,	*extremus*, extreme, outmost.
Inferus, lower,	*inferior*, lower,	*infimus*, *imus*, lowest.
(*Posterus*, later, next),	*posterior*, later,	*postremus* (*postumus*), last.
Superus, upper,	*superior*, upper,	*supremus*, *summus*, highest.

Propior, nearer, and *proximus*, nearest, are also worth noting, also *prior*, former, and *primus*, first. These have no positive adjective.

Sometimes in English we form our comparatives and superlatives by prefixing " more " and " most ", and this method is occasionally used in Latin, the adverb being *magis*, more, and *maxime*, most. This is especially common with adjectives that end in *-ius*. E.g. *magis dubius*, more doubtful; *maxime impius*, most wicked.

Examples :

Id postero die Flaminius senatui detulit.

Flaminius reported that to the senate on the next day.

In imo monte constiterunt.

They halted at the bottom of the hill (at the hill lowest).

In summo monte constiterunt.

They halted on the top of the hill (on the hill topmost).

Note *primum*, firstly, *primo*, at first (adverbs); similarly *postremum*, lastly, *postremo*, at last.

The positives of the adjectives in these sentences may be neglected at present : they are rarely used.

Latin Comparatives and Superlatives in English

You will notice that many Latin comparatives have become English words, e.g. *inferior* and *superior*. Others are

ulterior (further)
excelsior (higher)
junior (younger)
senior (older)
interior (further inside)

Similarly superlatives—e.g. *minimum, maximum.*

Latin Phrases

1. corruptio optimi pessima.
2. a fortiori.
3. a priori.

Tacitus (*adapted*) on the English Climate

Coelum imbribus ac nebulis foedissimum.

A Female Bluebeard

Inscripsit [1] tumulis septem scelerata virorum
    " Se fecisse " [2] Chloe.   quid pote [3] simplicius ? [4]
                                            —*Martial.*

Professor F. A. Wright has neatly turned this into a
limerick :—

" A much married lady was Sue ;
    She thought seven husbands her due.
        When the last one had gone,
        She inscribed on their stone
    ' Susan's work '—and quite natural too ! "

Catullus Pays Cicero a Compliment

Disertissime Romuli [5] nepotum,
quot sunt quotque fuere, [6] Marce [7] Tulli,
quotque post aliis erunt in annis,
gratias [8] tibi maximas Catullus
agit [8] pessimus omnium poeta,
tanto [9] pessimus omnium poeta
quanto [9] tu optimus omnium es patronus.

---

[1] Perfect of *inscribo*.
[2] Perfect Infinitive of *facio*.
[3] *pote = potest*.   Third singular of *possum*, " I am able ".
[4] *simplicior* is the comparative of *simplex*, " simple ".
[5] " Of Romulus ", the builder of Rome and founder of the Roman
race.   His " descendants " mean all Romans.
[6] *fuere*, for *fuerunt*.
[7] *i.e.* Marcus Tullius Cicero.
[8] *gratias agere*, " to thank ".
[9] *tanto . . . quanto*, " by so much . . . by how much "—" as . . .
so ".

Passage No. 3

At ille, ut [1] Karthaginem venit, multo aliter ac [2] sperarat [3] *rem publicam se habentem* [4] cognovit. namque diuturnitate externi mali tantum exarsit intestinum bellum, *ut* numquam in pari periculo *fuerit* Karthago, nisi cum deleta est. primo mercenarii milites, quibus adversus Romanos usi erant,[5] desciverunt : quorum numerus erat *viginti milium*.[6] hi totam abalienarunt [7] Africam, ipsam Karthaginem oppugnarunt.[7] *quibus* malis adeo sunt Poeni perterriti, ut etiam auxilia ab Romanis petierint eaque impetrarint.[8] sed extremo, cum prope iam ad desperationem pervenissent, Hamilcarem imperatorem fecerunt. is non solum hostes a muris Karthaginis removit, cum *amplius* centum milia facta essent armatorum, sed etiam *eo* compulit, *ut* locorum angustiis clausi plures fame quam ferro interirent.

[1] *Ut* with ind. means " as " or " when ".

[2] *Aliter ac :* " otherwise than ". Latin says, " otherwise and ".

[3] *Sperarat* for *speraverat.*

[4] *Res publica aliter se habet :* " the republic is in a different condition "; *literally,* " the republic is holding itself otherwise ".

[5] *Quibus usi erant: utor, uti, usus sum,* a deponent, takes the Ablative Case after it. It means " to use ". For Deponent Verbs see Lesson XXXVIII.

[6] *Viginti milium: mille* is an adjective, indeclinable, meaning " thousand "; but in the plural *milia* is a noun meaning " thousands ", and is declined : Nom. *milia,* Acc. *milia,* Gen. *milium,* Dat. and Abl. *milibus.* Thus : *mille equites,* adj., a thousand horsemen; *tria milia equitum,* three thousands of horsemen.

[7] *Abalienarunt, oppugnarunt: -arunt* for *-averunt.*

[8] *Impetrarint* for *impetraverint.*

N.B.—Consult Key for notes on the words in italics.

LESSON XXIII

PRESENT AND IMPERFECT SUBJUNCTIVE PASSIVE.— INDIRECT COMMAND OR PETITION

These two tenses are formed from the Active by the same changes as were explained in Lesson XXI. Thus :—

Amem	gives	*amer*	*Amēs*	gives	*amēris*
Moneam	,,	*monear*	*Moneās*	,,	*moneāris*
Regam	,,	*regar*	*Regās*	,,	*regāris*
Audiam	,,	*audiar*	*Audiās*	,,	*audiāris*
Amēmus	gives	*amēmur*	*Amētis*	gives	*amēmini*
Moneāmus	,,	*moneāmur*	*Moneātis*	,,	*moneāmini*
Regāmus	,,	*regāmur*	*Regātis*	,,	*regāmini*
Audiāmus	,,	*audiāmur*	*Audiātis*	,,	*audiāmini*

and similarly with the Imperfect Subjunctive.

Indirect Command or Petition

This is expressed quite differently in English and in Latin.   In English we say :—

> He advised him to do this.
> He ordered his soldiers to do this.

But Latin says :—

Monuit eum ut hoc faceret. He advised him that he should do this.

Militibus imperavit ut hoc facerent. He ordered the soldiers that they should do this.

Ut in these sentences does not mean " in order that ", nor yet does it mean " in such a way that ".   It introduces neither a clause of consequence nor a clause of purpose.   This is a new use altogether.   In fact in each case *ut* introduces a clause exactly equivalent to a noun or pronoun after the verb.   Thus in the second clause " to do this " is equivalent to " this " in " He commanded *this* to the soldiers ". This *Noun clause*, as we may call it, introduced by *ut* and having its verb in the Subjunctive, is always used in Latin after verbs of *commanding* or *entreating* and the like. Such a clause is called a Substantival clause (substantive equals noun), and this use of *ut* is called the Substantival use.

The *Rule* is : Verbs of entreating, commanding, decreeing, advising, persuading, striving, effecting, take a clause introduced by *ut* and followed by the Subjunctive in Latin. If there is a *not* or any other negative in the clause, instead of *ut* use *ne*. The tense of the Subjunctive follows the rule of Sequence of Tenses in Purpose clauses (*v.* Lesson XI).

Examples

I ask you to do this.	*A te peto ut hoc facias.*
I ask you not to do this.	*A te peto ne hoc facias.*
The senate decreed that he should do this.	*Senatus decrevit ut is hoc faceret.*
He made it his aim to defeat the enemy.	*Id egit ut hostes superaret.*
He effected that he should be sent into Spain as general (he brought it to pass that he was sent).	*Id effecit ut imperator in Hispaniam mitteretur.*

Here one example of each verb has been given. The principal parts of these verbs are given below :—

Peto, petīvi or *petii, petītum, petĕre,* to ask, to entreat.
Decerno, decrēvi, decrētum, decernĕre, to decree.
Ago, ĕgi, actum, agĕre, to do (*id ago,* I make it my aim).
Efficio, effēci, effectum, efficĕre, to effect.

Exceptions.—*Jubeo* (I bid) and *Veto* (I forbid) take the accusative and infinitive. E.g. *Te jubeo abire,* " I bid you go away ".

Books as Presents

Exigis ut nostros donem tibi, Tucca, libellos.
Non faciam : nam vis [1] vendere, non legere.
—Martial.

Passage No. 4

Omnia oppida abalienata, in his Uticam atque
Hipponem, valentissima totius Africae, restituit *patriae*.
neque eo fuit contentus, sed etiam fines *imperii* pro-
pagavit, *tota Africa* tantum otium reddidit, *ut* nullum
in ea bellum *videretur multis annis* fuisse.

Rebus his *ex sententia* peractis *fidenti animo* atque
infesto Romanis, quo facilius [2] causam bellandi
reperiret, effecit, ut imperator cum exercitu in
Hispaniam mitteretur, eoque secum duxit filium
Hannibalem annorum novem.[3] Erat praeterea cum eo
adulescens illustris, formosus, Hasdrubal ; de hoc ideo
mentionem fecimus, quod Hamilcare occiso ille exercitui praefuit resque magnas gessit, et *princeps* largitione
vetustos pervertit mores Karthaginiensium, eiusdemque
post mortem Hannibal ab exercitu accepit imperium.

LESSON XXIV

PERFECT AND PLUPERFECT SUBJUNCTIVE PASSIVE. —VERBS WITH DATIVE

These two tenses are combinations of the Perfect
Participle Passive and the Present and Imperfect

---

[1] Second singular of *volo*, " you wish ", *v.* Table of Verbs.

[2] *Quo facilius.* When there is a comparative adjective or adverb
in the Final clause, instead of *ut* Latin uses *quo*. Thus—

" By which he might find more easily."
" That he might find more easily."

[3] *Annorum novem.* This is a descriptive genitive, " his son nine
years old ".

Subjunctive respectively of the verb "to be".
Thus :—

Perfect Subjunctive.	Pluperfect Subjunctive.
Amatus sim	*Amatus essem*
Monitus sim	*Monitus essem*
etc.	etc.

Verbs Governing a Dative

Many *intransitive* verbs in Latin *take a dative*, because they require to have their sense completed by *indirect objects*. English requires us to translate them by a transitive verb, though that is not their true meaning.

E.g.,
Parco hostibus. I-am-sparing to the enemy, *i.e.* I spare.
Prosum urbi. I-am-of-advantage to the city, *i.e.* I benefit.
Praesum exercitui. I-am-at-the-head for the army, *i.e.* I command.
Impero militibus. I-give-orders to the soldiers, *i.e.* I order.

The main verbs in Latin taking a dative are comprised in the following lists :—

Confīdo, -ĕre...to trust (*lit.*, to be trusting to)

Faveo, -ēre...to favour (*lit.*, be favourable to)

Impero, -are...to give an order. *Eis imperat ut hoc faciant:* he orders them to do this

Invideo, -ēre...to envy. *Eis invideo :* I envy them (*lit.*, I am envious)

Mĭnor, -ari...to threaten. *Pueris minatur:* he threatens the boys

Obedio, -ire...to be obedient to

Pareo, -ēre...to obey. *Parentibus pareo :* I obey my parents

Persuadeo, -ēre...to persuade. *Eis persuadeo ut hoc faciant :* I persuade them to do this (*lit.*, I am persuasive of something to them)

Prosum, prodesse...to profit. *Prosum tibi :* I do you good.

Resisto, -ĕre...to resist. *Hostibus resistamus :* let us resist the enemy

Servio, -ire...to be of service to. *Regi servimus :* we serve a king.

Suadeo, -ēre...to advise. See *Persuadeo.*

Subvenio, -ire...to help. *Eis subvenio :* I help them (*lit.*, I come up helpfully)

Some of these verbs occasionally take an accusative of the thing and dative of the person.

Haec militibus imperat.
He gives these commands to the soldiers.
Mortem eis minatur.
He threatens death to them (" them with death " in English).
Haec tibi invideo.
I envy these things to you (I envy you these things).

There are of course many other verbs taking a dative, but they are less important. We have had already *cedo*, I yield to; and do not forget that the compounds of *sum*, save *possum*, take a dative.

Latin Quotations

1. Animo imperabit sapiens, stultus serviet.—*P. Syrus.*
2. Tempori parendum.
3. Victrix [1] causa deis placuit, sed victa [2] Catoni.

Passage No. 5

(With this passage we finish the Life of Hamilcar. There is only one thing to note in it before attempting the translation; the verb *mallet*, the last word, is the Imperfect Subjunctive of an irregular verb, *malle*, to prefer. It will be explained more fully in Lesson XXIX.)

At Hamilcar, *posteaquam* mare *transiit*, in Hispaniamque *venit*, magnas res *secunda* gessit *fortuna* : maximas bellicosissimasque gentes subegit, equis, armis, viris, pecunia *totam* locupletavit *Africam*. *hic* cum in Italiam bellum *inferre* meditaretur, *nono anno*

---

[1] Adjective, " conquering ".
[2] Past participle passive of *vinco*, " I conquer ".

postquam in Hispaniam venerat, in proelio pugnans adversus Vettones occisus est. huius perpetuum odium erga Romanos maxime concitasse [1] videtur secundum bellum Poenicum. namque Hannibal, filius eius, *assiduis* patris *obtestationibus* eo est perductus, ut *interire* quam Romanos non experiri mallet.

LESSON XXV

IMPERATIVE, INFINITIVE PASSIVE.—CONDITIONAL SENTENCES.—JUSSIVE SUBJUNCTIVE AND PROHIBITIONS

Turn to the Table now and learn the Imperative in each conjugation. The second person singular Present Imperative Active is always got by dropping *-re* of the Present Infinitive : *amare, ama ; monere, mone*, etc. The third person plural is always got by adding *o* to the same person of the Present Indicative : *amant, amantō ; monent, monentō*, etc., but this is rare.

The second person singular Present Imperative Passive is always the same as the Present Infinitive Active. Then change *-te* of the Imperative Active into *-minī* and add *r* to the remaining tenses, neglecting the forms ending in *-tote: amāte, amāminī ; amātō, amātor*, etc.

The Imperative expresses a command (*impero— -are*, " I command ")—

e.g. *Mihi pare*—" obey me " (addressed to one person).

Mihi parēte—" obey me " (addressed to two or more persons).

[1] Contracted for *concitavisse*.

Negative Commands (sometimes called Prohibitions) are expressed in two ways :—

> (1) By the Imperative of *nolo*, " I am unwilling ", i.e. *noli* (sing.) and *nolīte* (plur.) followed by the Infinitive (*v.* Table of Verbs).
>
> e.g. *Noli venīre, puer*—" don't come, boy ".
> *Nolīte venīre, pueri*—" don't come, boys ".
>
> (2) Less commonly by *ne* with the Perfect Subjunctive.
>
> e.g. *Ne, puer, hoc dixeris*—" don't say this, boy ".
> *Ne, pueri, hoc dixeritis*—" don't say this, boys ".

Jussive Subjunctive.

The Indicative mood states facts, the Subjunctive thoughts and suppositions. Therefore the Subjunctive is used to express wishes.

> e.g. *Bene regam*—" may I rule well ! "
> *Bene rex regat*—" may the king rule well ! "
> *Amemus*—" let us love ".

A negative wish is expressed by *ne* with the present subjunctive.

> e.g. *Ne nunc moriar*—" let me not die now !"

Wishes for the past (*i.e.* unfulfilled wishes) are expressed by *utinam* followed by the Imperfect or Pluperfect Subjunctive.

> e.g. *Utinam vivus esses*—" would that you were alive ! "
> *Utinam hic fuisses*—" would that you had been here ! "

Infinitive Passive

For the Present Infinitive Passive change the final *-e* of the Present Infinitive Active into *-ī*; but in the Third Conjugation change *-ere* into *-i*, thus : *regere, regi*.

The Future Infinitive Passive is formed from the Supine and the Present Infinitive Passive of *eo, iri*, to go : *amatum īrī*, " to be being gone for the purpose of loving ", that is, " to be about to be loved ".

Note that in such a sentence as *Dixit eum amatum iri* (he said that man was going to be loved) *amatum* governs *eum*, and does not agree with it.

Conditional Clauses

1. " If he had done this he *would have* paid the penalty."

This is what is called a conditional sentence, a sentence with a condition expressed in it, contained in the " if " clause.   On looking at it you will see that it refers to the past, and that it is implied that the condition was not fulfilled ; that is, he did not do it, and was not punished.   Such a sentence in Latin contains two Pluperfect Subjunctives :—

Si hoc fecisset poenas dedisset, which means " if he had done that, he would have been punished ".

2. Now consider this sentence :—

" If he were to do (*or* did) this he *would* be punished."

This sentence obviously refers to the Future.   If he were to act in a certain way in the future, he would pay the penalty in the future.   Such a conditional sentence has two Present Subjunctives in Latin :—

Si hoc faciat poenas det.

Never mind the fact that "would be" suggests an Imperfect Subjunctive. It refers to the future and must be Present tense in Latin.

3. Distinguish this carefully from a conditional sentence like that given in Lesson VI.

Si hoc fecerit poenas dabit.
If he does (shall have done) this he *will* pay the penalty.

Notice how much more exact Latin is than English in this last example. The time or the "if" clause precedes that of the main sentence, and therefore the *future perfect* tense is more logical than the present.

Note that "If . . . not" or "Unless . . ." is Nisi, and not Si . . . non.

Imperatives Familiar in English

1. Recipe.
2. Nota bene (N.B.).
3. Cave [1] canem.
4. Festina lente.
5. Vade mecum.
6. Carpe [2] diem.
7. Ave atque vale.
8. Noli [3] me tangere [4]

From the Prayer Book

1. Cantate Domino.
2. Benedicite,[5] omnia opera.
3. Venite exultemus [6] Domino.

Sir Christopher Wren's Epitaph in St. Paul's

Si monumentum requiris, circumspice.

---

[1] "beware of".
[2] *Literally*, "pluck".
[3] Imperative of *nolo*. *Literally*, "be unwilling" and so "don't".
[4] "to touch". [5] "Bless-ye." [6] "Let us rejoice."

A Drunkard's Promises

Omnia promittis, cum tota nocte bibisti;
  Mane nihil praestas.[1]   Pollio, mane bibe.
                    —*Martial.*

A Humble Invitation

Aude,[2] hospes, contemnere opes et te quoque dignum
Finge deo,[3] rebusque veni non asper egenis.
                    —*Verg. Aen.* VIII 364.

May She Meet the Wife!

Omnes quas habuit, Fabiane, Lycoris amicas
  Extulit.[4]   Uxori fiat [5] amica meae.—*Martial.*

Latin Phrases and Sayings

1. Exeat.[6]
2. Caveat emptor.
3. Aut bibat aut abeat.[7]   (Proverb.)
4. Ruat coelum, fiat [8] justitia.
5. Absit [9] omen.
6. Cedant arma togae.[10]—*Cicero.*
7. Dum vivimus, vivamus.
8. Requiescat in pace.   (R.I.P.)

---

[1] *praesto,* " I furnish or provide ".
[2] *aude*—imperative of *audeo.*
[3] *Dignus* governs an ablative.   In English we say " worthy of ".
[4] Irregular perfect of *effero,* " I carry outside "—*i.e.* " to burial ".
[5] Subjunctive of *fio,* " I become ".
[6] *Literally,* " let him (or her) go out ".   *exit*—" he goes out ",
exeunt—" they go out " (*v.* Table of Verbs).
[7] " let him go away " (from *ab-eo*).
[8] *Fio* is used as the passive of *facio* (*v.* Table of Verbs).
[9] Subjunctive of *absum,* " Let it be absent ! "
[10] The robe of a Roman senator, and so here used for the arts of
civil life.

Here are some lines of *Martial* on a rival, who is
bursting with envy because he is famous. " Then let
him burst " is his wish in the last line.

On a Rival

Rumpitur [1] invidia quidam, carissime Iuli,
   quod me Roma legit, rumpitur invidia.
rumpitur invidia quod turba semper in omni
   monstramur digito, rumpitur invidia.
rumpitur invidia tribuit quod Caesar uterque [2]
   ius mihi natorum,[3] rumpitur invidia.
rumpitur invidia quod rus mihi dulce sub urbe est
   parvaque in urbe domus, rumpitur invidia.
rumpitur invidia quod sum iucundus amicis,
   quod conviva frequens, rumpitur invidia.
rumpitur invidia quod amamur quodque probamur.
   rumpatur quisquis rumpitur invidia.

Passage No. 6 [4]

Cornelius Nepos, *Life of Hannibal*

(Passages 6–18)

His Hatred of Rome

Hannibal, Hamilcaris filius, Karthaginiensis. si
verum est, quod nemo dubitat,[5] ut populus Romanus

[1] " is being burst ", *i.e.* " is bursting ".
[2] Titus and Domitian, the two emperors reigning in Martial's
time.
[3] The father of three children at Rome had certain privileges.
[4] The preceding passages embrace the Life of Hamilcar. The
remaining passages contain the Life of his more famous son,
Hannibal. Don't be confused because the first sentence contains
no verb : it is a sort of heading to the Life—" Hannibal, the son of
Hamilcar, a Carthaginian ".
[5] *Quod nemo dubitat: quod* is the relative—" If it is true, *which*
no one doubts ".

omnes gentes virtute superarit,[1] non est infitiandum [2]
Hannibalem *tanto* [3] praestitisse ceteros imperatores
prudentia, *quanto* [3] populus Romanus *antecedat* fortitudine cunctas nationes. nam quotienscumque cum
eo congressus est in Italia, semper discessit superior.
quod nisi [4] domi civium suorum invidia debilitatus
esset, Romanos videtur superare potuisse.[5]   Sed mul-
torum obtrectatio devicit unius virtutem.

Hic autem velut hereditate [6] relictum odium
paternum erga Romanos *sic* conservavit, *ut* prius
animam quam id *deposuerit*, qui quidem, cum patria
pulsus esset et *alienarum opum* indigeret, nunquam
destiterit [7] animo bellare cum Romanis.

LESSON XXVI

POSSUM.—CONDITIONAL SENTENCES—*Continued*

There are seven common irregular verbs in Latin :—

Possum, I am able	*Volo*, I am willing
Eō, I go	*Nōlō*, I am unwilling
Ferō, I carry	*Mālō*, I prefer
Fiō, I become, I am made :	Passive of *facio*.

---

[1] *Ut...superarit :* this is a substantival clause subject to *verum
est*—" If *it* is true that the Roman people has surpassed ". *Superarit* is contracted for *superaverit*.

[2] *Infitiandum* is Gerund of *infitiari*, a deponent verb, " to deny ".

[3] *Tanto*, " by so much "; *quanto*, " by how much ".

[4] *Quod nisi : literally*, " as to which unless ". We should say,
" but if . . . not ".

[5] *Videtur superare potuisse : literally*, " *he* seems to have been
able to conquer ". We would say, " *it* seems *he* would have been
able to conquer ". Latin uses *videtur* personally, English impersonally, that is, without a person as subject. *Potuisse* is the Perfect
Infinitive of an irregular verb = to have been able. See Lesson
XXVI.

[6] *Velut hereditate :* " left as if by a legacy ".

[7] *Qui nunquam destiterit :* the relative here takes the Subjunctive
instead of the Indicative because it means " since he " (who since).

They are irregular only in the tenses derived from the Present stem, that is, in the Present, Imperfect and Future. For their conjugation *v.* Part III, Table of Verbs.

Turn now to the table and learn the conjugation of *possum*, I am able. It will help you to remember that *possum* is *pot-* + *sum*, the *t* being changed to *s* before the parts of *sum* that begin with *s*, and the *f* in the Perfect tenses being dropped. Thus Pos-sum, Pot-es, and Pot-ui (not pot*f*ui).

Note this verb has only a Present and Perfect Infinitive, and has no Participles, Gerund or Supines.

Conditional Clauses—*Continued*

" If he were now doing this he would now be paying the penalty."

This sentence refers to the Present, and it is implied that he is not now doing this, and is not now paying the penalty. This is expressed in Latin by two Imperfect Subjunctives :—

Si hoc faceret, poenas daret.

You remember if the Condition referred to the past, and its non-fulfilment was implied, we said two Pluperfect Subjunctives were used. These, however, may be either or both Imperfect Subjunctives, if you do not wish to talk of a completed, but of a continuous action or state. Thus " If he had been doing this he would have paid the penalty " would be *Si hoc faceret poenas dedisset*. Similarly " If he had done this he would have been paying the penalty " would be *Si hoc fecisset poenas daret*. And again *Si hoc faceret poenas daret* may mean, as above, " If he were doing this he would be paying the penalty " (present time) or " If he had been doing this he would have been paying the penalty ".   Only the context or the insertion of an adverb such as *nunc* or *tum* can tell you which is really meant.

Two Famous Lines

1. Tantum religio potuit suadere malorum.— *Lucretius*.
2. Possunt quia posse videntur.—*Virgil*.

Note.—*Religio* is nearer our " superstition " than " religion ".

Paula

Martial does not want to marry Paula as she is too old, or rather not old enough.   If she had been a little older, she might have been worth marrying in the hope of succeeding to her wealth after her death.

Nubere [1] Paula cupit nobis, ego ducere [2] Paulam
    nolo : anus est.   vellem,[3] si magis [4] esset anus.

Passage No. 7

Hannibal at 26 is made commander-in-chief of the Carthaginian army.   He conquers Spain and crosses the Alps.

Hic igitur, post Hamilcaris obitum, Hasdrubale imperatore suffecto, equitatui omni praefuit. hoc quoque interfecto exercitus summam imperii [5] ad eum

[1] " to marry ", of the bride.   *Lit.*, " to veil oneself ", for the bridegroom.
[2] " to marry ", of the man.   *Lit.*, " to lead ".
[3] Impf. subj. of *volo* (*v*. Table of Verbs).
[4] *magis*, " more ", comparative adv. of *magnus*.
[5] *Summam imperii*, " the total of the power ", " the chief control ".

detulit. id Karthaginem delatum publice [1] compro-
batum est. sic Hannibal minor septem et viginti
annis natus [2] imperator factus proximo triennio [3] omnes
gentes Hispaniae bello subegit : Saguntum, foederatam [4]
civitatem, vi expugnavit,[5] tres exercitus maximos
comparavit. Ex his unum in Africam misit, alterum
cum Hasdrubale fratre in Hispania reliquit, tertium [6]
in Italiam secum duxit. saltum Pyrenaeum transiit.
quacumque iter fecit, cum omnibus incolis conflixit :
neminem nisi victum dimisit. ad Alpes posteaquam
venit, quae Italiam ab Gallia seiungunt, quas nemo
umquam cum exercitu ante eum praeter Herculem
Graium transierat (quo facto [7] is hodie saltus Graius
appelatur), Alpicos conantes prohibere transitu [8] con-
cidit, loca patefecit, itinera muniit,[9] effecit ut ea [10]
elephantus ornatus [11] ire posset, qua antea unus homo
inermis vix poterat repere. hac copias traduxit in
Italiamque pervenit.

You should now be able to read a beautiful, though

[1] *Publice* : not " publicly ", but " in the name of the State ".
[2] *Minor quinque et viginti annis natus :* this is a very peculiar
Latin idiom meaning " less than five and twenty years of age ",
literally " born less than five and twenty years ".
[3] *Proximo triennio,* " within the next three years ".
[4] *Foederatam* is an adjective and implies that the State had a
special treaty of alliance with Rome.
[5] *Vi expugnare* means " to storm " (" to capture by force ").
[6] *Unum . . . alterum . . . tertium,* " one . . . another . . . the third ".
[7] *Quo facto :* This is not an Ablative Absolute. It means " from
that deed ", " by reason of that (which) deed ".
[8] *Prohibere transitu,* " to keep from the passage ". *Transitu* is
an Ablative of Separation.
[9] *Itinera muniit* is simply " made roads ", not " fortified roads ",
although *munire* means strictly " to fortify ".
[10] *Ea...qua,* " by that road by which "—both adverbs formed from
Ablative of pronouns.
[11] *Elephantus ornatus,* " an elephant with its equipment ".

untranslatable poem of *Catullus*, in which he pictures himself and Lesbia at the height of their love, showering kisses on each other, regardless of what the world may say.

Come, Live with Me and be My Love

Vivamus, mea Lesbia, atque amemus,
rumoresque senum severiorum
omnes unius aestimemus assis.[1]
soles occidere et redire possunt :
nobis cum semel occidit brevis lux,
nox est perpetua una dormienda.
da mi [2] basia mille, deinde centum,
dein mille altera, dein secunda centum,
deinde usque [3] altera mille, deinde centum.
dein, cum milia multa fecerimus,
conturbabimus [4] illa, ne sciamus,
aut ne quis malus invidere [5] possit,
cum [6] tantum [7] sciat esse basiorum.[7]

LESSON XXVII

EŌ.—CONDITIONAL SENTENCES.—*QUIN* AND *QUOMINUS*

Eō, īre, ĭi or īvi, ĭtum   .   . to go

Turn to the Table and learn this verb off by heart. Note again that only the Present stem tenses are

---

[1] *assis*, gen. of price. The " *as* " was a copper coin worth a little more than a farthing.
[2] Abbreviation for " *mihi* ".
[3] *usque*, " continuously ", " without interruption " (adv.).
[4] *conturbo*, " confuse ", *i.e.* mix them up and lose count. It was considered bad luck to count your blessings too accurately.
[5] *invidere*, more than " envy " here; " to cast an evil eye upon ".
[6] *cum*, since. *cum* with subjunctive often has a causal sense.
[7] *Lit.*, " so much of kisses ", *i.e.* " so many kisses ".

irregular. It is a very useful verb, since it forms many compounds. These always form the Perfect in -*ii*, not -*ivi* :—

Redĕŏ	*redĭi*	*redĭtum*	*redīre*	.	.	to return
Inĕŏ	*inĭi*	*inĭtum*	*inīre*	.	.	to enter
Abĕŏ	*abĭi*	*abĭtum*	*abīre*	.	.	to go away
Adĕŏ	*adĭi*	*adĭtum*	*adīre*	.	.	to approach

Conditional Sentences—*Continued*

There is a large class of conditional sentences in which nothing is implied as to the fulfilment of the condition. (*a*) " If he is doing this he is a fool ". In this sentence we neither imply that he is doing it, nor yet that he is not doing it. We simply say, " if he is, he is a fool ". Similarly in sentences like (*b*) " If he said this he was a fool ", (*c*) " If he was saying this he was a fool ". These in Latin, as in English, have the Indicative Mood.

(*a*) Si hoc facit, stultus est.
(*b*) Si hoc dixit, stultus erat.
(*c*) Si hoc dicebat, stultus erat.

Quin and *Quominus*

Eum inhibuit quominus rediret. He prevented him from returning.

Vix inhiberi potuit quin rediret. Scarce was he able to be prevented from returning (but that he should return).

Non dubium est quin hac mente semper futurus sim. There is no doubt but that I shall always be of this mind.

Nemo est quin hoc putet. There is no one but thinks this.

Non dubitavit quin hoc ita esset. He did not doubt but that this was so.

Non fieri potest quin hoc ita sit. It is impossible but that this is so (that this is not so).

They are used thus : *Quominus* with the Subjunctive after a verb of hindering is translated in English by " from " and the Participle. *Quin* is found only after negative verbs and phrases, *i.e.* verbs and phrases with a " not " expressed or implied, and is usually translated by " but " or " who . . . not ".

Note that Prohibeo is followed by a Present Infinitive (and not by Quominus or Quin).

Passage No. 8

Hannibal defeats P. C. Scipio at the Trebia.   He loses an eye and advances on Rome.

Conflixerat apud Rhodanum cum P. Cornelio Scipione consule eumque pepulerat.   cum hoc eodem Clastidii [1] apud Padum *decernit* sauciumque inde ac fugatum *dimittit.*   tertio idem Scipio cum collega Tiberio Longo apud Trebiam adversus eum venit.   cum iis manum conseruit : utrosque profligavit.   inde per Ligures [2] Appenninum [3] transit, petens Etruriam [4] hoc itinere [5] *adeo gravi morbo adficitur oculorum, ut* postea numquam dextro [6] aeque bene usus sit.

Qua valetudine cum etiamtum premeretur lecticaque ferretur, C. Flaminium consulem apud Trasumenum cum exercitu insidiis *circumventum occidit*, neque multo post C. Centenium praetorem cum delecta manu saltus

[1] At Clastidium, locative.
[2] *Ligures :* these were a tribe in the north of Italy, dwelling round the Gulf of Genoa.
[3] *Appenninum :* The great central range of Italy.   We talk of " the Apennines ", the Romans spoke of " the Apennine ".
[4] *Etruriam :* the district of Italy north of Rome and the Tiber.
[5] Note the way in which the meaning of *iter* varies—now " a road ", now " a march ", now " a journey ".
[6] *Nunquam dextro:* "He never had the proper use of his right eye". This disease, in fact, is said to have made the right eye blind.

occupantem. hinc in Apuliam pervenit. ibi *obviam ei venerunt* duo consules, C. Terentius et L. Aemilius. utriusque exercitus uno proelio fugavit, Paulum consulem occidit et aliquot praeterea *consulares*, in iis Cn. Servilium Geminum, qui superiore anno fuerat consul.

Hac pugna pugnata Romam profectus est nullo resistente. in propinquis urbi montibus moratus est. cum aliquot ibi dies castra *habuisset* et Capuam *reverteretur.* Q. Fabius Maximus, dictator Romanus, *in agro Falerno ei* se obiecit.

Notes.

Decernit, dimittit, adficitur : The present tense is used here, as often in Latin, to give vividness to the story. In English we should more naturally use the past tense, " he contended . . . he sent . . . he was affected . . ."

Adeo gravi morbo . . . ut : This is a consecutive clause introduced by *ut.*

Circumventum occidit : Latin uses a past participle and a finite verb : in English we use two finite verbs—" he surrounded and slew ".

Obviam ei venerunt : literally, " came in the way to him ". *Obviam ire* and *obviam venire* are regular Latin phrases for " to meet ".

Consulares : While a Roman held the chief magistracy he was consul. On the expiry of his year in office he became *consularis* or ex-consul.

Habuisset et reverteretur : Note the difference in the tenses, the first denoting a completed action, the second one in process of completion—continuous.

In agro Falerno : *ager* may mean a single field, or it may mean territory as here.

A Passage from the New Testament

The New Testament was originally written in Greek, but was translated several times into Latin. The most famous of the Latin translations was the *Biblia Sacra*

Vulgatae Editionis, now known as the "*Vulgate*", by St. Jerome in the 4th century A.D. This is a slightly simplified extract from Luke ii, verses 8–14.

Shepherds in the Fields

Erant in regione eadem pastores in agris excubantes [1] et custodientes noctu [2] gregem suum. Et Domini nuntius adstitit [3] eis, et Domini gloria circumfulsit [4] eos et timuerunt magno timore. Et dixit eis nuntius, " Nolite timere : ecce enim vobis gaudium magnum nuntio, quod toti populo erit : quia vobis hodie natus est servator, qui est Christus Dominus, in urbe Davidi. Et hoc vobis signum erit : invenietis infantem circumdatum incunabulis [5] et iacentem in stabulo.[6] " Et subito erat cum nuntio multitudo e caelesti [7] exercitu laudantes [8] Deum et dicentes,[8] " Gloria in altissimis Deo, et in terra pax in hominibus bonae voluntatis." [9]

LESSON XXVIII

FERO.—QUESTIONS, DIRECT AND INDIRECT

Now turn again to the Table and learn the Irregular verb *Fero*, I carry, I bring. It is irregular only in certain tenses. It is not irregular in the Imperfect and Future Indicative, nor in the Present Subjunctive. Its passive, too, is formed from the Active according to

[1] " sleeping out ".
[2] " by night ".
[3] " stood by them ".
[4] " shone around ".
[5] " swaddling-clothes ".
[6] " stable ".
[7] " heavenly ".
[8] plural, " men praising " in apposition to *multitudo*.
[9] " wish ", " will ".

the usual rules. This again is a very useful verb, forming many compounds :—

> *in + fero* gives *in-fĕro, in-tŭli, il-lātum, in-ferre,* to carry into.
> Note before *l, n* becomes *l.*
> *ad + fero* gives *af-fĕro, at-tŭli, al-lātum, af-ferre,* to carry to.
> Note the *d* changing to *f,* to *t,* to *l.*
> *ex + fero* gives *ef-fĕro, ex-tŭli, e-lātum, ef-ferre,* to carry out.
> Note the changes the preposition undergoes.

These are some of the common compounds, but you must notice the others as they occur. Try always to understand the force of the preposition with which the verb is compounded.

Questions

In English we mark a question by altering the order of the words, or by introducing the sentence by some interrogative word. The first method is not used in Latin. To show that a sentence is a question in Latin we put a little word *-ne,* or *num,* at the beginning of the sentence—*num* at the beginning, *-ne* after the first emphatic word. If the question expects the answer " yes ", *e.g.* Surely you have done it ? we employ *nonne.*

> *Librumne tulisti ?*   Have you brought the book ?
> *Num librum tulisti ?*   You haven't brought the book, have you ? (expecting the answer " no ").
> *Nonne librum tulisti ?*   Have you not brought the book ? (expecting the answer " yes ").

Indirect Questions

All these are direct questions. But " He asked me whether I had brought the book " is an indirect question —that is, a reported question. The following are some further examples of this :—

1. *A me petivit num librum tulissem* (or *librumne tulissem*).
2. *A me petivit quando librum laturus essem.*
3. *A me petivit quem librum ferrem.*

> 1. He asked me if I had brought the book.
> 2. He asked me when I would bring the book.
> 3. He asked me what book I was bringing.

We call words like *if*, *when*, *what*, interrogative particles, and these sentences always have one of these at the beginning. " If " may be *num* or *-ne*, but *-ne* must be put directly after the first word of the sentence and joined to it. It is never *si*, as of course it is not a condition, but equivalent to " whether ". " When " in such a sentence is not *cum*, but *quando*. " What ", of course, is some part of *quis*. The *interrogative* pronoun, " who ", " which ", " what ", is just the same as the relative given in Lesson XVI, but has *quis* and *quid* as well as *qui* and *quod* in the nominative singular masculine and neuter. *Qui* and *quod*, however, are used as adjectives with nouns ; *quis* and *quid* alone, as pronouns. These sentences must be introduced by an interrogative word, and must have their verb in the Subjunctive. The tense follows the usual rules of sequences :—

Present Subjunctive after Primary tenses } denoting con-
Imperfect Subjunctive after Historic tenses } tinuous action.

Perfect Subjunctive after both } denoting com-
Pluperfect Subjunctive after Historic tenses } pleted action.

Future Subjunctive. Future Participle + *sim* (or *essem*, in historic sequence).

Compare the following :—

A me petit { *num librum feram.* / *librumne feram.* } He asks me if I am bringing the book.

A me petit librumne tulerim. He asks me if I have brought the book.

A me petit num librum laturus sim. He asks me if I will bring the book.

Passage No. 9

Hannibal's army is entrapped by Q. Fabius Maximus, but H. extricates it at night by a trick without loss.

(In this passage there are frequent examples of *Participle + Finite verb* in Latin, equal to *two Finite verbs* in English.)

Hic clausus locorum angustiis noctu sine ullo detrimento exercitus se expedivit Fabioque, callidissimo imperatori, dedit verba.[1] namque obducta nocte sarmenta in cornibus iuvencorum deligata incendit eiusque generis multitudinem magnam dispalatam immisit.[2] quo repentino obiecto visu tantum terrorem iniecit exercitui Romanorum, ut egredi extra vallum nemo sit ausus. hanc post rem gestam non ita multis diebus [3] M. Minucium Rufum, magistrum equitum pari ac dictatorem imperio,[4] dolo productum in proelium fugavit. Tiberium Sempronium Gracchum, iterum consulem, in Lucanis absens in insidias inductum sustulit.[5] M. Claudium Marcellum, quinquies consulem, apud Venusiam pari modo interfecit. longum est [6] omnia enumerare proelia. quare hoc unum satis

---

[1] *Lit.,* " gave (empty) words ", so " tricked ".

[2] *Magnam dispalatam immisit:* let loose a great multitude, " having straggled ", or, perhaps, " having been scattered ", that is, " let loose far and wide ".

[3] *Non ita multis diebus:* Ablative of time within which.

[4] *Pari ac dictatorem imperio,* " with power the same as the dictator ".

[5] Irregular perfect of *tollo,* " take away ", so " destroy ".

[6] *Longum est:* Latin says " it is long " where we say " it would be long ".

erit dictum, ex quo intelligi possit,[1] quantus ille fuerit : [2] quamdiu in Italia fuit, nemo ei in acie restitit, nemo adversus eum post Cannensem pugnam in campo castra posuit.

Two Epigrams of Catullus

The first is on Cæsar, who was a contemporary of Catullus. Catullus did not like him, and was not afraid to say so. In the second line his contempt is suggested by his complete indifference whether Cæsar is dark or fair.

Indifference

Nil [3] nimium studeo, Cæsar, tibi velle [4] placere,
    nec scire utrum [5] sis albus an [5] ater homo.

The following epigram is the perfect expression of the bitter-sweet of love. Catullus has been disappointed in love and lost his respect for Lesbia, but cannot stop desiring her.

> To be wroth with one we love
> Doth work like madness in the brain.
>   —*Coleridge.*

Odi [6] et amo : quare id faciam, fortasse requiris.
    nescio, sed fieri [7] sentio et excrucior.[8]
    I hate yet love her. Will you ask me why ?
    I know not. But I feel. 'Tis agony.

[1] *Ex quo possit* = *ut ex eo possit*, " that it may be perceived " : a *qui* Final clause. See Lesson XXXIII.
[2] *Quantus ille fuerit :* Indirect question.
[3] *nil*—abbrev. for *nihil*, " not at all ".
[4] inf. of *volo*.
[5] *utrum...an*, " whether...or ".
[6] *Odi*—perfect of a defective verb, " I hate ".
[7] *fieri*—Inf. of *fio*, used as a passive of *facio*, " to be done, to happen ".
[8] *excrucior*—" I am being tortured ".

A Christmas Hymn

This hymn appears to have been written in the seventeenth century, but we do not know by whom. The well-known English translation, " O come, all ye faithful " dates from the nineteenth century.

> Adeste,[1] fideles,
> laeti triumphantes;
> Venite, venite in Bethlehem :
> natum videte
> regem angelorum :
> Venite adoremus Dominum.
>
> Deum de Deo,
> Lumen de lumine
> Parturit Virgo Mater,
> Deum Verum,
> genitum [2] non factum.
> Venite adoremus Dominum.
>
> en grege relicto,
> humiles ad cunas,[3]
> vocati pastores approperant.
> et nos ovanti [4]
> gradu festinemus
> Venite, adoremus Dominum.
>
> stella duce,[5] Magi
> Christum adorantes,

[1] *adeste*, imperative second pers. plur. of *adsum*, " be present ".
[2] *genitum*, past partic. pass. from *gigno*, " born ".
[3] *cunas*, " cradle ".
[4] *ovanti*, " rejoicing ".
[5] *stella duce*, " under the leadership of a star ". *Lit.*, " a star being leader "—ablative absol. (*v.* Lesson XIV).

aurum, thus,[1] myrrham,[2] dant munera.
  Jesu infanti
  corda praebeamus :
Venite adoremus Dominum.

  aeterni [3] parentis
  splendorem aeternum,
velatum sub carne videbimus,
  Deum infantem,
  pannis [4] involutum,
Venite adoremus Dominum.

  cantet nunc hymnos,
  chorus angelorum ;
cantet nunc aula caeleitium,
  Gloria
  in excelsis Deo !
Venite adoremus Dominum.

LESSON XXIX

VŎLO, NŌLŌ, MĀLŌ AND VERBS WITH INFINITIVE

The three verbs *volo*, I am willing, *nolo*, I am not willing, *malo*, I prefer (I am more willing), are so much alike that they had better be learned together.

Nolo is simply *non* + *volo*, as you will see by a look at the present tense. Sometimes the *non* is kept entire, sometimes the *v* of *volo* is simply changed into *n*. Thus *nonvis, nonvult*; but *nolumus, nolunt*.

Similarly *malo* is simply *ma-* (for *magis*, more) and *volo*, " I am more willing ", that is, " I prefer ".

[1] *thus*, " incense ".
[2] *myrrham*, " myrrh ".
[3] *aeterni*, " eternal ".
[4] *pannis*, " rags ".

Note all three form the Imperfect Indicative alike by adding *-ebam*, etc.; the Perfect Indicative by adding *-ui*, *-uisti*, *-uit*, etc.; the Future Indicative by adding *-am*, *-es*, *-et*, etc.; the Present Subjunctive by adding *-im*, *-is*, *-it*, etc., to the Present stem; and the Imperfect Subjunctive by adding *-m*, *-s*, *-t*, etc., to the Infinitive. They all lack the Passive voice.

Note that this is often known as the Prolate Infinitive.

Verbs with the Infinitive in Latin

Not every verb which is followed by an Infinitive in English takes an Infinitive in Latin. If you think of the English form of a Latin Final or Consecutive or Substantival clause, or of the Supine construction after verbs of motion, you will at once see that this is so. In fact you must always be careful when putting an Infinitive after a Latin verb. The verbs which take this in Latin belong to three great classes :—

1. Verbs which denote Possibility or the Reverse.
2. Verbs which denote Beginning or Ceasing.
3. Verbs which denote Desire or Endeavour.

There are a good many more which do not come under these heads, but these are the commoner ones. The following list gives some of the Latin verbs :—

1. *Possum*, I am able, I can : *Non possumus haec facere*, we cannot do this.

2. *Coepi, incipio*, I begin : *Praeesse exercitui coeperat*, he began to be at the head of the army. See note on *odi* (p. 151).

3. *Cupio*, I desire : *Cupio haec cognoscere*, I desire to know these things.

Volo, nolo, malo.

Conor, I attempt.

Statuo, I resolve : *Romanis bellum inferre statuit*, he resolved to attack the Romans.

Of the others the more common are :—

Debeo, I ought : *Inimicis ignoscere debemus*, we ought to pardon our enemies.

Videor, I seem.

Scio, I know } *Scio (disco) hoc facere*, I know (I am learning) how
Disco, I learn }   to do this.

Odi, I hate (only used in the Perfect Tenses, the Perfect having a present meaning. Similarly *coepi*).

In translation, then, when you come across one of these verbs, you must always look for an Infinitive to complete the meaning.

Passage No. 10

Hannibal is recalled to Carthage, and is defeated by Scipio at Zama.

Hinc invictus patriam defensum [1] revocatus bellum gessit adversus P. Scipionem, filium eius Scipionis, quem ipse primo apud Rhodănum, iterum apud Padum, tertio apud Trebiam fugaverat. cum hoc exhaustis iam patriae facultatibus cupivit in praesens [2] bellum componere, quo valentior [3] postea congrederetur. In colloqium convenit : condiciones non convenerunt.[4] post id factum paucis diebus apud Zamam cum eodem conflixit : pulsus (incredibile dictu) [5] biduo et duabus noctibus Hadrumētum pervenit, quod abest Zama

[1] Supine : " to defend ".

[2] *In praesens :* " for the present ".

[3] *Quo valentior :* when a Final clause has an adjective or adverb in the comparative degree in it, *quo* is used instead of *ut*.

[4] *Condiciones non convenerunt*, " the terms did not come together, fit, suit ".

[5] *Incredibile dictu: Dictu* is the second Supine. The phrase means " unbelievable in the telling ". *Dictu* is really the ablative of an old noun of the Fourth Declension, as are all such second Supines.

circiter milia [1] passuum trecenta.   in hac fuga Numidae,
qui simul cum eo ex acie excesserant, insidiati sunt ei :
quos non solum effugit, sed etiam ipsos oppressit.
Hadrumeti [2] reliquos e fuga collegit : novis dilectibus
paucis diebus multos contraxit.

Cum in apparando acerrime esset occupatus, Karthaginienses bellum cum Romanis composuerunt. ille
tamen exercitui postea praefuit resque in Africa gessit
usque ad P. Sulpicium [3] C. Aurelium consules.

Note.—As regards the place-names, the Rhône is the
river in the south of France, the Po is in the north of
Italy, the Trebia is its tributary.   Zama is a town near
Carthage in the north of Africa, and Hadrumetum is in
the same quarter.

LESSON XXX

HINTS ON TRANSLATING VERSE.—TWO PASSAGES FROM OVID

Hints on Translating Verse

There are two important differences between Latin
and English poetry.   English poets make great use of
rhyme : Latin poetry, as the Romans wrote it, is
always rhymeless.   In English, the accent or beat falls
on the heavier syllables and the number and arrange-
ment of the beats determines the metre :—

> Téll me whére is Fáncy bréd,
> I'n the heárt or i'n the heád,
> Hów begót, how nóurishéd ?

[1] " A thousand Roman paces " is roughly an English mile.
[2] Locative.
[3] *Usque ad P. Sulpicium :* " right on up to ".   We should say,
" up till the time of ".

In Latin metre is determined by the *length* of syllables, which is a different matter. There is not space here to go into the intricate rules which determine whether a syllable is long or short. They are set out in full in the chapter on Prosody in Kennedy's *Revised Latin Primer*. Here are three of the most important :—

1. A syllable is short when it contains a short vowel followed by a single consonant or by another vowel : *păter, pŭer.*

2. A syllable is long when it contains a long vowel or a diphthong : *frāter, mēnsāe, nēmo.*

3. A vowel short by nature becomes long by position when it is followed by two consonants or by *x* or *z* : *mōllĭă, sŭpplēx*, but it can be either long or short if followed by a consonant and "*r*", e.g., *gr, tr*, etc.

Note.—When a word ends with a vowel and is followed by a word beginning with a vowel, the first vowel is elided in scansion, e.g. *metusque aberant* below.

4. Final *a* is sometimes short, sometimes long. The nominative of the first declension (*mensă*) is short, but the ablative " by a table " (*mensā*) is long. To know this is a great help in translating verse. If you know the rules of scansion, you will be able to tell (which you cannot do in prose) whether a final *a* of a first declension noun is short or long, and therefore whether it is nominative or ablative.

Latin poetry becomes not only more interesting, but more easy to translate, if you understand something of its scansion.

You have already had several extracts from Martial, who wrote most of his epigrams in a two-line metre called the *Elegiac* (because a Greek poet invented this metre for the writing of elegies).

It consists of two lines, of which the first (called the *Hexameter*—" hex " is Greek for " six ") has six feet. Each foot, except the fifth and sixth, consists *either* of three syllables (a long syllable followed by two short) called a *dactyl* from the Greek word " dactylon "—a " finger ", and scanned lōng-short-shŏrt, like " terrible " in English—*or* of two syllables, both long, called a " spondee ", because long long, – –, like the English " bamboo ". The first four feet can be either dactyls or spondees, but the fifth foot is always a dactyl, and the sixth has only two syllables.

Here is a Hexameter in English. Notice how it scans, and it will help you to scan a Latin one.

Dōwn ĭn ă	deep dārk	dēll săt ăn	ōld sōw	chewin' ă	bean-stalk.
Pārtŭrĭ-	*ŭnt mŏn-*	*tēs, nās-*	*cĕtŭr*	*rĭdĭcŭl-*	*ŭs mus.*

The second line is shorter, and consists of five feet, and is called the *Pentameter* (" pente " is Greek for " five "). It is divided into two halves of two and a half feet each. The second half always consists of two dactyls + one extra syllable. Thus :—

Lōng, shŏrt shŏrt | lōng, shŏrt, shŏrt | lōng (or short)

e.g., In English—" mīnd ŏf ă | rhĭnŏcĕr|us ".

or in Latin—" *lit-er-a* | *dicta per*|*it* ".

The first half of the pentameter consists of two dactyls or spondees, or one of each, followed by one extra long syllable, thus :—

Āll mĕn ălīke hate slōps.

In the following elegiac couplet *seven* words are missing. They each consist of the *same four letters*, placed in different order. What are the seven words? It should help you to discover them if you bear in mind how the elegiac couplet scans. The number and " quantity " (*i.e.*, whether long or short) of the missing syllables is given to help you :—

N.B.—The termination of *quondam* is elided before the first letter of the missing word which follows, which shows that the missing word begins with a vowel.

A Puzzle

"*Sit* . . . . *sub* . . . ." *cecinit quond(am)* . . . . *ad* . . . .;
    " . . . .", *poeta* . . . ., " *sit meus* " *inquit*,[1] " . . . ."

The missing words are given in the Key in Part III.
The following elegiac couplet is an attempt to put into Latin the following tongue-twister to illustrate pronouns. Try not only to translate it, but to scan it :—

> *He said that that that that man said was that that that man thought.*

Dixit homo nobis illud, quod dixerit ille,
    Illud idem (verum est !) esse quod iste putet.

The passage for translation on p. 159 is written in Hexameters. Each line consists of six feet, and each foot consists of a dactyl ($-\,\cup\,\cup$), or a spondee ($-\,-$). The last foot always consists of two long syllables or of a long syllable followed by a short. A pause, or cæsura, usually occurs in the third foot of each line, though

[1] (he) said.

sometimes in the fourth foot as in the first line below, *i.e.*, after *fidem*. According to these rules the first lines of the passage will be scanned thus :—

Spōntĕ sŭ|ā, sĭnĕ | lēgĕ, fĭd|ēm||rēct|ūmquĕ cŏ|lĕbānt.
Pōenă mĕ|tūsq(e) ăbĕr|ānt,||nēc|sūpplēx|tūrbă tĭm|ēbăt
Iūdicis|ōră sŭ|ī,||sĕd ĕr|ānt sĭnĕ|vīndicĕ|tūtī.

If possible, you should ask some classical friend to read aloud to you so that you may gain some idea of the music of Latin verse.

In translating verse you must apply the same general principles as in translating prose, but you must take into account the essential differences in the language and style of both. If you consider a passage of English poetry you will find in it expressions not normally used in prose. Take, for instance, the first verse of Keats' *Ode to a Nightingale*—

> My heart aches, and a drowsy numbness pains
>   My sense, as though of hemlock I had drunk,
> Or emptied some dull opiate to the drains
>   One minute past, and Lethe-wards had sunk :
> 'Tis not through envy of thy happy lot,
>   But being too happy in thine happiness,—
>   That thou, light-wingèd Dryad of the trees,
>   In some melodious plot
> Of beechen green and shadows numberless,
>   Singest of summer in full-throated ease.

Here Keats uses words with special poetic value— *Lethewards*, *beechen*; he prefers the second person singular forms; he inverts the natural prose order—

shadows numberless. In Latin verse, also, the poet modifies language to suit his needs. Words are often given figurative meaning : *fetus*, in the passage you are to translate, means literally " offspring ", but here is used for the " offspring " or " fruit " of the arbutus tree—*arbuteos fetus*. Inanimate things are personified or half-personified. In the sentence beginning *Nondum caesa suis* . . . the pine tree is made the subject, as though it acted of itself, and the sentence might be literally translated—" Not yet had the pine, hewn down on its own mountains, descended to the watery waves that it might visit a foreign land ". The poet means that men had not yet made wooden boats in which to sail abroad, but he prefers the other form because it evokes a more vivid image. Sometimes a singular form is used with a plural meaning, as here, in the phrase *militis usu*, where *militis* means " soldiers ", or, collectively, " soldiery ", or a plural form has singular meaning, as *iudicis ora*, " the face of the judge "; a plain noun is frequently replaced by a descriptive phrase : instead of the oak, Ovid writes of " Jove's spreading tree "—*patula Iovis arbore*—for the oak was sacred to Jove.

The chief difficulty in translating verse is in the word-order, and it is necessary to notice inflections and gender with especial care. In the sentence *Nondum caesa suis* . . . the participle is widely separated from its noun *pinus* in the next line; *suis* is separated from *montibus* by a clause. This unusual order is usually justified by something besides the requirements of metre. Here it points the contrast between *suis* (its own) and *peregrinum* (foreign), and you must try to bring out the contrast in your translation. *Fossae* (two lines later) is the subject of *cingebant*, *gentes* the subject of *peragebant*; both subjects gain emphasis by their position at the end of the line. *Tellus* has the same emphatic position; *ipsa immunis, intacta, saucia* all agree with it, and it governs *dabat*. *Zephyri* comes after the verb it governs and is followed by its object *natos . . . flores*. From this you will see the importance of reading the sentence through several times, and picking out the main verb, subject, and object in due order. Once you do this by habit, the word-order will no longer present difficulties. How can you tell that *patula* in l. 14 is ablative? Scan it, and you will see that the final -*a* is long.

Use your imagination boldly in translating verse; if a passage cannot be literally translated, then translate more freely, if you can do so without infringing the rules of grammar. Finally, in deference to the original, let your translation be in the best English at your command—polished, idiomatic, elegant.

The passage is taken from *Ovid*, who lived from 43 B.C. to A.D. 18. He was a brilliant and successful poet, but he incurred the disfavour of the Emperor Augustus, and was banished to the wild, remote shores of the Black Sea. Much of his verse is left to us, including the *Metamorphoses*, or Transformations, so named because they are legends of people changed into a different form. In this passage, chosen from the beginning of the poem, he imagines the happy Golden Age, when the world was young.

I. Aurea Aetas. The Golden Age

Sponte sua, sine lege, fidem rectumque colebant.
Poena metusque aberant, nec supplex turba timebat
iudicis ora sui, sed erant sine vindice tuti.
Nondum caesa suis, peregrinum ut viseret orbem,
montibus in liquidas pinus descenderat undas,   5
nullaque mortales praeter sua litora norant.[1]
Nondum praecipites cingebant oppida fossae ;
non galeae, non ensis erant ; sine militis usu
mollia securae peragebant otia gentes.
Ipsa [2] quoque immunis rastroque intacta nec ullis 10
saucia vomeribus, per se dabat omnia tellus ;
arbuteos fetus montanaque fraga legebant,
cornaque et in duris haerentia mora rubetis,
et quae deciderant patula Iovis arbore glandes.
Ver erat aeternum : placidique tepentibus auris   15
mulcebant Zephyri natos sine semine flores.
Mox etiam fruges tellus inarata ferebat,
nec renovatus [3] ager gravidis flavebat aristis :
flumina iam lactis, iam [4] flumina nectaris ibant,
flavaque de viridi stillabant ilice mella.   20

—*Metamorphoses*, Book I.

[1] *norant : novi* (perfect of *nosco*) gives the present meaning—
" know ", so the pluperfect will mean " knew ". *Norant* is a contracted form of *noverant*.

[2] *Ipsa* is by its position emphatic, and means " of her own
accord ". The same idea is repeated in *per se* in the next line.

[3] *nec renovatus :* These words go closely together. The negative
affects *renovatus*, but not the rest of the sentence.

[4] *iam . . . iam . . .* usually means " now . . . again . . .", and
so here comes to mean " in one place . . . in another . . ."

Vocabulary

aeternus, -a, -um...eternal

arbor, -is, f....tree

arbuteus, -a, -um...of the arbutus tree

arista, -ae, f....ear of corn

aura, -ae, f....air

caedo, cecidi, caesum, -ere...hew down

cingo, cinxi, cinctum, -ere...surround

colo, colui, cultum, -ere...cultivate, study, practise

cornum, -i, n....wild cherry

decido, -cid-, -ere...fall

descendo, -scendi, -scensum, -ere ...descend

ensis, -is, m....sword

flaveo, -ere...be yellow

flavus, -a, -um...yellow

flos, floris, m....flower

flumen, -inis, n....river

fossa, -ae, f....ditch, trench, moat

fragum, -i, n....wild strawberry

frux, frugis, f....fruit, produce

galea, -ae, f....helmet

glans, glandis, f....acorn

gravidus, -a, -um, heavy

haereo, haesi, haesum, -ere...cling

ilex, ilicis, the ilex tree or holm-oak

immunis, is, e...without compulsion, free

inaratus, -a, -um...unploughed

intactus, -a, -um...untouched

iudex, -icis, judge

Iuppiter, Iovis...Jupiter or Jove (father of the gods)

liquidus, -a, -um, liquid, flowing

mel, mellis, n....honey

metus, -us, m....fear

mollis, -e...soft, gentle

montanus, -a, -um...of the mountain

mortalis, -e, n....mortal

morum, -i, n....blackberry

mulceo, mulsi, mulsum, -ere, stroke, touch gently

nectar, -is, n....nectar (the drink of the gods)

novi (perf. of *nosco,* get to know) ...know

orbis, -is, m....circle; (in the poets) land

os, oris, n....mouth; face (as here)

patulus, -a, -um...spreading

perago, -egi, -actum, -ere...pass, go through

peregrinus, -a, -um...foreign

pinus, -i (or *-us*), m....pine

placidus, -a, -um, placid, gentle

praeceps, -ipitis, steep, precipitous

rastrum, -i, hoe, mattock

rectus, -a, -um...right, here used as noun—righteousness

renovatus, -a, -um...renewed (of land) having lain fallow

rubeta, -orum, n.pl....brambles

saucius, -a, -um...wounded

securus, -a, -um,...free from care

semen, seminis, n....seed

spons, spontis, f....free-will

stillo, -are...drip

supplex, -icis...suppliant

tellus, -uris, f....earth

tepens, -entis...warm

turba, -ae, f....crowd

tutus, -a, -um...safe

unda, -ae, f....wave

usus, -us, m....use, necessity

ver, veris, n....spring

vindex, -icis...defender

viso, visi, visum, -ere...visit

vomer, -eris, m....ploughshare

Zephyrus, -i, m....West wind

2. Here is another passage from *Ovid*, describing how Persephone (called by the Romans Proserpina), the daughter of Zeus and Demeter, was snatched away by Pluto in his chariot while she was picking flowers with her companions in Sicily, and made queen in the lower world. The story originally comes from the Homeric Hymn to Demeter and was retold by Ovid. Tennyson treated the theme in his " Demeter and Persephone " and Milton alludes to it in " Paradise Lost ":—

> Not that fair field
> Of Enna, where Proserpin gathering flowers,
> Herself a fairer flower, by gloomy Dis
> Was gathered—which cost Ceres all that pain
> To seek her through the world.

The Rape of Persephone

Persephone, solitis ut erat comitata [1] puellis,
  Errabat nudo per sua prata pede,
Valle sub umbrosa locus est aspergine [2] multa
  Uvidus ex alto desilientis aquae,
Tot fuerant illic, quot habet natura, colores,
  Pictaque dissimili flore nitebat humus.
Quam simul aspexit, " Comites, accedite ", dixit,
  " Et mecum [3] plenos flore referte [4] sinus ".
Carpendi studio paulatim longius itur,[5]
  Et dominam casu nulla secuta [6] comes.
Hanc videt et visam patruus velociter aufert,[7]
  Regnaque caeruleis in sua portat equis.—*Ovid.*

[1] " accompanied by " (dat.).   [2] " spray ".
[3] For " *cum me* ".   [4] 2nd plur. imperat. of *refero* (bring back).
[5] *Lit.* " it is gone ". Pres. pass. of *eo*, here used impersonally. We should say, " they go ".
[6] Perf. of *sequor* (see Lesson XXXVIII). Understand *est*, " (she) followed ".   [7] 3rd sing. pres. indic. of *aufero*, " carries away ".

Passage No. 11

Peace talks fail. Hannibal recalled to Carthage and given supreme command.

His enim *magistratibus* [1] legati Karthaginienses Romam venerunt, qui senatui populoque Romano gratias *agerent* [2] quod cum iis pacem fecissent, ob eamque rem corona aurea eos *donarent* [3] simulque peterent, *ut* [4] obsides eorum Fregellis essent captivique redderentur. his ex senatus consulto responsum est : munus eorum gratum acceptumque esse; obsides, quo loco rogarent, *futuros*, [5] captivos non *remissuros*, [5] quod Hannibalem, cuius opera susceptum bellum foret, inimicissimum nomini Romano, etiam nunc cum imperio apud exercitum haberent itemque fratrem eius Magonem. hoc responso Karthaginienses cognito Hannibalem domum et Magonem revocarunt. huc ut rediit, *rex* [6] factus est, postquam *praetor* [6] fuerat, anno secundo et vicesimo : ut enim Romae consules, sic Karthagine quotannis annui bini reges creabantur. in

[1] Abl. abs. " these men being magistrates ", *i.e.,* " in the time of . . ."

[2] *Qui . . . agerent* : this is a " *qui* Final " clause. *Qui = ut ei; gratias agere,* to return thanks.

[3] *Donarent,* literally, " to gift them with a crown ". *Donarent* and *peterent* are also final Subjunctives after *qui.*

[4] *Ut redderentur* : Substantival clause after *peterent.*

[5] *Futuros . . . remissuros* : Don't be misled by the omission of *esse* after these words. This is very common in Accusative and Infinitive constructions.

[6] *Rex . . . praetor* : Nepos is here using the term *rex,* strictly " king ", for the name of the two supreme magistrates at Carthage, actually called *suffetes. Praetor* was the name of a magistrate at Rome of less rank than a consul, who was the chief magistrate. Again Nepos is using it for the corresponding magistrate at Carthage. The Carthaginians had of course different names for their magistrates, and quite a different constitution from that at Rome. The name of their chief magistrate was *Suffete.*

eo magistratu pari diligentia se Hannibal praebuit, ac fuerat in bello.

Note.—From *munus* to *Magonem* is *Oratio Obliqua*—that is, *Reported Speech*. In the Subordinate clauses here you will find Subjunctives where you expect Indicatives, and in the Principal clauses *Infinitives*. Thus you would have expected *rogarent* to be *rogabant*: translate as if it were. *Susceptum foret* you would have expected to be *susceptum esset*: translate it as if it were. Note that *forem, fores, foret, foremus, foretis, forent* is another form of *essem, esses, esset*, etc. For *secundus, vicesimus* and *bini* see Table of Numerals in Part III.

LESSON XXXI

FIŌ.—VERBS OF FEARING

The Passive of *facio*, I make, which, remember, is a verb of the Third Conjugation, would naturally be *facior*, but this is not found in Latin. The Passive is *fīō, factus sum, fĭĕrī*. This verb again is only difficult in the Present stem tenses. It means, *I am made* or *I become*. Turn now to the Table and learn it before proceeding.

Verbs of Fearing

There is what may seem a rather strange construction in Latin after verbs of fearing, but it is logical when you think it out.

1. *Vereor ut* (or *ne non*) *veniat* means " I fear that he *may not* come ".
2. *Vereor ne veniat* means " I fear that he *may* come ".

Latin seems to put the statement in exactly the opposite way to English. Where we have " that not "

it has *ut* or *ne non*; where we have " that " it has *nē*.
The Roman thought thus :—

(1) " I am afraid. What is it I fear? I do hope he
will come."

Vereor ut veniat.

(2) " I am afraid. I do hope he won't come. May
he not come."

Vereor ne veniat.

So *ne* introduces the fear that something is going to
happen, and *ut* (or *ne non*) the fear that something may
not happen after all.

These are Substantival *ut* clauses. If the verb of
fearing is *historic* in tense, you have the Imperfect
Subjunctive :—

Verebar ne veniret. I was afraid that he would come.
Verebar ut (or *ne non*) *veniret.* I was afraid that he would not come.

But remember that " I fear to do wrong " is *vereor
peccare*; " I am afraid to cross the river ", *vereor
flumen transire.*

Passage No. 12

*Envoys from Rome arrive at Carthage demanding
Hannibal's surrender. He escapes in a ship to Antiochus,
king of Syria, with whom he plans another attack on
Italy.*

Namque effecit ex novis vectigalibus non solum ut
esset pecunia, quae Romanis ex foedere penderetur, sed
etiam superesset, quae in aerario reponeretur. deinde
anno post, M. Claudio L. Furio consulibus, Roma

legati Karthaginem venerunt. hos Hannibal ratus [1]
sui exposcendi gratia [2] missos, priusquam iis senatus
daretur,[3] navem ascendit clam atque in Syriam ad
Antiochum [4] profugit. hac re palam facta Poeni
naves duas, quae eum comprehenderent,[5] si possent [6]
consequi, miserunt : bona eius publicarunt, domum a
fundamentis disiecerunt, ipsum exulem iudicarunt.

At Hannibal anno tertio, postquam domo profugerat,
L. Cornelio Q. Minucio consulibus, cum quinque navibus
Africam accessit in finibus Cyrenaeorum, si forte
Karthaginienses ad bellum Antiochi regis spe fiduciaque
inducerentur,[7] cui iam persuaserat, ut cum exercitibus
in Italiam proficisceretur. huc Magonem fratrem
excivit. id ubi Poeni resciverunt, Magonem eadem,
qua fratrem,[8] absentem adfecerunt poena.

Note.—The two *quae* clauses at the beginning of this
passage are examples of the Final *qui* construction :
" money such as to be paid ", etc. Remember *pecunia*
is also subject of *superesset.*

[1] *Ratus :* this governs the Accusative and Infinitive, *hos . . .
missos esse.*
[2] *Sui exposcendi gratia,* " for the sake of demanding him ".
[3] *Priusquam . . . daretur,* " before the senate was given to them ".
Senatum dare is Latin idiom for giving an audience of the senate to
any one. *Daretur* is Subjunctive because Hannibal fled intentionally before the audience could be given (see Lesson XXXIV).
[4] *In Syriam ad Antiochum :* We say " to Antiochus in Syria ";
Latin says, " into Syria, to Antiochus ".
[5] *Quae comprehenderent : qui* Final construction.
[6] *Si possent,* " if they should be able ".
[7] *Si forte . . . inducerentur : Si forte* in primary time takes the
Present Subjunctive, in secondary the Imperfect, meaning " in the
hope that ", literally, " if by chance ".
[8] *Eadem, qua fratrem,* " with the same penalty with which ".

LESSON XXXII

IMPERSONAL VERBS.—PASSIVE OF DATIVE VERBS

There are certain verbs in Latin which can only be used in the third person singular and in the Infinitive. They never have a personal subject : hence they are called Impersonal Verbs. Compare " it rains " in English. We say, I pity you, I may do this; Latin says *Miseret me tui, licet mihi hoc facere*, It pities me of you, it is allowed to me to do this.

Note these examples :—

(*a*) Impersonal Verbs taking the dative and Infinitive :—

Eis licet hoc facere.   They may do this.   (It is permitted to them to do this.)
Eis libet hoc facere.   They are pleased to do this.   (It is pleasing to them to do this.)

(*b*) Impersonal Verbs taking the genitive :—

Interest civium regem bene regere.   It is the interest of the citizens that the king should rule well.
Refert militum imperatorem esse peritum.   It concerns the soldiers that the general should be skilful.

Interest is the third person singular of *intersum*.

(*c*) Impersonal verbs taking the accusative of the person and genitive of the cause.

> *Miseret me*, it pities me; that is, I pity.
> *Poenitet me*, it repents me; that is, I repent.
> *Pudet me*, it shames me; that is, I am ashamed.
> *Taedet me*, it wearies me; that is, I am tired of.

Example :—

> *Pudet me huius facti.*   I am ashamed of this deed.

You might also have,

Pudet me hoc fecisse.   It shames me to have done this, *or*
Pudet me quod hoc feci.   It shames me because I have done this.

(*d*) Impersonal Verbs taking the Accusative and Infinitive :—

> *Oportet me*, it behoves me; that is, I ought.
> *Decet me*, it becomes me.
> *Juvat me*, it delights me; that is, I delight.

Examples :—

Oportet me hoc facere. I ought to do this. (It behoves me to do this.)

Oportuit me hoc facere. I ought to have done this. (It behoved me to do this.)

Note.—If you say " it concerns me (you, etc.) to do this " and translate by *interest* or *refert*, you use not *mei*, *tui*, but *mea*, *tua*—the ablative singular feminine of the adjective instead of the pronoun. *Refert* was originally *re fert*, and *mea*, *tua*, etc., agree with *re*.

These are not all the Impersonal verbs, but they will enable you to recognise the construction when you see it. This Impersonal construction is the only one that can be employed in the Passive of verbs which take a dative in the Active :—

> *Invidetur mihi.* I am envied. (It is envied to me.)
> *Parcitur mihi.* I am spared, and so on.

Remember you may use these Impersonal verbs in the third person singular of all the tenses and in the Infinitive, and these are the only parts you can use. If you cannot form any of the tenses turn to the Vocabulary.

My Wish Is My Law

Si libet, licet. *Lit.*, " If it is pleasing it is lawful ".

Passage No. 13

Antiochus is defeated.   Hannibal flies to Crete.

Illi [1] desperatis rebus cum solvissent naves ac vela
ventis dedissent, Hannibal ad Antiochum pervenit.
de Magonis interitu duplex memoria prodita est :
namque alii naufragio, alii a servulis ipsius interfectum eum scriptum reliquerunt.[2]   Antiochus autem
si tam in gerendo bello consiliis eius parere voluisset,
quam in suscipiendo instituerat, propius Tiberi quam
Thermopylis de summa imperii [3] dimicasset.   quem
etsi multa stulte conari videbat, tamen nulla deseruit
in re.   praefuit paucis navibus, quas ex Syria iussus
erat in Asiam ducere, iisque adversus Rhodiorum [4]
classem in Pamphylio [5] mari conflixit.   quo [6] cum
multitudine adversariorum sui superarentur, ipse, quo
cornu rem gessit, fuit superior.

Antiocho fugato, veritus ne dederetur, quod sine
dubio accidisset,[7] si sui fecisset potestatem, Cretam ad

----

[1] Note that *illi* is subject of *solvissent* and *dedissent*.

[2] *Scriptum reliquerunt,* " have left it written " : followed by
Accusative and Infinitive.

[3] *De summa imperii,* " concerning the sum total of empire ",
" concerning the empire of the world ".   Antiochus had formed a
great power in Asia and had crossed into Greece bent on conquest ;
but he delayed too long, and gave the Romans time to send an
army across into Greece which routed him at Thermopylae in 191
B.C.   He then fled back to Asia.

[4] *Rhodiorum :* the Rhodians inhabited the island of Rhodes, off
the south-west coast of Asia Minor.

[5] *Pamphylio :* the Mediterranean near Pamphylia, on the south
coast of Asia Minor.

[6] *Quo :* understand *mari,* " in which sea ".

[7] *Quod . . . accidisset :* Conditional sentence in Past time; non-
fulfilment of condition implied.

Gortynios venit, ut ubi, quo se conferret,[1] consideraret.
vidit autem vir omnium callidissimus in magno se fore [2]
periculo, nisi quid [3] providisset, propter avaritiam
Cretensium : magnam enim secum pecuniam portabat,
de qua sciebat exisse [4] famam. itaque capit [5] tale
consilium.

LESSON XXXIII

QUI AND SUBJUNCTIVE

1. *Legati Romam venerunt qui senatui gratias agerent.*
Ambassadors came to Rome to (who might) return thanks to the
senate.

This might have been put thus :—

Legati Romam venerunt ut senatui gratias agerent.
Ambassadors came to Rome in order that they might return
thanks, etc.

Qui, then, in the above sentence equals *ut ii*, and the
Subjunctive is the ordinary one found in Final clauses.
The tense employed will be the same as if *ut* had been
used instead of *qui*.

In an ordinary clause introduced by *qui* you would
have the Indicative :—

Legati Romam venerunt qui Carthagine missi erant.
The ambassadors came to Rome who had been sent from
Carthage.

---

[1] *Quo se conferret,* " Where am I to betake myself ? " is a Deliberative question. This, even in the direct form, has its verb in
the Subjunctive, *Quo me conferam,* " Whither am I to betake myself ?"
Put indirectly, it becomes Present or Imperfect Subjunctive according to the sequence. Here we have secondary sequence, hence the
Imperfect Subjunctive.

[2] *Fore :* remember this is another form for *futurum esse.*

[3] *Quid :* with *si* or *nisi,* " any one ", " anything ".

[4] *Exisse :* contracted for *exiisse,* which again is for *exivisse (exire).*

[5] *Capit :* this ought strictly to be *cepit,* " took ", but the Present
is put for effect. It is called the Historic Present.

2. Again, in the sentence *Non is sum qui hoc faciam,* I am not the sort of man to do this (literally, I am not he who would do this), *qui* is really equal to *ut ego*, and *is* to *talis*. The *qui* clause, then, is equivalent to an *ut* Consecutive clause; it expresses a consequence, and therefore its verb is in the Subjunctive Mood—*qui* Consecutive. The tense will be the same as after *ut* Consecutive. *Qui* with the Subjunctive is also used after *dignus* (worthy). E.g., *Dignus est qui regat* is the Latin for " he is worthy to rule ".

3. Sometimes it has a *causal* sense equivalent to " in that he ", " because he ". E.g., *Erras qui hoc feceris,* You are wrong who (since you) have done this.

Similarly *qui* sometimes means " although I " (you, etc.) and is followed by a Subjunctive :—

> *Ego qui hoc dixissem condemnatus sum.*
> I although I had said this was condemned.

This of course could also have been translated :—

> *Ego quamvis hoc dixissem condemnatus sum.*

Always be on the look-out, then, for the verb after *qui* in translating, and if it is Subjunctive Mood see which of these shades of meaning is appropriate. Observe, however, the effect of *Oratio Obliqua* on *qui* clauses : see Lesson XXXVI.

What to Read

Hoc lege quod possit dicere vita " meum est ".
> —*Martial.*

Read this, which life can say " is mine ".
(Literally : " *the sort of thing which life can* ", etc.)

Passage No. 14

*How Hannibal tricks the Cretans to save his treasure.
He plans to overthrow Eumenes, King of Pergamum and
friend of Rome.*

Amphoras complures complet plumbo, summas
operit auro et argento. has praesentibus principibus
deponit in templo Dianae,[1] simulans se suas fortunas
illorum fidei credere. his in errorem inductis, statuas
aëneas, quas secum portabat, omni sua pecunia complet
easque in propatulo [2] domi abjicit. Gortynii templum
magna cura custodiunt, non tam a ceteris quam ab
Hannibale, ne ille inscientibus iis tolleret secumque
duceret.

Sic conservatis suis rebus Poenus, illusis Cretensibus
omnibus, ad Prusiam in Pontum [3] pervenit. apud
quem eodem animo fuit erga Italiam, neque aliud
quidquam egit quam regem armavit et exercuit
adversus Romanos. quem cum videret domesticis
opibus minus esse robustum, conciliabat ceteros reges,
adiungebat bellicosas nationes. dissidebat ab eo Pergamenus [4] rex Eumenes, Romanis amicissimus, bellum-
que inter eos gerebatur et mari et terra : quo magis
cupiebat eum Hannibal opprimi.

[1] *Diana :* the Roman goddess of the moon, goddess also of open-
air pursuits—the chase and so forth.
[2] *Propatulum :* this denotes the open space in front of the house
—the courtyard.
[3] *Pontus :* a district and kingdom of Asia Minor on the Black Sea.
(*Pontus Euxinus* is the Latin name for the Black Sea, or simply
Pontus.)
[4] *Pergamenus :* this means " belonging to Pergamum ", a city in
Mysia, a district in the north-west corner of Asia Minor.

Passage No. 15

He invents a secret weapon—poisonous snakes hidden in jars.

Sed utrobique [1] Eumenes plus valebat propter Romanorum societatem; quem si removisset, faciliora sibi cetera fore [2] arbitrabatur. ad hunc interficiendum talem iniit rationem. classe paucis diebus erant decreturi. superabatur [3] navium multitudine : dolo erat pugnandum, cum par non esset armis. jussit quam plurimas [4] venenatas serpentes vivas colligi easque in vasa [4] fictilia conjici. harum cum effecisset magnam multitudinem, die ipso, quo facturus erat navale proelium, classiarios [5] convocat iisque praecipit, omnes ut in unam Eumenis regis concurrant navem, a ceteris tantum satis habeant [6] se defendere. id illos facile serpentium multitudine consecuturos. [7] rex autem in qua nave veheretur, ut scirent, se facturum : [8] quem si aut cepissent aut interfecissent, [9] magno iis pollicetur

---

[1] *Utrobique,* " on both sides ", that is, " by land and by sea ".

[2] When you put *Si hunc removero, faciliora mihi cetera erunt* after a Past verb of saying, it becomes (*Dixit*) *si hunc removisset, faciliora sibi cetera fore.* The Future Perfect Indicative becomes Pluperfect Subjunctive, and the Future Indicative becomes Future Infinitive.

[3] *Superabatur,* " he was being overcome ", " he was inferior ".

[4] *Quam plurimas. Quam* with the superlative means " as — as possible ". *Vasa,* gen. *vasorum,* neut. plur. Second Declension. In the singular the Nominative is *vas,* gen. *vasis,* and the noun belongs to the Third Declension.

[5] *Classiarios,* " the men belonging to the fleet ", " the marines ".

[6] *Satis habere,* " to consider it sufficient "; *tantum,* here " only ".

[7] *Consecuturos* is Future Infinitive after a verb of saying understood before *id;* so *facturum.*

[8] *Facturum ut scirent,* " he would cause them to know ". An *Ut* Substantival clause.

[9] For *cepissent* and *interfecissent* compare *removisset* at the beginning, and note.

praemio fore.[1] tali cohortatione militum facta classis ab utrisque in proelium deducitur. quarum acie constituta, priusquam signum pugnae daretur, Hannibal, ut palam faceret [2] suis, quo loco Eumenes esset, tabellarium [3] in scapha cum caduceo [4] mittit.

LESSON XXXIV

TEMPORAL CLAUSES

If the English sentence begins with " when " and refers to past time, use *cum* with the Subjunctive. If you use *ubi* you will have the Indicative after it. You will also use the Subjunctive always both in Present and Past time if *cum* means " since ". Remember also the peculiar construction illustrated in Lesson VI.

> When I reach Rome I shall do this.
> *Ubi Romam advenero, hoc faciam.*

In sentences like " He did this before the enemy came ", the word " before " is translated by *priusquam* or *antequam*, and these take the Indicative when only the idea of time is denoted, and when the " *before* " clause actually took place : *Hoc fecit prius quam (ante quam) hostes venerunt.* But if you want to bring out the meaning thus, " He did this before the enemy should

---

[1] *Magno praemio fore :* This is what is called the Predicative Dative. Latin says, " He promises that will be for a great reward to them " : we say, " He promises that will be a great advantage to them ", or " will bring a great reward to them ". Similarly we say, " This was a great loss to him " : Latin says, *Hoc ei magno damno fuit,* " This was for a great loss to him ".

[2] *Palam facere,* " to make plain, to disclose ". *Palam* is an adv. meaning " openly ".

[3] *Tabellarius* is a letter-carrier or courier, and the *scapha* was a light skiff.

[4] *Caduceo :* This *caduceus* is the herald's staff, equivalent to our flag of truce.

come ", meaning that he was looking forward to their coming and wishing this to be done before that, you would employ the Subjunctive : *Hoc fecit prius quam hostes venirent,* " He did this before the enemy came ", meaning " might come ".

Sometimes the *prius* and *quam* are separate, thus : *Hoc* prius *fecit* quam *hostes venirent.* There is no change in meaning, however.

Note these two sentences :—

He wished to see Caesar before Cicero came. *Caesarem videre voluit priusquam Cicero* veniret. [Subjunctive because we don't know whether Cicero came or not.]

He happened to see Caesar before Cicero came. *Caesarem forte vidit priusquam Cicero* venit. [Indicative because Cicero definitely came.]

In the second sentence there is no intention expressed, in the first there is.

While

In a sentence like " While he was writing I was reading " you say in Latin, *Dum scribebat ille ego legebam*; but where you say " While he was writing I killed him ", Latin says, very strangely, *Dum scribit eum interfeci.* We may put the Rule thus : If " while " with its verb denotes a longer period at some point in which a certain thing happens, Latin uses a Present Indicative in the " while " clause even in historic time, and sometimes even in Oratio Obliqua.

With the Subjunctive again *dum* and *donec* mean " until ", and denote purpose in addition to time. Thus :—

Manebam dum (or *donec*) *ille veniret.* I was waiting until he should come (intentionally).

Maneo dum (or *donec*) *ille veniat.* I am waiting till he comes.
[Implying intention, and no certainty that he will come.]
Manebam forte donec ille venit. I happened to wait until he came
(*lit.*, I waited by chance). *Venit* is Indicative because he actually came.

A Famous Sentence from St. Augustine's Confessions

Fecisti nos ad te, Domine, et inquietum est cor
nostrum, donec requiescat in te.

'Arry

Here is another poem of *Catullus* on a Roman cockney
'Arry, whose aitches ruffled the wild Ionian Sea. If
'Arry wanted to say " extras " he would say " hextras "
and for " ambush " " hambush ".

Chommoda dicebat, si quando commoda [1] vellet
    dicere, et insidias [2] Arrius hinsidias,
et tum mirifice sperabat se esse locutum,
    cum quantum poterat [3] dixerat [4] hinsidias.
credo,[5] sic mater, sic Liber avunculus eius,
    sic maternus avus dixerat atque avia.
hoc misso in Syriam requierant [6] omnibus aures :
    audibant [7] eadem haec leniter et leviter,
nec sibi postilla metuebant talia verba,
    cum subito affertur [8] nuntius horribilis,
Ionios fluctus, postquam illuc Arrius isset,[9]
    iam non Ionios esse sed Hionios.

[1] *commoda*, additions to soldiers' pay, " extras ".
[2] *insidias*, ambush.
[3] *quantum poterat*, as much as he could—*i.e.*, " with all the strength
of his lungs ".
[4] *cum...dixerat*, with plup. ind. means " whenever ".
[5] *credo*, ironical, " I expect ".
[6] *requierant* for *requieverant*, plup. of *requiesco*, " had begun to
take a rest ".   [7] *audibant* for *audiebant*.
[8] Pres. ind. pass. from *affero*, " bring to ".
[9] *isset*, contraction for *iisset*, " had gone ".

Passage No. 16

*How Hannibal discovers the ship of Eumenes, and
uses his surprise weapon.*

Qui ubi ad naves adversariorum pervenit epistolamque ostendens se regem professus est quaerere, statim ad Eumenem deductus est, quod nemo dubitabat, quin aliquid de pace esset scriptum. tabellarius, ducis nave declarata suis, eodem, unde erat egressus, se recepit. at Eumenes soluta epistola nihil in ea repperit, nisi quae ad irridendum eum pertinerent.[1] Cuius etsi causam mirabatur neque reperiebat, tamen proelium statim committere non dubitavit. horum in concursu Bithynii Hannibalis praecepto universi navem Eumenis adoriuntur. quorum vim rex cum sustinere non posset, fuga salutem petit : quam consecutus non esset, nisi intra sua praesidia se recepisset, quae in proximo litore erant collocata. reliquae Pergamenae naves cum adversarios premerent acrius, repente in eas vasa fictilia, de quibus supra[2] mentionem fecimus, conjici coepta sunt.[3]

LESSON XXXV

NUMERALS

Occasionally through this book a Roman number has been introduced. It will be convenient here to give a few hints as to their use. The tables of Numerals,

[1] *Nisi quae ad irridendum eum pertinerent:* " unless such as pertained to laughing at him ", " jeering remarks ". The Subjunctive is a consecutive one.

[2] *Supra,* adv. " above ".

[3] *Coepta sunt :* note that *coepi* is used in the Passive when combined with a Passive Infinitive.

given in Part III, should be learned off by heart sooner
or later. Don't try to do them all at once : take so
many a day for a week or two, and continually revise
them.

The *Cardinal numeral adjectives*, as they are called—
one, two, three, etc.—are all, except the first three,
indeclinable up to two hundred—that is, the same form
is used whether the noun is masculine, feminine or
neuter, and in all cases.

Ducenti, -ae, -a, two hundred, *trecenti, -ae, -a,* three
hundred, and so on up to nine hundred, are declined like
boni, -ae, -a.

Unus is declined like *solus, -a, -um* (see Lesson XVI).

Duo and *Tres* are declined thus :—

	Masc.	Fem.	Neut.	Masc. & Fem.	Neut.
Nom.	Du-o	du-ae	du-o	Tres	tria
Acc.	Du-o *or* du-ōs	du-as	du-o	Tres	tria
Gen.	Du-ōrum	du-ārum	du-ōrum	Trium	trium
Dat. } Abl. }	Du-ōbus	du-ābus	du-ōbus	Tribus	tribus

Mille, a thousand, is an indeclinable adjective in the
singular, but a noun governing the genitive in the
plural : *mille naves,* a thousand ships ; *duo millia* (or
milia) *hominum,* two thousands of men.

Where we say twenty-three, thirty-five, the Romans
said three and twenty, *tres et viginti* ; five and thirty,
quinque et triginta ; but above a hundred they used the
same form of expression without " and " : one hundred
(and) one, *centum unus* ; two hundred (and) nine,
ducenti novem ; three hundred (and) thirty-five, *trecenti
triginta quinque.*

The *Ordinal numerals* answer the question " which in

order? " that is, they mean first, second, third. They are all declined like *bŏnus*. In the twenty-first year, *uno et vicesimo anno*. (Note the use of *unus* instead of *primus* in this case.)

The *Distributive numerals* are used to denote so many apiece. Thus, We gave them two books each. *Eis binos libros dedimus* (literally, two-each books).

Nouns in Latin which have a singular meaning in the plural require these numerals to make their meaning plural. Thus, " two camps " is *bina castra*; " two letters ", *binae litterae*, but *duae epistolae*.

The *Numeral adverbs* answer to our once, twice, thrice, three times, twenty times, etc. : *Ter hoc fecit*, thrice he did this.

Passage No. 17

*The trick succeeds. Eumenes and his fleet flee.
Rome sends envoys to hunt out Hannibal.*

Quae iacta initio risum pugnantibus concitarunt,[1] neque quare id fieret poterat intellegi.[2] postquam autem naves suas oppletas conspexerunt serpentibus, nova re perterriti, cum, quid potissimum vitarent,[3] non viderent, puppes verterunt seque ad sua castra nautica rettulerunt. sic Hannibal consilio arma Pergamenorum superavit, neque tum solum, sed saepe alias [4] pedestribus copiis pari prudentia pepulit adversarios.

[1] *Concitarunt :* contracted for *concitaverunt*.
[2] *Poterat intellegi :* Impersonal construction : " nor was it able to be perceived ".
[3] *Vitarent :* Deliberative Subjunctive : not " what they were avoiding ", but " what they were to avoid ".
[4] *Alias :* adv. " at other times ".

Quae dum in Asia geruntur,[1] accidit [2] casu ut legati Prusiae Romae apud [3] T. Quintium Flamininum consularem cenarent, atque [4] ibi de Hannibale mentione facta, ex iis unus diceret eum in Prusiae regno esse. id postero die Flamininus senatui detulit. patres conscripti, qui Hannibale vivo [5] numquam se sine insidiis futuros existimarent, legatos in Bithyniam miserunt, in iis Flamininum, qui ab rege peterent, ne inimicissimum suum secum haberet sibique [6] dederet. his Prusia negare ausus non est : illud recusavit, ne id a se fieri postularent,[7] quod adversus [8] ius hospitii esset : ipsi, si possent, comprehenderent : [9] locum, ubi esset, facile inventuros.

LESSON XXXVI

ORATIO OBLIQUA

Re-read, in conjunction with this lesson, Lessons XV and XVI.

If you report a man's words exactly as he said them, you are said to use the *Oratio Recta* ; but when the words are quoted indirectly with the " I's " and " You's " changed to " He's " and so forth, you are said to use the *Oratio Obliqua* or Indirect Statement.

---

[1] *Geruntur :* note the tense, Present Indicative, as always with *dum* when it means " while ".

[2] *Accidit :* Impersonal, " it happened ".

[3] *Apud :* often used in this sense, meaning " at the house of ".

[4] *Accidit casu ut . . . atque,* " it happened that they were dining . . . and one said ". Two Substantival clauses.

[5] *Hannibale vivo :* Ablative Absolute.

[6] *Que,* here = " but ".

[7] *Ne . . . postularent :* a command becoming Subjunctive in the *Oratio Obliqua* after *recusavit :* " Let them not demand ".

[8] *Adversus,* prep. with acc., " against ".

[9] *Comprehenderent :* also represents a command.

Thus in Passage No. 15—" Do ye all attack the ship of
King Eumenes alone, and count it enough merely to
defend yourselves from the rest. You will easily
manage that through the number of the serpents. I
will see that you know in what ship the king is sailing "
—these represent Hannibal's exact words. This is
Oratio Recta. But, " He told them all to attack the
ship of Eumenes only, and count it enough merely to
defend themselves from the rest. They would easily
manage that through the number of the serpents. He
would see that they knew in what ship the king was
sailing "—this is *Oratio Obliqua.*

Often, in Latin, long passages are found introduced
by a verb of saying, and containing thereafter no verbs
in the Indicative Mood, but only Infinitives and Subjunctives. Remember in such passages that the
Infinitives represent the principal verbs of the *Oratio
Recta,* and the Subjunctives, as a rule, the verbs of
subordinate clauses, whether in the actual words these
had Indicative or Subjunctive Mood. *Commands,*
however, in the Imperative Mood become Subjunctive
in such passages. Thus, *In regem Eumenem concurrite,*
would be if reported, (*Dixit*) *in regem Eumenem con-
currerent,* (He said) Let them attack King Eumenes.[1]

The pronouns *ego, tu, nos, vos,* of course, just like I,
you, we, ye, in English, disappear in such a passage,
and only *se, ille, is,* are found—the pronouns of the
third person.

---

[1] Note that " I deny " and " I say that . . . not " are both
translated by *nego,* not by *dico . . . non. Example : Urbs non
capta est* (The city has not been captured). *Negat urbem captam
esse* (He says that the city has not been captured).

Examples

These examples should be carefully read over and examined :—

I see the men who have attacked the town	(He said) he saw the men who had attacked the town.
Video homines qui oppidum oppugnaverunt.	(*Dixit*) *se homines videre qui oppidum oppugnavissent.*
I see the men who are attacking the town.	(He said) he saw the men who were attacking the town.
Video homines qui oppidum oppugnant.	(*Dixit*) *se homines videre qui oppidum oppugnarent.*
I see the men who are about to attack the town.	(He said) he saw the men who were about to attack the town.
Video homines qui oppidum oppugnaturi sunt.	(*Dixit*) *se homines videre qui oppidum oppugnaturi essent.*
When I come to Rome I shall see Caesar.	(He said) when he came to Rome he would see Caesar.
Ubi Romam venero Caesarem videbo.	(*Dixit*) *se ubi Romam venisset Caesarem visurum esse.*

If the verb of saying had been in the Present tense (*dicit*), where in the above sentences you have the Pluperfect Subjunctive you would have the Perfect, where you have the Imperfect you would have the Present, and where you have the Future Participle with *essent* you would have the Future Participle with *sint*.

Passage No. 18

Hannibal's house is surrounded.   Rather than fall into the hands of the Romans he takes poison.

Hannibal enim uno loco se tenebat in castello, quod ei a rege datum erat muneri,[1] idque sic aedificarat, ut in omnibus partibus aedificii exitus haberet, scilicet

---

[1] *Muneri* is called a Predicative Dative. We say " had been given as a gift ", Latin says " had been given for a gift ".

veritus ne usu veniret,[1] quod accidit. huc cum legati
Romanorum venissent ac multitudine domum eius
circumdedissent, puer [2] ab ianua prospiciens Hannibali
dixit plures praeter consuetudinem armatos apparere.
qui imperavit ei, ut omnes fores aedificii circumiret ac
propere sibi nuntiaret, num eodem modo undique
obsideretur. puer cum celeriter, quid esset, renunti-
asset omnesque exitus occupatos ostendisset, sensit id
non fortuito factum, sed se peti neque sibi diutius vitam
esse retinendam. quam ne alieno arbitrio dimitteret,
memor pristinarum virtutum venenum, quod semper
secum habere consuerat, sumpsit.

Sic vir fortissimus, multis variisque perfunctus [3]
laboribus, anno acquievit septuagesimo.

LESSON XXXVII

ORATIO OBLIQUA (Cont.)

In this Lesson we shall give a few examples showing
how Conditional Sentences appear in *Oratio Obliqua* :—

1. FUTURE CONDITIONS

Direct Form	*Indirect Form*
If he does this he will be punished.	(He said) if he did this he would be punished.
Si hoc fecerit poenas dabit.	(*Dixit*) *si id fecisset poenas eum daturum esse.*

N.B.—*Hoc* of the Oratio Recta becomes *id* in the Oratio Obliqua.

---

[1] *Veritus ne usu veniret,* " fearing lest in experience (in actual
life, actually) that might come which came ".

[2] *Puer,* here " slave boy ".

[3] *Perfunctus : perfungor* takes the ablative case after it, where
you would expect the accusative. *Fruor,* I enjoy, *potior,* I get
possession of, *vescor,* I feed upon, *utor,* I use, take a similar ablative.

If he were to do this he would be punished.	(He said) if he were to do this he would (should) be punished.
Si hoc faciat poenas det.	(*Dixit*) *si id faceret poenas eum daturum esse.*

2. PAST CONDITIONS

If he had done this he would have been punished.	(He said) if he had done this he would have been punished.
Si hoc fecisset poenas dedisset.	(*Dixit*) *si id fecisset poenas eum daturum fuisse.*

Note that a Future Participle with the Perfect Infinitive instantly points to a condition referring to the past, and of which you imply the non-fulfilment.

Now turn back and examine Passage No. 11, in which there is a very good specimen of the *Oratio Obliqua* : " The Senate said, ' Your gift is pleasing and accepted ; the hostages will be where you ask ; we shall not send back the captives, because you are keeping Hannibal, by whose means the war has been undertaken, even now in supreme authority over the army '." *Gratum acceptumque esse*, in Hannibal's actual words were *gratum acceptumque est* ; *rogarent* was *rogant ;* *futuros* was *erunt ; remissuros* was *remittemus ; susceptum foret* was *susceptum est ; haberent* was *habent.*

In Passage No. 15 an example of a Conditional sentence in *Oratio Obliqua* is found. Turn now and examine it.

Quem si aut cepissent aut interfecissent magno iis pollicetur praemio fore.

He promises that if they had taken or slain him it would be for a great reward to them. (*Pollicetur* is Historic Present, practically equal to *pollicitus est*.)

His actual words were : " If you take him or slay him it will be a great reward to you ".

Si hunc ceperitis aut interfeceritis magno vobis praemio erit.

Passage No. 19

This passage is taken from Julius Caesar's *Commentaries on the Gallic War*, which give his own record of the period when he was proconsul or governor in Gaul. The province was wild, and but half-conquered; he had to face continual rebellions, in which the Gauls of the north were helped by their neighbours in Britain. His first expedition to this country was one of exploration, and this passage gives some of his notes on the appearance and customs of the Ancient Britons.

The Britons

Ex his omnibus longe sunt humanissimi, qui Cantium incolunt, quae regio est maritima omnis, neque multum a Gallica different consuetudine. Interiores [1] plerique frumenta non serunt, sed lacte et carne vivunt pellibusque sunt vestiti. Omnes verò se Britanni vitro inficiunt, quod caeruleum efficit colorem, atque hoc [2] horribiliores sunt in pugna aspectu; capilloque [3] sunt promisso atque omni parte corporis rasa praeter caput et labrum superius. Uxores [4] habent deni duodenique inter se communes, et maxime fratres cum fratribus parentesque cum liberis; sed, qui sunt ex iis nati, eorum habentur liberi, quo primum virgo quaeque deducta est.—Caesar, *Gallic War*, V. xiv.

[1] *Interiores :* " those further inland ".
[2] *hoc :* ablative expressing measure—" all the more horrible in appearance ".
[3] *capillo . . . promisso . . . omni parte . . . rasa :* ablatives of description.
[4] *Uxores habent deni duodenique :* Not " they have ten or twelve wives in common ", but " ten or twelve men have wives in common ". The custom was apparently to ensure children for each of them.

Vocabulary

aspectus, -us, m....appearance
caeruleus, -a, -um...blue
Cantium, -i, n....Kent
capillus, -i, m....hair
caput, capitis, n....head
caro. carnis, f....flesh
communis, -e...in common
deduco, -duxi, -ductum, -ere...lead away, marry
deni, -ae, -a...(distributive numeral), ten each, by tens
differo, distuli, dilatum, differe... differ
duodeni, -ae, -a...(distributive numeral), twelve each
frumentum, -i, n....corn
humanus, -a, -um...human, civilised
incolo, incolui, incultum, -ere... inhabit
inficio, -feci, -fectum, -ere...dye
labrum, -i, n....lip

lac, lactis, n....milk
liber, -i...child
longe, adv....by far
maritimus, -a, -um...maritime
parens, -entis...parent
pars, partis, f....part
pellis, -is, f....skin
plerique...the majority
praeter...besides, except
promissus, -a, -um...long
quisque (declined like *quis* with the suffix *-que* added)... each
rado, rasi, rasum, -ere...scrape, shave
regio, regionis, f....region
uxor, -is, f....wife
vero...indeed
vestio, -ivi, -itum, -ire...clothe
virgo, virginis, f....maiden
vitrum, -i, n....woad

LESSON XXXVIII

CONJUNCTIONS.—DEPONENT VERBS

Conjunctions

These, as has been already pointed out, join words or sentences. They may be simple Connectives like *et*, *atque*, *-que*, " and ". More commonly, however, they have some special meaning. Thus we have conjunctions denoting :—

Time : e.g., *cum* (when), *postquam* (after that), *antequam* (before that), *priusquam* (before that), *ubi* (when), *donec* (until), *dum* (while), etc.

Place : *ubi* (where), *quo* (whither), *unde* (whence).

Reason : *quod* (because), *quare* (why), *cum* (since).

Purpose : *ut* (in order that), *ne* (lest).

Result : *ut* (so that).

Condition : *si* (if), *nisi* (unless).

Concession : *etsi, quamquam, quamvis, licet* (although).

Comparison : *ut* (as), *quasi* (just as).

Deponent Verbs

Many Latin verbs are *passive in form* but *active in meaning*. E.g., *hortor*, " I exhort "; *hortatus sum*, " I have exhorted "; *hortari*, " to exhort ".

They are called deponents because they have " put down "—*i.e.*, away—some of their parts—*i.e.*, the active voice. They are conjugated like ordinary passive verbs, but of course a deponent cannot have a passive voice. *Hortor* means " I exhort ". If you want to say in Latin " I am exhorted ", you have to use a different word.

There are, however, two exceptions to the above rule :—

1. Most deponent verbs still keep their active voice forms for the present and future participle, future infinitive and the gerund—e.g., *morior* " I die ", *moriens* " dying ", *moriturus* " about to die ", *moriturus esse* " to be about to die "; *moriendum* (gerund).

2. Their gerundives are passive both in form and meaning. E.g., *hortandus*, " fit to be exhorted ". *Milites hortandi sunt* would mean " the soldiers must be cheered up ".

Remember that the past participle is passive in form, but generally active in meaning—e.g., *veritus*, " having feared ".

You will find the commonest ones in the alphabetical list of Latin verbs in Part III, arranged alphabetically among the active verbs. You can spot them because they all end in -*or*. I suggest that you go through the list underlining all the deponent verbs and learning by heart their principal parts. This is well worth doing, because they are exceedingly common in Latin, and it will save you much trouble later in translation if you become familiar with them now. Note that some of them are irregular.

Examples of Deponent Verbs from Horace

1. *Parturiunt montes, nascetur ridiculus mus.*
   The mountains labour, there will be born a ridiculous little mouse.
2. *Video meliora proboque, deteriora sequor.*
   I see a better (way) and approve; I follow the worse.
3. *Dulce et decorum pro patria mori.*
   It is sweet and honourable to die for one's country.

The Joys of Literature

Haec studia [1] adolescentiam [2] alunt, senectutem oblectant, secundas [3] res ornant, adversis [4] perfugium [5] ac solatium praebent, delectant domi, non impediunt foris,[6] pernoctant [7] nobiscum, peregrinantur,[8] rusticantur.[9]—*Cicero.*

This might be translated freely as follows :—

Reading gives food to our youth, and diversion to our old age. It crowns success and offers a haven of consolation in failure. It gives pleasure in the home, and is no handicap in the world outside. Through sleepless nights, in our travels abroad and in the seclusion of the country, it is an unfailing companion.

[1] *studia*, literary studies.
[2] *adolescentiam*, youth.
[3] *secundus*, prosperity—literally, prosperous things.
[4] *adversis*, in adversity.   Understand *rebus*.
[5] *perfugium*, refuge.
[6] *foris*, out of doors—*i.e.*, in business.
[7] *pernoctant*, pass the night.
[8] *peregrinantur*, travel abroad (deponent verb).
[9] *rusticantur*, live in the country.

Passage No. 20

This next passage is very different in style and subject from those you have already read. *Suetonius*, from whose writings it is taken, was the Emperor Hadrian's secretary in the second century A.D. He wrote biographies of the Roman emperors, and in them made good use of all the palace gossip that came his way. The details he gives of their private lives are odd and often very entertaining, and he is always at pains to show the real man behind the almost mythical figure of the Emperor. From him we know the colour of Caesar's eyes and the drastic measures Nero took to perfect his singing voice, and in this passage he describes the plain diet of Augustus, the first and greatest of the Roman Emperors.

The style is easy and familiar, and you should aim at translating it into easy natural English. There are a number of unfamiliar words, which have been given in a list at the end.

Suetonius on Augustus

Cibi [1]—nam ne haec quidem omiserim—minimi erat atque vulgaris fere. Panem et pisciculos minutos et caseum manu pressum et ficos virides maxime appetebat : vescebaturque et ante cenam quocumque tempore et loco, quo stomachus desiderasset.[2] Verba ipsius ex

---

[1] *Cibi . . . minimi erat atque vulgaris fere.* Literally, " He was of very little food and plain for the most part ", *i.e.*, " He ate very little, and for the most part plain food ". This is a rather curious use of *est* and the genitive.

[2] *Desiderasset :* a shortened form of the pluperfect subjunctive *desideravisset.*

epistulis sunt : " Nos in essedo palmulas gustavimus."
Et iterum : " Dum lectica ex regia domum redeo, panis
unciam cum paucis acinis uvae duracinae [1] comedi."
Et rursus : " Ne Judaeus quidem, mi Tiberi, tam
diligenter sabbatis ieiunium servat quam ego hodie
servavi, qui [2] in balneo demum post horam primam
noctis duas buccas comedi priusquam ungui inciperem."
Ex hac inobservantia nonnumquam vel ante initum [3]
vel post dimissum convivium solus cenitabat, cum pleno
convivio [4] nihil tangeret.

Vocabulary

acinus, -i, m....berry

appeto, -ivi, -itum, -ere, reach after, desire (here, like)

balneum, -i, n....bath

bucca, -ae, f....cheek, mouth, mouthful

caseum, -i, n....cheese

cena, -ae, f....supper, dinner

cenito, -are, be accustomed to dine

cibum, -i, n....food

*comedo, -edi, -esum, -ere...*eat

convivium, -i, n....feast

demum...at last

desidero, -are...desire

essedum, -i, n....chariot, carriage

fere...nearly, almost

ficus, -i, m....fig

gusto, -are, taste, eat a little of

ieiunium, -i, n....fast

Iudaeus, -i, m....Jew

incipio, -cepi, -ceptum, -ere... begin

inobservantia, -ae, f....carelessness

maxime, very greatly, especially

minutus, -a, -um...tiny

nonnumquam...sometimes

palmula, -ae, f....date

panis, -is, m....bread

pisciculus, -i, m....small fish

regia, -ae, f....palace

servo, -are...keep, observe

sabbata, -orum, n.pl....Sabbath

tango, tetigi, tactum, -ere...touch

uncia, -ae, f....ounce

unguo, unxi, unctum, -ere... anoint

vescor, vesci (deponent)...eat, feed

viridis, -is, -e, green

vulgaris, -is, -e...common, plain

---

[1] *Uvae duracinae :* a bunch of grapes, that is to say, too hard for making into wine, but suitable for eating.

[2] *Qui :* this refers of course to *ego.* It is awkward to use the relative in this way in English and it is best to translate it by " for ".

[3] *Initum . . . dimissum :* Past participles passive agreeing with *convivium.* Latin uses a participle where we prefer to use an abstract noun or a clause.

[4] *Pleno convivio :* literally " when the banquet was full ". Translate—" While the banquet was in progress ".

LESSON XXXIX

ADVERBS.—MAGIC SQUARES.—SUGGESTIONS FOR FURTHER STUDY

If we know the corresponding adjective it is very easy in Latin to make the adverb. Thus in adjectives of the first class you simply add *-ē* to the stem, as—*durus*, hard, *dur-ē* (hardly), stubbornly; *liber*, free, *liber-ē*, freely.

Benĕ, well, *malĕ*, badly, are very common and should be noted on account of their exceptional quantity, and *benĕ* for its exceptional form also.

But adjectives of the second class form adverbs by adding *-iter* to the stem; when the adjective is like *ingens* simply by adding *-er*. Thus we get *ferox*, fierce, *ferociter*, fiercely; *prudens*, prudent, *prudenter*, prudently.

There is a large class of adverbs, however, in *-ō*, which, by the rule given above, should be in *-ē*. As *falso*, falsely (*falsus*); *necessario*, necessarily (*necessarius*); *subito*, suddenly (*subitus*).

Some Latin Adverbs Common in English

				Literal Meaning
Tandem	.	.	.	At length
Verbatim	.	.	.	Word for word
Alibi	.	.	.	In some other place
Alias	.	.	.	Otherwise
Passim	.	.	.	On all sides

Comparison of Adverbs

If you can compare the corresponding adjective, the adverb gives no trouble. The comparative of the adverb is simply the neuter singular of the comparative adjective. The superlative is obtained from the superlative of the adjective by changing *-us* into *-ē* :—

Liber, free, *liberē*, freely, *liberius*, *liberrime*.
Durus, hard, *durē*, hardly, *durius*, *durissime*.
Prudens, prudent, *prudenter*, prudently, *prudentius*, *prudentissime*.

Just as there are a few adjectives compared irregularly, so there are a few adverbs. Thus we have :—

Bene (*bonus*), well,   *melius*, better,   *optime*, best.
Male (*malus*), badly,   *pejus*, worse,   *pessime*, worst.
Multum (*multus*), much,   *plus*, more,   *plurimum*, most.
Magnopere (*magnus*), greatly, *magis*, more,   *maxime*, most.
Non multum (*parvus*), little, *minus*, less,   *minime*, least.
Diu, long,   *diutius*, longer,   *diutissime*, longest.
Saepe, often,   *saepius*, oftener,   *saepissime*, oftenest.
                                potius, rather,   *potissimum*, especially.

QUADRATA MAGICA

The four Latin words in each square are the same whether read across or downwards. You have had them all in the book, except : *arare*, First Conj., "to plough"; *aper—apri*, a wild boar.

1.

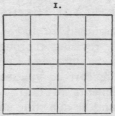

1. Quid est in mari ?
2. Saepe sic rogo.
3. Quid est nobis cunctis **carum ?**
4. Primus incola terrae (not an actual Latin word).

2.

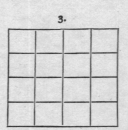

1. Quid nocte nobis lucem
    dat ?
2. A viro ducta femina.

3. Haec res est, quae significat.
4. Quid facit agricola in agris
    in hieme ?

3.

1. Periculosum animal.
2. " I place " Latine.

3. Causalis est coniunctio.
4. Urbs sita in Italia.

SUGGESTIONS FOR FURTHER STUDY

You are now assumed to have worked carefully through this book, revising thoroughly according to some of the methods suggested in the Introduction. If this assumption be correct, you may be said to have mastered the rudiments of Latin. You now know enough grammar, and have a wide enough vocabulary, to begin to read Latin for yourself, and if your main object in learning Latin is to be able to read it intelligently and easily, you need not trouble about studying any more grammar in grammar books. You will learn grammar in the best possible way by reading much and carefully.

If you wish to continue translation from English into Latin, or are preparing for an examination which requires it, there are a number of *Latin Prose Composition* books available, of which one of the best and most recent is *An Outline of Latin Prose*, by Vincent and Mountford (Oxford University Press), but if you prefer one with a key, there is Macmillan's *Latin Course*, Part III.[1] There are several good Latin grammars. Kennedy's *Revised Latin Primer*, for instance, sets out all necessary grammar very clearly. At this stage you should, if possible, obtain some outside help or, at any rate, arrange for your versions to be read by someone who knows Latin. If you cannot join an evening class, you may be able to take one of the correspondence courses now widely advertised.

If, however, you have no aim save to read Latin for pleasure, it is best to set English–Latin aside. Steady practice in reading will rapidly improve your mastery of vocabulary and grammar. You will need a dictionary, but the grammar given in this book will be sufficient for reference.

Before beginning to read on your own account you should make sure of the Irregular Verbs. Time spent on them at the beginning will be amply repaid in time

[1] Flecker and Macnutt's *Complete Latin Course* (Longmans, 2 vols.) gives fuller explanation of syntax and the way to write Latin than most books, but it has no key.

saved during your reading. Turn to the list in Part III. Get a bit of paper about the size of this page, and cover up the whole of the page, leaving only the first part of each verb exposed : *abdo*, *abigo*, and so on. Try, if you can, to put in *abdidi*, *abditum*, *abdere* (to hide); move down your paper to see if you are right ; then try to put in *abegi*, *abactum*, *abigere* (to drive away). Work through the whole of these verbs in this way time after time. By-and-by cover up all but the English meaning on the right-hand side of the page, and try to fill in all the rest. You will never regret the time you spend in mastering this list.

Julius Caesar's *Commentaries on the Gallic War* have for years been regarded as the easiest actual Latin to begin on. Books IV and V, which include his expeditions to Britain, are especially interesting. But Caesar's sentences are frequently long and involved, and you will probably find it easier to read him in a simplified version, such as Part III of *Latin for To-day* (Ginn), which covers most of the Gallic War and has excellent maps, or in a little book, such as *Caesar in Britain*, by Pantin (Macmillan). Many people find Caesar's *Civil War* more interesting, especially Book I, which deals with the war in Spain, or the last seven chapters of Book III, which is his own, though brief, account of his doings in Egypt with Cleopatra. Another of the easier Latin prose-writers is Cornelius Nepos, whom you have already met in this volume. Others of his *Lives* include Greek Generals, such as Miltiades, Themistocles, and Alcibiades. Easier Latin still is the Vulgate or other Latin translations of the Bible. If you prefer to embark on Cicero, whose prose style was the model for centuries and had a profound influence on English writers, such as Dr. Johnson and Burke, you will find his rhetoric a good contrast to Caesar's plainness. Of his speeches, the *Pro Archia*, a defence of the poet's function in the world, or the *Pro Lege Manilia*, a panegyric on Pompey, or the speeches against Catiline are among the easiest. His *De Amicitia* and *De Senectute* are good examples of his polished essay-writing, but they don't tell you a great deal about either friendship or old age. Many readers find his *Letters* more interesting, but they are difficult for beginners. Another interesting letter-writer is Pliny, who lived under the Empire, and whose description of the eruption of Vesuvius, for instance, is thrilling to read and not difficult. A simplified selection of his letters by C. E. Robinson (Allen & Unwin) in the Roman World Series has been edited for beginners with all the help in notes and vocabulary that you will need.

It is a good plan to alternate prose and verse in your reading. The greatness of much Latin poetry cannot be questioned, but very little of it is easy reading for beginners. For centuries Ovid has been the way into Latin poetry for schoolboys. His *Metamorphoses*, of which you have read an extract, are pleasant and tolerably easy, and Book XIII is a good one on which to begin. But Ovid is not everyone's meat, and there is much to be said for beginning Latin poetry with Catullus, a contemporary of Caesar and Cicero, and a poet as human as Burns and as frank as any poet of to-day in expressing his deepest thoughts and feelings. There is an edition of his easiest poems intended as a first Latin poetry book in the Roman World Series (Allen & Unwin).

You might then like to go on to Virgil. His *Aeneid* is the epic story of the foundation of Rome, and should be read as a whole, even if you read parts in translation. Perhaps the best book to begin on in the original is Book II, which describes the fall of Troy, or Book IV, the tragedy of Dido and Aeneas. There are many translations, of which perhaps the best in prose is by Mackail (Macmillan). There is a very readable translation into blank verse by Rhoades in the World's Classics. Many people, however, prefer Virgil's *Georgics*. If you have any liking for bees, read the Fourth. The story of Orpheus and Eurydice, in the same book, is not difficult, and is Latin poetry at its greatest.

Another of the great books of the world are the Odes of Horace, but he is difficult and untranslatable. The edition by Page (Macmillan) is among the best. If you prefer an anthology of Latin poetry, *A Book of Latin Poetry*, by E. V. Rieu (Methuen), can be warmly recommended. It is pure gold, and the notes are exactly what a modern reader needs, but so rarely gets in editions of classical authors. This selection of poems from Ennius to Hadrian is a model of its kind, and an excellent bedside book.

The advantages and disadvantages of using translations in the learning of Latin are debatable. Cribs are still discouraged at schools, because too great a reliance upon them tempts the student to make the English words fit the Latin. In fact you will find it difficult to see the Latin as it really is if you look at an

English translation first.   Moreover, the habit of relying
upon a translation weakens the ability to comprehend
Latin at sight.   On the other hand, good translations,
especially in the absence of a good teacher, can
frequently help the student to a fuller understanding of
the Latin.   If you want translations, the Loeb Classical
Texts, which you will find in the better municipal
libraries, give English and Latin versions side by side.
They vary considerably in their merit, but they are
handy, and include most of the authors you will want
to read.   Many Latin authors are also translated in the
Everyman Library.

If you want an introduction to other Latin authors,
there is Mackail's *Latin Literature*—a stimulating and
brilliant book.   *The Writers of Rome*, by Wight Duff
(Oxford), is a shorter but sound guide.   There is no
need to confine yourself to classical Latin.   Apuleius'
diverting story of the *Golden Ass* is waiting for you,
and the lovely *Vigil of Venus*; and if you would
explore later literature, there is Helen Waddell's
collection of Mediaeval Latin Lyrics.   You may then
like to return to the Classical Age and dip into some of
the great writers which are generally considered to be
too difficult for beginners, such as Lucretius, whose epic
poem, *De Rerum Natura*, contains the germs of the
atomic theory, as well as a courageous defence of
scientific truth against superstition, or Tacitus, the
Carlyle of Ancient Rome, who " wrote history in flashes
of lightning ".

Though in your reading you must struggle at times
with difficulties of syntax and grammar, never forget
that you are also studying literature.   Try to get some

understanding of the Roman background. Even the slight account of the rise and fall of Rome, which is given in Wells' *Short Outline of World History*, will make you better able to appreciate the authors you are reading, or *The Ancient World*, by T. R. Glover, which has been republished in the Pelican series. A fuller account of Roman history, and not less interesting, will be found in C. E. Robinson's *History of Rome* (Methuen).

But perhaps the best book on the achievement of Rome and its legacy to, and influence on, the modern world is *The Roman Commonwealth*, by R. W. Moore (English Universities Press). A slighter, but not less good book, is *Rome*, by Warde Fowler, in the Home University Series. *Everyday Life in Ancient Rome*, by Treble and King (Oxford Press, 3s.), gives a short but vivid account of the way the Romans lived.

There are many historical novels which bring the Romans to life. Naomi Mitchison's novel, *The Conquered*, will give you a better understanding of Caesar, for it tells the story of a Gallic rising from the standpoint of the conquered Gauls. John Buchan's biographies of Julius Caesar and Augustus are well worth reading. Robert Graves' novels, *I Claudius* (reprinted as a Penguin), and *Claudius, the God*, give a vivid picture of life under the Empire, while for a better understanding of the intellectual life of imperial Rome you might read Pater's *Marius the Epicurean*.

PART II

ENGLISH-INTO-LATIN EXERCISES

Exercise 1 (b)

Write down the forms for these English phrases in Latin :—

1. The friendship of the sailors of Italy. 2. The inhabitants of Spain. 3. Of the inhabitants of Italy. 4. By the anger of the sailor. 5. By the victory of the poets. 6. To the islands. 7. For the sailors of Spain and Italy. 8. The shore of Italy.

The following exercise is now to be turned into Latin. To add a little to the interest I have tried to tell you consecutively a few facts about the life of Hamilcar Barca, a famous Carthaginian general, who fought against the Romans.

Exercise 2 (b)

(Words in italics are not to be translated.)

1. Barca is arming *the* inhabitants *of* Spain. 2. *He* was trying at first to win *the* friendship *of the* inhabitants. 3. *He* was defeating many times *the* people of this land. 4. *He* does not love Italy now, nor used *he to* love *it*. 5. *He* was warring with *the* inhabitants *of* Italy, and *he* was ablaze *with* boldness and anger. 6. *He* was fighting in *the* island *of* Sicily. 7. *The* inhabitants *of* Italy, however, were defeating Barca. 8. *He* then asks for *their* friendship and obtains *it*. 9. Now *he* is renewing *his* wrath against Italy. 10. *You* hope for victory, O Barca.

Exercise 3 (b)

Turn into Latin :—

1. We love Philip's sons. 2. Philip's sons used to love the
horses. 3. Philip gives horses to his sons. 4. Where are the
horses of Philip now ? 5. They are in the fields. 6. The goats
and horses belong to (*say* are of) the sons of Philip. 7. With
his horses and his goats and his sons, Philip is in the fields.

Exercise 4 (b)

(Words in italics are not to be translated.)

The Carthaginians fought with *the* Romans three times.
At first *they* fought in Sicily, and *by the* aid *of the* winds *the*
Carthaginians often defeated *the* sailors *of the* Romans.   But at
last near Sicily *the* Roman sailors defeated *their* opponents.
The Carthaginians after that no longer hoped for victory and
refused to renew *the* war.   *They* then asked-for *the* friendship
of their enemies and obtained *it*.   Accordingly *the* Carthaginians
and *the* Romans were no longer enemies.

Exercise 5 (b)

Words in italics do not have separate words in Latin.)

Dear *to* me is *the* cypress in my garden.   For *its* leaves are
full-of-shade.   *It* is tall and old, but *it* was always beautiful.
In autumn *it* is loveliest.   After-that *it* seems rough and
gloomy.   Then *I* am wretched when *I* am looking *at it*, for a
great sadness seems *to* be in my mind.   For many years *I* have
loved my cypress, and *I* shall love *it* for-ever (*say* always).

Exercise 6 (b)

1. They had attacked a large number of Carthaginians in
this place. 2. If we attack this place the Spaniards will renew
the war. 3. When ye have estranged Spain from the Carthaginians, ye will attack Africa. 4. After we have extended
our empire we shall preserve it with great stubbornness.

5. We had hesitated to preserve the Romans when they were in great danger. 6. I had hesitated to approve Barca's plan. 7. After we conquer Africa we shall extend our empire to Spain. 8. We shall refuse to attack the Romans because they have won our friendship. 9. When I have armed the Spaniards I shall fight with the Gauls. 10. In this place we had fought with Philip for many years.

Exercise 7 (b)

1. It is the duty of a commander-in-chief to preserve the limits of the Empire. 2. Ye were pondering in mind the renewal of (to renew) the peace. 3. O Hannibal, you enriched Africa with steeds and money. 4. In autumn the sky is beautiful. 5. The ships of the Romans attacked the Carthaginians near the islands. 6. The Romans, a people of great valour, used to govern all other races. 7. It is incumbent upon a chief to defeat the enemy. 8. To make peace is the privilege of the commander-in-chief. 9. No longer shall we fight with the Romans with ships. 10. When we conquer the fleet of the Carthaginians we shall make peace.

Exercise 8 (b)

1. Caius, by surname Caesar, sailed with large forces to Malta. 2. By land and sea we have defeated the fleets of the Romans. 3. It is not in-keeping-with-my-valour to make peace (see footnote 2, Ex. 8 (a), page 54). 4. We have ratified the peace with a treaty. 5. Ye have violated the treaty, O Carthaginians. 6. We are sailing to Caesar at Rome with great gifts (see footnote 1, Ex. 8 (a), page 55). 7. From Rome to London is a long voyage. 8. The animals of the sea are very big. 9. Man surpasses all animals in virtue. 10. He was renewing the iron-head of his spear.

Exercise 9 (b)

1. However, at Zama the Romans defeated their enemies. 2. For many years, indeed, Pompeius lived at Rome. 3. A

great multitude of the enemy attacked the Romans at break of day. 4. At Carthage the Carthaginians were meditating war. 5. Caesar and Pompey surpassed all other Romans in greed of glory. 6. At Athens there are many beautiful statues. 7. In this way Hannibal had won the friendship of the States of Italy. 8. We were fighting for one year in Africa with a small tribe. 9. Men overcome the greed of money by love of virtue. 10. It is not in-keeping-with-my-custom to attack warlike nations.

Note.—In sixth sentence of Exercise 9 (*b*) say " many *and* beautiful ", and so always in Latin. *Cf.* sixth sentence in Exercise 9 (*a*).

Exercise 10 (*b*)

1. The Romans attacked the Carthaginians while exploring the territory (*omit* while). 2. For already they had estranged all the States. 3. Then with a huge multitude of men the enemy attacked Caesar. 4. However, we shall always value the brave man at a greater price (*for* brave men *use simply masculine of adjective*). 5. We indeed love our wives with a passionate love. 6. The fiery steeds of the Carthaginians will soon attack and put to flight the enemy. 7. Ye have estimated virtue highly, but money more highly still. 8. We shall not only rout the enemy from the walls, but attack their city also. 9. The soldiers estimated at a low value the designs of the brave general. 10. Generals give great rewards to brave soldiers.

Exercise 11 (*b*)

1. Accordingly Caesar with a large army sailed to Britain to attack his enemies. 2. At daybreak we routed a band of the enemy with our cavalry. 3. The magistrates thereafter prepared an army that the enemy might not attack the city. 4. The enemy are stirring up the Gauls to seize the defile by night. 5. With her armies Rome (*say* Romans) conquered the world (*say* all nations *or* races). 6. With their horns goats attack their enemies. 7. The magistrates on the next day dined at home. 8. For Caius had sailed from Rome in the third month. 9. They accordingly arm themselves to preserve

their homes.   10. We approved of this plan that we might avoid a disaster.

Exercise 12 (b)

1. Then his hopes were high, but sad his thoughts.   2. Accordingly, since he had routed the first line, he attacked the second.   3. For to-day we shall doubtlessly rout the enemy's line-of-battle.   4. The enemy were standing in battle array. 5. However, the commonwealth was in great danger, since the Gauls had routed their legions.   6. For they had attacked the Roman legions with the greatest hope.   7. When they had prayed the gods many prayers, they renewed the battle. 8. Many were his thoughts as he looked on the Roman line-of-battle.   9. For with the greatest good-faith Hannibal had made peace.

Exercise 13 (b)

1. But when the Romans conquer those races they will surrender.   2. He sailed to that island by night to sacrifice victims to Jove most high and holy.   3. After the seizure of the defile they explored the fields.   4. Those actions at first stirred up laughter in the *combatants* (translate by dative of Present Participle of the verb *to fight*).   5. Next he routed the legions stationed on the shore.   6. Being accordingly about to attack Rome he prepared a strong army.   7. He suddenly routed the enemy (when they were) about-to-attack the camp secretly.   8. For we have sailed to Africa that we may recover the estranged cities.   9. Where are the conquered forces? They are about to seek peace.   10. How many out of that large army are likely to look upon (*specto*) their fatherland again ?

Exercise 14 (b)

1. We were waging war with the Romans many years. 2. We shall see the line of battle of the enemy on the third day.   3. They will conquer and hold all the world beneath their sway.   4. Ye are leading large forces against the Romans. 5. Before the arrival of the Romans we were waging war with-ill-success (*say* badly) by sea and land.   6. When we were

waging war we always conquered our enemies. 7. But at last we almost came to despair. 8. They were coming to Rome, the strongest city of Italy. 9. We shall carry out important (great) operations (things) with success (with favourable fortune). 10. With undying hatred for the Romans Hannibal is leading an army into Italy.

Exercise 15 (b)

1. He says this man will make an end of this war. 2. He says these men are making an end of this war. 3. These men say those have made an end of these wars. 4. If Catulus refuses to end this war we shall leave Sicily. 5. This man is coming to Africa to end the war and destroy Carthage. 6. The Vettones will slay him while fighting in battle. 7. The bystanders say this woman is brave. 8. He says he will leave Rome to-morrow. 9. On-the-point-of-departure from Sicily he made peace with Catulus. 10. We shall arrive in Rome at daybreak.

Exercise 16 (b)

1. Catulus himself had said he would not end the war. 2. Catulus alone had said he himself had ended the war. 3. If Catulus says he will end the war, we shall sail at once to Rome. 4. We ourselves had thought they were about to return home alone with great disgrace. 5. Those who come to Rome look at the beautiful buildings. 6. Hannibal himself said he alone had removed the enemy from the walls of Carthage. 7. Which-of-the-two said the Romans were slaying the captives? 8. The one said this was so : the other said-it-was-not-so (denied). 9. We had seen the man who (see Note at end of Vocabulary 16) had restored to his country the strongest towns in Africa (say of Africa). 10. Neither said that Caesar gave this province to him alone.

Exercise 17 (b)

1. Yon man was defending Eryx so bravely that the Romans had no hope of success. 2. That man is defending Eryx with

such bravery that the Romans do not think they will take it.
3. He was defending your city in such a manner that the
Romans had no hope of victory.   4. He was so bold as to
say (*say* that he was saying) he would not surrender your
town.   5. The Romans were waging war so badly that they
were losing all their towns.   6. The bravery of that man was
so great that he used to conquer all his opponents.   7. He is so
wise that he sees these things are false.   8. So great a war
broke out that the Carthaginians were losing the towns of
Africa.   9. Which of the two is bold enough to fight with that
man yonder (*say* is so bold that he may fight)?   10. He said
they had lost the empire of all Africa.

Exercise 18 (*b*)

1. The Carthaginians were so terrified that they asked aid
even from the Romans and obtained it.   2. Since, O Carthaginians, ye had lost everything in Sicily ye made peace.
3. You defended Eryx so bravely that we retreated.   4. When
they resolved to make an end of the war they entrusted the
business to Hamilcar.   5. He was so fired with the lust for
war that he refused to leave Sicily.   6. Some were ablaze with
the desire of ruling, others with the desire for (of) money.
7. When he discovered these things were useless for fighting
he destroyed them.   8. So many mercenaries had revolted
that the Carthaginians were in despair.   9. Let-us-leave [1] to
others the desire for warfare (of warring).   10. By sparing the
property of others we shall win their love.

Exercise 19 (*b*)

1. Just now there are many Carthaginians in Sicily.   2. We
were a long time at Rome.   3. If I am (see Note at end of
Vocabulary 19) at Rome I shall come to see you.   4. When
you are (see Note at end of Vocabulary 19) at Rome you will
see the Capitol.   5. He is hastening that he may be at Rome on
that day.   6. Cassius was slain after the battle by his slave

[1] "Let us leave" is first person plural of the Present Subjunctive,
a common meaning.

with a dagger. 7. Antonius had been loved by Cleopatra. 8. When they are defeated by the Romans they will certainly retire from Sicily. 9. If we are defeated in this battle by Scipio we shall certainly be in great danger. 10. When the mercenaries had revolted Carthage was in great peril.

Exercise 20 (b)

1. He defended Eryx in such a manner that he made an end of the war in that place. 2. So great a war had blazed forth that Carthage was never in like danger. 3. Since a hundred thousand of armed men had been brought together (*say* had been made : *facio*) he resolved to attack the enemy. 4. Italy was being harassed by a large number of the enemy. 5. So fiercely did they fight that the town was preserved. 6. Shut in by the narrowness of the position (*say* places), more were slain by famine than by the steel. 7. Ye [1] have been at Rome, but we [1] have not been in Greece. 8. Before the capture of the city (*say*, Before the city taken : *capio*) by the enemy, a large number of them were slain. 9. I had been for many years in Corinth for the purpose of seeing the statues. 10. They were so terrified by these woes that they surrendered.

Exercise 21 (b)

1. Affairs in Sicily are being carried on badly both by land and by sea. 2. No opportunity of doing harm will be given to the enemy. 3. On the contrary, when an opportunity is given (Ablative Absolute), the enemy will be attacked (*lacesso*). 4. Affairs were being carried on well in Sicily. 5. War must be waged in that spot by us. 6. Men must not injure their friends. 7. We must leave Sicily within a few days. 8. The Romans must never yield to the enemy. 9. Eryx must be defended by the Carthaginians. 10. If affairs are going on badly in Sicily we shall depart from that island. 11. We shall resolve to make an end of this war. 12. If our fleet is con-

[1] The pronouns are here emphatic by contrast and are therefore inserted in Latin. Ye = *vos*; we = *nos*.

quered by the Roman consul we shall make peace (remember the tense of " is conquered ").

Note.—No vocabulary is given in this exercise, nor in any succeeding one. The words are mainly taken from the preceding Latin passage, and many of the phrases are closely modelled on it.

Exercise 22

1. I was ablaze with greed for war : you thought we must pay regard to peace.   2. He gave these gifts to us, to you those.   3. You are the wisest of us all, I am the bravest.   4. Having been subdued they surrendered to us.   5. My fatherland is very dear to me, although worn out by the disasters of war.   6. He (that man) is wiser than you.   7. He is sending these gifts to the wisest man of the Romans.   8. I was ablaze with keener passion for war than you.   9. This task is the easiest of all, that the most difficult.   10. He is very like his father (genitive) ; his brother is more like his mother (genitive).   11. I will rather perish amid the ruins of my country.   12. He said he would go home in (with) the deepest disgrace.   13. Thereafter we had made peace with this design.   14. He and his men laid down their arms and left Sicily (*Latin says,* arms having been laid down left).

Exercise 23

1. He was entreating them to do those things.   2. I have entreated them to do these things.   3. They made it their aim to send an army into Spain.   4. We shall bring it to pass that we are sent into Spain as generals.   5. We have found our country in a much different condition from what we expected.   6. He gathered together mercenary soldiers that he might use them against the Romans.   7. We have attacked Carthage itself that all Africa may be alienated.   8. He will drive them to such a point that more will be perishing by famine than by the steel.   9. The senate decreed that Carthage should be attacked and destroyed.   10. The senate decrees that Carthage is to be attacked and destroyed.   11. The senate will decree

the destruction of Carthage (*say* that Carthage may be, etc.).
12. He attacked Carthage in order that he might destroy it.
13. He entreated him not to send him to Rome. 14. He
ordered the soldiers to remove the enemy from the walls.
15. He has ordered the soldiers to leave Italy at once.

(Tell in each sentence whether you are using a Final,
Consecutive or Substantival Subjunctive.)

Note.—" *That not* " *in a Consecutive clause is* "*ut non*"; in
the other two, *ne*. Similarly " that never " is *ut nunquam*,
" that none " *ut nullus*, but in the Final and Substantival
clauses *ne unquam*, *ne quis*.

Exercise 24

1. Catulus commanded the Carthaginians to leave Sicily.
2. He came-to-the-aid of the estranged towns (*subvenio*).
3. I was envying Hannibal his supreme command over the
army. 4. The chief by his bounty did much good to the
Carthaginians (*say* benefited many things : *multa* and dative).
5. We will restore to our country the strongest towns of all
Africa. 6. We shall never be slaves to Hannibal and the
Carthaginians. 7. He said he would never be a slave to the
Romans (*say* he denied he would ever). 8. He has restored
such peace to Africa that there seems to have been no war
within many years. 9. He was sent with an army to Spain
that he might find more easily a pretext for war. 10. You are
taking with you your son nine years of age. 11. He mentioned
this man because he accomplished many great deeds. 12. We
will oppose our foes by land and by sea. 13. Hannibal
threatens the Romans with perpetual war (*say* threatens
perpetual war to the Romans). 14. He came to Spain with
an army that he might the better accomplish these things.
15. When he had accomplished these things in accordance
with his wish he set out for home.

Exercise 25

1. If his affairs had been restored he would have renewed
the war (see Passage No. 2). 2. If he had conquered them by

his valour they would have surrendered (see Passage No. 2).
3. If Catulus had said he would not end the war, the Romans
would have left Sicily.   4. If his affairs were to be restored, he
would renew the war.   5. If he conquers them by his valour
they will surrender.   6. If he should conquer them by his
valour they would surrender.   7. If Catulus were to refuse to
end the war they would leave Sicily.   8. If Catulus refuses to
end the war they will leave Sicily.   9. The second Punic war
seems chiefly to have been stirred up by the undying enmity
of this man for the Romans.   10. Carry out great exploits,
subdue the most warlike races, and enrich Africa with men and
money.   11. He said Africa would be enriched with steeds and
men.   12. He said he was meditating carrying on the war
into Italy.   13. He says Africa is being enriched with men and
money.   14. They were slain in the ninth year after they came
into Spain.   15. Love your enemies.

Exercise 26

1. We shall be able to conquer the Romans.   2. They were
able to conquer all nations.   3. Ye were able to surpass all
nations in valour.   4. Thou canst not kill thine enemy.
5. We had been able utterly to subdue the valour of one man.
6. You will have been able to lay down your hatred for the
Romans.   7. He says he can kill his enemies.   8. He says he
can surpass all races in valour.   9. He says Hannibal could
have surpassed all generals in forethought.   10. If Hannibal
were here now he would be conquering Italy.   11. If Hannibal
had been in that battle he would have defeated the enemy.
12. If Hannibal had not surpassed all generals in skill, he
would not have been the greatest general of all (if not = *nisi*).
13. If we had been doing this we would have suffered the
severest punishment (paid the heaviest (*gravissimus*) penalty).
14. If you[1] had done this, you would have been suffering the
most severe (*gravissimus*) penalties.   15. If he had been wise
he would not have been doing that.

[1] Use the singular.

Exercise 27

1. There is no doubt but that he is returning.   2. There was no doubt but he was returning.   3. It is impossible that he is not departing.   4. It was impossible that you were not departing.   5. There was no one but thought the enemy were departing.   6. There is no one but is now entering the city.   7. If he was approaching Rome he was making a mistake.   8. If he is entering the house he is a fool.   9. I shall go to Rome if he will go to Carthage.   10. If he is doing this there is no good in it (*say* nothing of good, *nil boni*).

Exercise 28

1. They are asking him whether he will bring them their books.   2. They are asking him if he is bringing much money with him.   3. They are asking him if he has brought much money with him.   4. We asked them if they had brought any money with them (*say* anything of money, *quid pecuniae*).   5. We asked them if they were bringing any money with them.   6. We asked them if they would bring much money with them.   7. If you bring (*duco*) with you all the cavalry, you will win the day (you will conquer, simply).   8. He asked me if I would go with him to the camp.   9. Hamilcar asks Hannibal if he will go with him to the camp.   10. He has gone away to bring the cavalry.   11. We asked him when he would return to Rome.   12. I do not know what books he is bringing with him from Italy.   13. The soldiers did not know whether that was being approved of in-the-name-of-the-State.   14. Within the next three years, the Carthaginians subdued all the nations of Spain.

Exercise 29

(For Vocabulary, look back to Passages Nos. 7 & 8.)

1. They have begun at last to cross the defile of the Pyrenees.   2. He preferred to send one of these armies into Africa.   3. Hannibal has brought it to pass that an elephant with its equipment is able to go by that way.   4. He attempted to

join battle with Publius Cornelius Scipio at the river Po.
5. They ought to leave one army in Spain and lead the other
into Italy (the one . . . the other, *alter . . . alter*). 6. They
ought to have left one army in Spain and led the other into
Italy (*say* " were owing to leave " : Latin makes *debeo* Past,
and the Infinitive Present tense). 7. We know how to lay
open the country and make roads. 8. It seems that Hannibal
crossed the Alps by the Graian defile (*say* Hannibal seems to
have, etc.). 9. It is said that Hannibal routed (*profligo*) the
inhabitants of the Alps (*Alpici*) in trying to prevent his
passage (*say* Hannibal is said). 10. On this journey they were
afflicted with so serious a disease that half the army (*say*
" half of the army ", using *dimidium*, half) perished (*intereo*).

(The following are five sentences on Indirect questions.
Remember " whether . . . or not " is *utrum . . . necne*.)

11. They do not know whether Hannibal has made for
Etruria or not. 12. I cannot tell whether Hannibal wishes
this or not. 13. He asked if he was unwilling to go into Spain
and would prefer to remain at Carthage. 14. We shall ask
them when they prefer to do this. 15. You have told us what
the enemy were wishing.

Exercise 30

(For Vocabulary, look back to Passage No. 8.)

1. He stayed in the mountains near the city for the purpose
of holding his camp there. 2. He set out for Rome to fight
this battle. 3. He wished to send forward Caius Centenius
the praetor, for the purpose of seizing the defile. 4. He won
great glory by routing the enemy in one battle. 5. We
would have preferred to appoint decemvirs for the purpose of
drawing up laws. 6. He has done this that Hannibal may be
willing to end the war. 7. He wished to march quickly for
the purpose of surrounding the enemy. 8. When he was
weighed down by a serious disease he preferred to be carried
in a litter. 9. He marched into Apulia to meet the consuls
(use Supine, or *ad* and Gerund). 10. With none to oppose he
advanced on Rome to storm the city. 11. Quintus Fabius

Maximus wished to throw himself in his path.   12. They were
unwilling to advance on Rome to attack the city.   13. He
did this in order that the consul might be unwilling to leave the
city.   14. He returned to Capua to attack the Romans.
15. He surrounded the consul and his army and slew them.

Exercise 31

Note that verbs like " to be ", " to become ", " to be
named ", " to be chosen ", take the same case after as before
them.

1. I fear that Caesar may not become king.   2. I was
afraid that Caesar might not become king.   3. They were
afraid that Caesar would cross the river.   4. They are afraid
that Caesar may cross the river.   5. Caesar was afraid to
become king.   6. Caesar is afraid to become king.   7. Caesar
is afraid to cross the river.   8. Caesar was afraid of crossing
the river.   9. By cultivating virtue we shall become happy.
10. Within not so many days these men will become consuls.
11. After this achievement I shall become a very clever
general.   12. Caesar said that that man had been made
consul by treachery.   13. Caesar says he has no fear of
Cicero's becoming consul (*say* lest Cicero may become).   14.
Men become good generals by practising military matters.
15. From this it is possible to see how great a general he
became.

Exercise 32

(For Vocabulary, look back to Passage No. 10.)

1. He pitied the son of the general whom he had routed at
the Rhône.   2. I ought to defend my fatherland when called
back home.   3. He ought to have defended his fatherland
when called home.   4. I am delighted to have ended so great
a war.   5. They are glad because they have collected those
who remain from the rout (they are glad to have collected).
6. The Romans were ashamed at having been defeated at
the Trebia by Hannibal.   7. I know the Romans were ashamed
of their defeat on the Trebia (*say* to have been defeated, *or*

because they, etc.). 8. He knew the Romans had repented of the destruction of Carthage (because they had destroyed : Pluperfect Subjunctive explained in Lessons XXXVI and XXXVII.) 9. You may be consul at Rome and not be-at-the-head-of an army. 10. He might have been king at Carthage if he had wished. 11. It was his pleasure to remain at Hadrumetum collecting the remnants of his army (say *reliquos*). 12. It was the interest of the soldiers to obey the commands of Hannibal faithfully; it is ours to defeat Hannibal himself. 13. It concerns all of us to do what is right. 14. He said he had been permitted to prepare an army by fresh levies. 15. The Numidians repented of having set an ambush for Hannibal. 16. They have been persuaded to do this. 17. The fields will be injured by the Carthaginians. 18. If the fields are injured by the Carthaginians we shall send ambassadors to Rome. 19. The king will be obeyed by all good citizens (say, *optimus quisque,* " each best man "). 20. The soldiers were commanded to depart from the city within three days.

Exercise 33

(For Vocabulary, see Passage No. 11.)

1. Ambassadors are coming to Rome to return thanks to the senate and people of Rome. 2. Ambassadors have come to Rome to return thanks to the senate and people of Rome. 3. Ambassadors went to Rome to seek peace from the Romans. 4. Ambassadors will go to Rome to seek peace from the Romans. 5. The Carthaginians are not the sort of men to make peace. 6. The Romans were not the sort of men to ask for (*peto*) peace. 7. I, since I had come too late (*serius*), did not see my father. 8. Although you have been the cause of this war we shall keep you in authority over the army. 9. They, since they had been recalled, returned home. 10. They, since they have been recalled, will return home. 11. They besought them to keep their captives at Fregellae. 12. They gave them a golden crown because they had made peace with them.

Exercise 34

(For Vocabulary, see Passage No. 13.)

1. When he had weighed anchor and set sail, two ships were sent to seize him.   2. When he has weighed anchor and set sail, we shall send two ships to seize him.   3. He was slain by a slave before he had written the letter.   4. The slave has been ordered to slay him before he writes the letter.   5. On the rout of Antiochus, he fled before the Romans could seize him.   6. While he was writing a letter to his mother in Rome, the slave slew him.   7. While his men were being overcome by the multitude of their opponents, Hannibal was routing those with whom he had engaged.   8. While he was journeying from Carthage to Crete, pirates (*latrones*) attacked him (either *dum* or Present Participle).   9. Hannibal waited until the fleet of the Rhodians joined battle.   10. He was unwilling to halt (*consistere*) until he should get to the Gortynii in Crete.   11. While Hannibal was with Antiochus he was successful in all his battles.   12. This would undoubtedly have happened had he put himself in the power of the Romans.   13. He resolved to depart before he should come into great danger on account of the avarice of the Cretans.   14. So long as Antiochus was willing to follow out (*say* obey) Hannibal's advice, he was successful in war.   15. In despair, Hannibal came to Antiochus in Syria.

Exercise 35

(For Vocabulary, see Passage No. 14.)

1. They had filled three hundred and sixty-five jars with lead.   2. Two hundred and twenty-nine jars had been filled with gold and silver.   3. He gave three apples to the boy.   4. He said he would have given (himself to have been about to give) two hundred ships to Hannibal.   5. Rome was founded in the year B.C. 753 (*say* in the 753rd year before Christ having been born).   6. The battle of Cannae was fought in B.C. 216.   7. Hannibal lived for seventy years.   8. Caesar had given two ships to each leader.   9. We shall give them two hundred sesterces each.   10. Darius set sail for Europe with more than

a thousand ships.   11. Three times the Romans charged the
enemy, but at last they were routed.   12. I have seen the city
of Rome twenty times ere this.   13. Hannibal came down from
the Alps into Italy with twenty-five thousand men.   14.
For sixteen years under the leadership of Hannibal, Carthage
waged war with Rome.   15. In B.C. 202, at Zama, the Romans
utterly-conquered the Carthaginians (use *devinco*).

Exercise 36

(For Vocabulary, see Passage No. 15.)

1. He said that Eumenes had more power through the
alliance with the Romans.   2. He said that those men would
come together on the day on which he was intending to fight
by sea.   3. He said he saw those who were fighting in this
naval battle.   4. He said he had seen those who were fighting
in this naval battle.   5. He said he would take care that they
knew in what ship the gold was being carried.   6. He thought
if he removed this man all would be easy for him.   7. He said
he had seen the general who had fought so long (*tamdiu*) with
the Romans.   8. He says he has seen the messenger who was
sent with the herald's wand to Eumenes.   9. He says those
who are attacking the ship of Eumenes are being routed.   10.
He says that those who attack the ship of Eumenes will be
routed (" who attack " in Latin becomes " who may have
attacked ").   11. Hannibal sends the messenger before the
signal for battle can be given.   12. He said Hannibal sent the
messenger before the signal for battle could be given.   13. He
said Hannibal had sent the messenger before the signal for
battle had been given.   14. He said Hannibal sent the letter-
bearer to show his men where the king was.   15. He said he
had commanded them all to attack the ship of Eumenes alone.

Exercise 37

(For Vocabulary, see Passage No. 16.)

1. He said he would not secure that unless he betook himself to the protection of his own troops (*say* within his own
forces).   2. He said he would not secure that unless he were

to betake himself to the protection of his own troops. 3. He said he would not have secured that unless he had betaken himself to the protection of his own troops. 4. He said he would not be a fool if he were doing that. 5. He promised that if they took or slew him there would be a great reward for them. 6. He asserted that if they had taken or slain him there would have been a great reward for them. 7. He said that if they were to slay him there would be a great reward for them. 8. He said if he had not sought safety in flight he would have been slain (*say* it to have been about to be . . . that (*ut*) he should be slain : *i.e.*, future participle with perfect infinitive followed by *ut* with Imperfect Subjunctive). 9. He said if they should not seek safety in flight they would be slain. 10. He says if they do not seek safety in flight they will be slain (Future Perfect after Primary tense becomes Perfect Subjunctive). 11. He says if they had not sought safety in flight they would have been slain. 12. He says if they had not been fools they would not have been doing that. (Keep same tense of Subjunctive as in direct form.) 13. Although he was marvelling at the reason of this, yet he did not hesitate to join battle. 14. No one doubted but that he had brought some message concerning peace. 15. Having thus made known the ship to his own side he returned to the same place whence he had come.

Exercise 38

(For Vocabulary, see Passage No. 18.)

1. The throwing of these things suddenly produced laughter in the combatants. 2. They were so terrified by the strange occurrence that they could not see what especially to avoid. 3. Ill-success is the mark of a bad general. (Ill-success = to wage war badly.) 4. Although they saw Antiochus making many very foolish attempts they on no occasion deserted him (see Passage No. 13). 5. Since he saw he was not strong enough (*say* too little strong) in the resources of his own kingdom, he won over all other princes (see Passage No. 14). 6. A fierce war was being waged (*say* a war was being waged

fiercely) between them both by land and sea : therefore Hannibal was the more eager for his overthrow (see Passage No. 14). 7. He said he would very easily find the place where he was. 8. He ordered the soldiers to bring him word speedily whether he was beset on all sides. 9. The boy very quickly reported that all the outlets were seized. 10. The Carthaginians perceived this was no chance occurrence, and their empire could no longer be maintained. 11. I will bring you word quickly what it is. 12. If you had ordered us we would easily have found where he was (from *facilis* you expect *faciliter*, but the adverb is *facile*). 13. He saw that they had not come by chance, but were seeking him. 14. Mindful of his former valour, he took the poison not to lose his life at the bidding of another. 15. The messengers reported that an unusual number of armed men were in sight.

PART III

KEY TO THE PASSAGES FOR TRANSLATION IN LESSONS XX TO XXXIX

(Keys to the other passages and extracts will be found in the next section.)

Passage No. 1

Literal Version

HAMILCAR, father of Hannibal, by surname Barca, a Carthaginian, in the first Punic war, but in the last times, quite a young man, in Sicily, began to be in command of the army. When (although) before the arrival of him both by land and by sea the affairs of the Carthaginians were being carried on badly, he himself, when he was present, never to the enemy yielded, nor gave a place of injuring, and often on the contrary, a chance having been given, attacked and ever departed superior (victor). Which having been done, when almost everything in Sicily the Carthaginians had lost, he (that man) so defended Eryx that a war in that place was not seeming to have been waged. Meanwhile the Carthaginians by means of a fleet at the Aegatian Islands by Caius Lutatius consul of the Romans having been defeated, resolved to make of the war an end and that matter entrusted to the judgment of Hamilcar.

Second Version

Hamilcar, the father of Hannibal, by surname Barca, a Carthaginian, near the end of the first Punic war, took over the command of the army in Sicily (while) quite a young man. Although before his arrival the Carthaginians were faring badly both by land and sea, he himself when he was present never yielded to the enemy nor gave them a chance of doing him harm. On the contrary, often when a chance had been given, he attacked (them) and always came off the victor. And on this being done (by doing this), although the Carthaginians had lost almost everything in Sicily, he so defended Eryx that the war did not seem to have been fought in that spot. Meanwhile the Carthaginians on their defeat at the Aegatian Islands by Caius Lutatius, consul of the Romans, with a fleet, resolved to end the war and entrusted that business to the discretion of Hamilcar.

N.B.—Make absolutely certain that you know every word in this before going on—parts of verbs, stems of nouns, etc. Use freely the Table of Irregular Verbs.

Passage No. 2

Literal Version

That man (Hamilcar) although he was blazing with the greed of warring, yet thought he must pay-regard-to peace, because he was perceiving that his fatherland, worn out by expenses, longer to endure the calamities of war was not able. With this design he made peace, in which so great was his boldness, since Catulus was

denying that he the war would end unless he (Hamilcar)
with his men, who had held Eryx, their arms having
been left should leave Sicily, that, his fatherland lying
prostrate, he himself said he would rather perish than
with so great disgrace (he would) return home : for
(he said) it not to be of his valour the arms received
from his fatherland against the enemy to surrender to
his foes.   To the obstinacy of this man Catulus yielded.

Notes

Nisi decederent : Catulus said, " I will not end, unless they shall
be departing ".   This " shall be departing " becomes Imperfect Subjunctive when the words are reported; just as in English they
become " he would not end unless they should depart ".

Note the pronouns *ipse* subject to *dixerit, se* referring to *ipse* but
the subject of *periturum.*   *Se, suus* always refer to the subject of
the main verb, here to *dixerit.*

Second Version

Although he was ablaze with eagerness for war, yet
he thought he must pay regard to peace because he felt
that his fatherland, worn out by the expense, could not
longer endure the disasters of the war.   With this
design he concluded peace.   In this, such was his
boldness, when Catulus refused to end the war, unless
he and his men who had held Eryx should lay down
their arms and leave Sicily, that he said he would rather
perish amid his country's ruins [1] than return home with
such dishonour; for it was not in keeping with his
valour to surrender to his foes the arms he had received
from his fatherland against the enemy.   Catulus
yielded to his obstinacy.

[1] *Succumbente patria :* his fatherland lying low, Ablative Absolute.
This may be translated very freely as above.

Passage No. 3

Literal Version

But that man, when he came to Carthage, by much otherwise than he had hoped, found the State holding itself. For by the length (duration) of the foreign evil, so great an internal war blazed out that never in like danger Carthage was unless when it was destroyed. At first, the mercenary soldiers, whom they had used against the Romans, revolted; of whom there was a number of twenty thousands. These estranged all Africa, attacked Carthage itself. By which evils, so were the Carthaginians terrified, that even aids from the Romans they sought and obtained them. But at last, when almost now to despair they had come, they made Hamilcar general. That man, not only the enemy from the walls of Carthage removed, when more than a hundred thousand of armed men had been made, but even drove them to that point that, by the narrowness of the places shut in, more (men) by famine than by steel were perishing.

Notes

Ut : note this use of *ut,* meaning " when ", taking the Indicative.
Rempublicam se habentem : accusative after *cognovit.*
Ut . . . fuerit : This is of course a Consecutive clause. Note *tantum.*
Viginti milium : a Descriptive Genitive, describing *numerus.*
Quibus malis : Latin says " By which evils "; we would say " By these evils ".
Adeo . . . ut . . . petierint : Consecutive Subjunctive again.
Amplius : an adverb meaning " more ". You might expect the ablative after it, since " than " is omitted; but in Latin this adverb often has no effect on the case of the number with it. *Amplius centum milia* (not *centum milibus*), more (than) 100,000 (*centum,* a hundred, is indeclinable).
Eo . . . ut : This is again a Consecutive clause : *eo,* " to that point ", " to such a point ", . . . *ut,* "that".

Second Version

But when he came to Carthage, he found the state of his country far different from what he had expected. For through the duration of their misfortunes abroad, so serious an internal war had risen, that Carthage was never in like danger unless when it was destroyed. At first the mercenary soldiers, whom they had employed against the Romans, revolted. The number of these was twenty thousand. These alienated the whole of Africa (and) attacked Carthage itself. The Carthaginians were so panic-stricken at these disasters that they even sought aid from the Romans and obtained it. But at last when now they were reduced almost to despair, they made Hamilcar commander-in-chief. He not only removed the enemy from the walls of Carthage, although more than a hundred thousand armed men had come together, but even drove them to such a pass that, shut in by the straitened nature of the position, more were perishing by famine than by steel.

Passage No. 4

Literal Version

All the estranged towns, among these Utica and Hippo, the strongest of all Africa, he restored to his fatherland. Nor with that was he content, but he even extended the bounds of (her) empire, in all Africa so great repose made that in it no war seemed within many years to have been. These matters, in accordance with his wish, having been accomplished, with a confident heart and hostile to the Romans, by which the more easily a cause of warring he might find, he effected that as general with an army into Spain he should be sent, and thither with himself he took his son Hannibal of nine years. There was besides along with him a young man, distinguished, handsome, Hasdrubal; concerning this man therefore we have made mention because Hamilcar having been slain, he was in command of the army, and great things carried out, and first by bribery the ancient manners of the Carthaginians corrupted, and of the same man after the death, Hannibal from the army received the command.

Notes

Patriae : Dative of the Recipient, the one who receives.

Imperium means firstly " absolute authority ", then " dominion ", " sway ", and almost like our " empire ".

Tota Africa : Note the Ablative of Place without the preposition *in*.

Ut . . . videretur : a Consecutive *ut* clause. Latin says " no war seemed to have been "; we should say " it seemed as if there had been no war ".

Multis annis : Ablative of the Time within which, as often in Latin : " within many years ".

Ex sententia mea, sua, nostra : Latin phrases for " in accordance with my, his, our view, opinion, wish ", etc.

Fidenti animo : Ablative of Description.

Secum : after the personal pronouns, *me, te, se, nobis, vobis,* you place *cum,* meaning " along with ", instead of before them; *mecum,* " along with me ", *tecum,* etc. Note *se* here because referring to the subject of the main verb, *duxit.*

Princeps (= *primus,* first) is in apposition with the subject of *pervertit.*

Largitione : Ablative of Means, " by means of bribery ".

Second Version

He restored to his country all the towns that had been lost, among these Utica and Hippo, the strongest in all Africa. And he was not content with that, but also extended the limits of her sway, and restored such profound repose in all Africa, that it seemed as if there had been no war in it for many years. On the satisfactory completion of these affairs, with a confident heart full of enmity towards Rome, he secured his despatch to Spain with an army as commander-in-chief. Along with him he took thither his son Hannibal, nine years of age. There was besides along with him a distinguished and handsome youth, Hasdrubal. Of this man we have made mention for this reason, because (that) when Hamilcar was slain, he took command of the army and performed great exploits, and was the first to corrupt by bribery the ancient character of the Carthaginians; and after the same man's death, Hannibal received from the army the supreme command.

Passage No. 5

Literal Version

But Hamilcar, after the sea he crossed and into Spain came, great exploits performed with favourable fortune : the greatest and most warlike races he subdued, with horses, arms, men, money all Africa he enriched. Here when into Italy the war to carry he was deliberating, in the ninth year, after into Spain he had come, in battle fighting against the Vettones, he was slain. Of this man, the continual hatred towards the Romans especially, to have stirred up the second Punic war (seems). For Hannibal the son of him, by the continual entreaties of his father, to that point was brought that to perish than the Romans not to try he was preferring.

Notes

Posteaquam = *postquam*, after (conjunction).

Transiit . . . venit : note Latin using the Perfect where we rather employ the Pluperfect.

Secunda fortuna : an Ablative of Description, " with success ".

Totam locupletavit Africam : note the order—adjective, verb, noun. This is for variety, to avoid two accusatives coming together. Similarly *secundum bellum Poenicum*, " second war Punic ", to avoid two adjectives coming together.

Hic is probably the adverb " here ". It might be nominative masculine singular, " this man ".

Inferre is the Present Infinitive of an irregular verb, " to carry into ". It is explained on p. 143.

Nono anno, "within the ninth year", Ablative of Time within which.

Assiduis patris obtestationibus : note the order—adjective, genitive, noun.

Eo : as before (Passage No. 3, end), " to that point ", " to such a pass ", etc.

Ut . . . mallet : Consecutive clause after *eo*, hence Subjunctive. *Mallet* is Imperfect Subjunctive of an irregular verb, *malo*, I prefer (see Lesson XXIX).

Interire, as also *transire* (line 1), are compounds of an irregular verb, *eo*, *ivi*, *itum*, *ire*, which is explained on p. 139.

Second Version

But Hamilcar, after crossing the sea and coming into Spain, performed great exploits with success (carried out important operations with success): subdued very strong (and) very warlike nations, (and) enriched the whole of Africa with horses, arms, men, (and) money. Here, while he was planning the carrying of the war into Italy, in the ninth year after his arrival in Spain, he was slain in battle against the Vettones. His undying hatred for the Romans seems to have been the chief cause of the second Punic war. For Hannibal, his son, was brought to such a state by his father's continual entreaties that he preferred to perish than not make trial of the Romans (that is, make trial of the might of Rome).

Passage No. 6

Literal Version

Hannibal, son of Hamilcar, a Carthaginian. If it is
true, which no one doubts, that the Roman people all
nations in virtue has surpassed, it must not be denied
(there is not a denying) Hannibal by so much to have
surpassed all other generals in forethought, by how
much the Roman people surpasses in bravery all
nations. For as often as with it he engaged (fought) in
Italy, always he departed superior. As to which,
unless at home of his own citizens by the envy he had
been weakened, the Romans he seems to conquer to
have been able. But of many the disparaging utterly
conquered of one the valour. This man, as though by
a legacy left, the hatred of his father towards the
Romans so preserved, that sooner his life than that he
laid down; who indeed, when from his country he had
been driven and of foreign resources was in need, never
ceased in mind to war with the Romans.

Notes

Tanto . . . quanto : these are Ablatives of Measure of Difference.
Antecedat : this is Subjunctive in Oratio Obliqua—that is, in an
adjective clause after a verb of saying (*infitiandum*). In Oratio
Recta, plain straightforward statement, it would be Present Indicative. Thus : *Oratio Recta*, I see the man who is selling fish ;
Oratio Obliqua, He says he sees the man who is selling fish. The
verb " is selling " in the second clause would be Subjunctive : *Dicit
se hominem videre qui pisces venditet.*
Sic . . . ut . . . deposuerit : Consecutive Subjunctive.
Alienarum opum indigeret : indigeo, " be in want of ", takes a
genitive case where you might expect the *accusative*. It also sometimes has the ablative.

Second Version

Hannibal, son of Hamilcar, a Carthaginian. If it is true, as no one doubts, that the Roman people has surpassed all nations in valour, it must not be denied that Hannibal as far excelled all other commanders in forethought as the Roman people surpasses all nations in bravery. For as often as he engaged in battle with them in Italy, he always came off victorious. And had he not been weakened by the jealousy of his own countrymen at home it seems as if he would have been able to overcome the Romans. But the detraction of many utterly overcame the valour of one. This man, however, so preserved his father's hatred for the Romans, left as it were by a legacy, that he sooner laid down his life than that. Since, indeed, when he had been driven from his country and was in need of the resources of strangers, he never ceased to wage war in mind with the Romans.

Passage No. 7

He therefore, after Hamilcar's death, Hasdrubal being chosen commander-in-chief, took-the-command of all the cavalry; when this man also was slain, the army presented the supreme authority to him. That fact being reported at (to) Carthage was approved of in the name of the State. So Hannibal, at less than twenty-seven years of age, became general, and within the next three years subdued in war all the peoples of Spain. He stormed Saguntum, a treaty state, and prepared three very large armies. Of these he sent one into Africa, another with Hasdrubal, his brother, he left in Spain, the third he took with him into Italy. He crossed the pass of the Pyrenees. Wheresoever he marched he came into conflict with all the inhabitants. He let no one go, unless vanquished. After he came to the Alps, which separate Italy from Gaul, which no one had ever crossed with an army before him, save the Greek Hercules (from which action that is to-day called the Greek Pass), he routed the men of the Alps in attempting to prevent his passage (keep him from the pass), opened up the country (the places), made roads, and brought it to pass that an elephant with its equipment was able to go by that way by which, before that, one unarmed man was scarcely able to crawl. By this way he led his forces across and came into Italy.

Notes

Karthaginem : accusative after a verb of motion; no preposition because it is the name of a town.

Factus . . . subegit : literally, "having become . . . he subdued". In English we prefer, as in the translation, two finite verbs.

Effecit ut : note that this is a substantival clause after *ut*.

Passage No. 8

He had engaged-in-battle at the Rhône with Publius Cornelius Scipio, the consul, and had routed him. With this same man at Clastidium, near the Po, he contends and sends him thence wounded and routed. A third time the same Scipio, with his colleague, Tiberius Longus, came against him at the Trebia. With them he joined battle : and overthrew them both. Thence through Liguria he crossed the Apennines, making-for Etruria. On this march he is affected with so severe a disease in the eyes that he never after that had equally good use of his right eye.

Although he was even then oppressed with this sickness and was being carried in a litter, he surrounded and slew Caius Flaminius, the consul at Trasumenus, together with his army, and, not long after, Caius Centenius, a praetor, who was holding the passes with a chosen band.   Hence he came into Apulia.   There two consuls met him, Caius Terentius and Lucius Aemilius. He routed the armies of each in one battle, slew Paulus, the consul, and several ex-consuls besides, among them Cnaeus Servilius Geminus, who had been consul in the preceding year.

After this battle he set out for Rome, with no one offering any resistance.   He halted in the mountains near the city.   After he had held his camp there for several days and was on his way back to Capua, Quintus Fabius Maximus, the Roman dictator, threw himself in his way in the Falernian territory.

Passage No. 9

Here though shut in by the narrowness of the places (position) he extricated himself by night without any loss to (of) his army, and baffled Fabius, although he was a very clever general.   For when night came on (Ablative Absolute) he bound faggots to the horns of his oxen and set them on fire, and let loose far and wide a great multitude of that description.   And when the sudden sight presented itself he caused such panic among the Roman army that no one dared to come outside the rampart.   Within not so many days after this achievement, he craftily lured Marcus Minucius Rufus, master of the horse, whose power was equal to the dictator's, into battle and routed him. Tiberius Sempronius Gracchus, consul for the second time, he drew into an ambush, while he was away among the Lucanians and slew. He slew Marcus Claudius Marcellus, five times consul, at Venusia in a similar manner. It would be tedious to enumerate all his engagements. Wherefore it will be sufficient to say this only (literally, this one thing will be enough having been said), from which it may be seen how great he was : as long as he was in Italy no one opposed him in battle; no one after the battle of Cannae pitched his camp against him in the open (level) ground (in the plain).

Notes

Vallum : the Romans made their camps in the form of a square with a ditch on every side, and behind the ditch a rampart of earth topped by a palisade (*vallum*).

Dictator : in times of difficulty the Romans, who usually were governed by two magistrates called consuls, used to appoint a supreme official called dictator, who had under him, but in this case equal to him, a master of the horse—that is, commander of the cavalry.

Passage No. 10

Hence, though unsubdued, having been recalled to defend his native land, he waged war against Publius Scipio, son of that Scipio whom he himself, first at the Rhône, a second time at the Po, a third time at the Trebia, had routed. With this man, in the present exhaustion of his country's resources, he desired meanwhile to make peace, that afterwards when stronger he might engage him. He came to a parley : the terms were not agreed on. Within a few days after that action he joined battle with him at Zama. He was routed and, wonderful to relate, within two days and two nights came to Hadrumetum, which is about 300 miles from Zama. During this retreat (flight) the Numidians, who had left the battle at the same time with him, set an ambuscade for him. These he not only escaped, but crushed the men themselves. At Hadrumetum he gathered the remaining men from their flight (the men left from the rout) : within a few days by fresh levies he gathered together many men.

Although he had been very actively engaged in making preparations the Carthaginians ended the war with Rome. He however after that was in command of an army and performed exploits in Africa up to (the time of) the consuls Publius Sulpicius and Caius Aurelius.

Key to Missing Words

" Sit MORA sub RAMO " cecinit quondam OMAR ad ORAM ;
  " ROMA ", poeta MARO, " sit meus ", inquit " AMOR ".

" Let there be delay beneath a bough," sang once
  Omar to the shore; " Let Rome ", said the poet
  Maro, " be my love ".

Note. Maro, i.e. *Vergilius Maro.*

The next couplet scans as follows :—
  Dīxǐt hŏmō nōbīs ǐllūd, quŏd dīxěrit ǐllě,
    Ĭllŭd ǐdēm (vēr(ūm)ēst !) ēssě quŏd ǐstě pǔtet.

The Golden Age

Of their own will, without the compulsion of law, men
practised faith and righteousness. Punishment and
fear were not there; no suppliant crowd feared the face
of its own judge : they were safe without a defender.
Not yet had the pine tree, felled on its native hills, gone
down to the flowing waves, that it might sail to see a
foreign land; mortals knew no shores save their own.
Not yet were towns begirt with steep moats; there
were no helmets nor swords; without need of soldiery,
the nations free from care passed their time in gentle
ease. Without compulsion, untouched by the hoe,
unwounded by any ploughshare, the earth of herself
gave all things. Men gathered arbutus berries and
mountain strawberries, wild cherries and blackberries
clinging to the harsh brambles, and acorns that had
fallen from Jove's spreading tree. Spring was eternal :
the soft west winds with their warm breath caressed
the flowers that grew unsown. Anon the unploughed
earth bore fruit, and the unfallowed field was yellow
with the heavy ears of corn; rivers of milk flowed
there, and there rivers of nectar, and the yellow honey
dripped from the green ilex.

Notes

natos sine semine flores : literally, flowers born without seed.
mella : The ancients believed that honey was a kind of dew, left on
the leaves and flowers and gathered up by the bees. In the Golden
Age as the poets imagined it, it was so plentiful that men could
gather it for themselves.

Notice the liquid music of the last line, made by the repetition of
l—an effect which is quite lost in translation.

The Rape of Persephone

Persephone as she was accompanied by her usual maidens wandered in her meadows with bare feet. In a shady valley there is a spot wet with much spray of water dancing down from a height. There were as many colours as nature possesses and the earth shone painted with all kinds of flowers. As soon as she saw it, "Come, my companions," she said, "and with me fill your laps with flowers." In their keenness for picking they strayed a little too far, and by chance no companion followed the mistress. Her uncle sees her and no sooner seen than he carries her off swiftly and takes her on grey steeds to his kingdom.

Passage No. 11

For during the office of these men Carthaginian ambassadors came to Rome, to return thanks to the senate and Roman people because they had made peace with them, and to give them on account of that a golden crown and at the same time to ask that their hostages might be (kept) at Fregellae and that the prisoners should be restored. To this in accordance with a decree of the senate the reply was made : their gift was pleasing and was accepted; the hostages would be (kept) in the place in which (literally in what place) they were asking, they would not send back the prisoners because (the Carthaginians) were keeping Hannibal, a most bitter enemy to the Roman name, by whose instrumentality the war had been undertaken, even now in supreme authority over their army and likewise his brother Mago. On hearing of this reply the

Carthaginians called Hannibal and Mago home. When he returned hither, he was appointed king (supreme magistrate) in the twenty-second year after he had been praetor. For as there were consuls at Rome, so at Carthage, each year two kings keeping-office-for-a-year (*annui*) used to be appointed. In that office Hannibal showed the same diligence he had shown in war (literally showed himself of equal diligence as he had been in war : *pari diligentia*, Ablative of Description).

Passage No. 12

For he brought it to pass by means of fresh taxes, not only that there was money to be paid to the Romans in accordance with the treaty, but also money over, to be put back (*or* laid by) in the treasury. Then one year after, when Marcus Claudius and Lucius Furius were consuls, ambassadors came from Rome to Carthage. Hannibal, thinking these had been sent for the purpose of demanding his surrender, before they got audience of the senate, embarked on a ship secretly and fled to Syria to Antiochus. On this becoming known, the Carthaginians sent two ships to seize him if they could catch up with him. They confiscated his goods, razed his house to the ground, (and) adjudged him to be an exile. But Hannibal in the third year after his flight from home, when Lucius Cornelius and Quintus Minucius were consuls, with five ships, drew near to Africa in the territory of the Cyrenaeans, if perchance (in the hope that) the Carthaginians by hope and confidence in King Antiochus might be induced to join the war. He had already persuaded Antiochus to advance with his armies into Italy. Hither he summoned his brother Mago. When the Carthaginians got to know that, they inflicted the same penalty on Mago in his absence as on his brother.

Passage No. 13

When they, despairing of their fortunes, had weighed anchor and set sail (literally, released the ships and given the sails to the winds), Hannibal made his way to Antiochus. Concerning the fate of Mago two tales are told (a twofold memory has been handed down) : (for) some have left it written that he perished by shipwreck, others by-the-hands-of his own slaves. Antiochus, however, if he had given the same obedience to Hannibal's (his) counsels in waging war as he had begun to do in undertaking it, would have contended for the Empire of the world nearer Tiber than Thermopylae. And although he (Hannibal) saw him making many foolish attempts, yet on no occasion did he desert him. He was in command of a few ships, which he had been ordered to take from Syria into Asia, and with them he engaged-in-battle against a fleet of Rhodians in the Pamphylian Sea. And although his own men were being overcome by the number of their opponents, he himself, in the wing on which he acted, was victorious. On the rout of Antiochus, fearing lest he should be given up (to the Romans), which doubtless would have happened had he placed himself in his power (if he had made power of himself), he came to the Gortynii in Crete, to consider there whither to betake himself. Now being the most cunning of all men he saw he would be in great danger unless he should have taken some precaution on account of the greed of the Cretans.   For he was carrying with him a great amount of money concerning which he knew a report had gone abroad.   Accordingly he takes (took, adopted : Historical Present) a plan of this sort.

Passage No. 14

He fills several jars with lead, (and) covers the tops with silver and gold.   These in the presence of the chiefs he places in the temple of Diana, pretending to trust his fortunes to their good faith.   The chiefs being deceived he fills the brazen statues which he was carrying with him, with all his money, and casts them forth in the open space before (of) his house.   The Gortynii guard the temple with great care, not so much from others as from Hannibal, to prevent him lifting (his property) and taking (it) away with him without their knowledge.   So the Carthaginian, having secured his possessions and tricked all the Cretans, came to Prusias in Pontus.   With him he preserved the same sentiments towards Italy (he was of the same mind), nor did he do anything else save arm the king and stir him up against the Romans.   And since he saw that this prince was not strong enough in the resources of his own kingdom (was too little strong in home resources) he won over to his side all the other princes, and formed alliances with the most warlike races.   The Pergamene king, Eumenes, a very great friend of the Romans, kept aloof from him, and war was waged between them both by land and sea.   Therefore Hannibal was the more eager for his overthrow. (By which Hannibal was more desirous for him to be overwhelmed.)

Passage No. 15

But both on land and sea Eumenes was stronger by reason of his alliance with Rome. Hannibal thought if he had removed him, all that was left (all other things) would be easier for himself. For slaying this man he entered on the following plan. In a few days there was likely to be a naval battle (they were about to contend with the fleet). He was at a disadvantage in the number of his ships. He must fight with cunning since he was not equal in arms. He ordered as many poisonous serpents as possible to be gathered alive and to be put into earthenware vessels. When he had got together a great number of these, on the very day on which he intended to fight the naval battle, he calls together the sailors and enjoins on them to make their attack on the ship alone (*unam*) of Eumenes the king, (and) to consider it sufficient merely to defend themselves from the rest. They would easily attain that end by the great number of the serpents. He would see, he said, that they knew in what ship the king was sailing. If they either took or slew him, he promised they would be given a large reward. The soldiers having been thus exhorted, the fleet on both sides was led into battle. On their line of battle being arranged, before the signal for fight was given, Hannibal, to disclose to his men the position of Eumenes, sends a messenger in a small-boat with a herald's staff.

Passage No. 16

When he came to the enemy's ships, and showing the letter, asserted that he was seeking the king, he was at once conducted to Eumenes, because no one doubted but that he had some message about peace (something had been written concerning peace).   The letter-bearer, having shown the general's ship to his own men, betook himself to the same place whence he had come.   But Eumenes, on opening the letter found nothing in it save mocking remarks (what pertained to making a fool of him), and although he marvelled what the cause of this might be without finding (nor did he find), yet he did not hesitate to join battle forthwith.   In this attack (attack of these men) the Bithynians, by reason of Hannibal's injunction, attack the ship of Eumenes in-a-body (*universi*).   Since the king could not bear up against the force of these, he seeks safety in flight, which he would not have secured had he not retreated within the lines of his own troops (within his own forces), who had been drawn up on the neighbouring shore.   Since the remaining Pergamene ships were pressing their opponents too severely, suddenly the earthenware vessels, of which we have made mention above, began to be hurled upon them.

Passage No. 17

The discharge of these (which having been thrown) at first roused laughter among the combatants, nor could it be seen why that was being done (nor could the purpose of this be understood).   However, after they saw their ships filled with serpents, terrified by the strange circumstance, since they could not see what most especially to avoid, they turned their sterns round and betook themselves to the quarters of the fleet (to their own naval camps). Thus by his wisdom, Hannibal overcame the arms of the Pergamenes; not then only, but on many another occasion on land (with land forces) he routed his opponents with equal skill. While these things were going on in Asia, the ambassadors of Prusias happened to be dining in the house of (*apud*) Titus Quintius Flamininus, an ex-consul at Rome, and there, mention having been made of Hannibal, one of them happened to say that he was in the realm of Prusias. On the next day Flamininus laid that information before the senate. The senators, since they thought that they would never be free from secret plots while Hannibal was alive, sent ambassadors to Bithynia, among them Flamininus, to ask the king not to keep with him their greatest enemy and (but) to surrender him to them. Prusias dared not say no to these: he made the following refusal (saying), let them not ask that to be done by him which was against the rights of hospitality. Let them seize him themselves, if they could: they would easily find out where he was. (*Note.*—The direct words of Prusias were: " Ask not that to be done by me which is against the rights of hospitality. Seize him yourselves if you can. You will easily find the place where he is." Note the changes on turning it into *Oratio Obliqua*.)

Passage No. 18

For Hannibal stayed in one place in a fort which had been given to him by the king as a gift, and had built it in such a way that he had outlets in all parts of the building, fearing doubtless lest that might actually occur which came to pass. When the envoys of the Romans had come hither and had surrounded his house in great numbers (with a crowd), a boy looking forth from the door told Hannibal that an unusual number of armed men were in sight. He ordered him to go round all the doors of the dwelling and bring word quickly to him whether it was beset in the same manner on all sides. When the boy had quickly brought back word what was the state of the case (literally, what was), and had shown that all the outlets were seized, he felt that that had not been done by chance, but that it was himself they were seeking and that he should no longer live. That he might not lay his life down at the bidding of another, mindful of his former glorious deeds (virtues), he took the poison which he always had been accustomed to have with him. So one of the most valiant of men (literally, a very brave man), after the accomplishment of many and manifold labours, passed away in his seventieth year.

Passage No. 19

Of all these, by far the most civilised are those that inhabit Kent, which is entirely a maritime district, and there they do not differ much from Gallic custom. Those who live further inland for the most part do not sow corn, but live on milk and flesh, and are clad in skins. All the Britons, indeed, dye themselves with woad, which produces a blue tint, and they are all the more horrible in appearance when in battle; they wear their hair long, and every part of the body shaved except the head and upper lip. Wives are held in common between ten or twelve of them, brothers chiefly joining with brothers, and parents with children; but the children that are born from among them are counted as the children of those to whom each maiden had first been married.

Passage No. 20

He ate very little food—for I would not pass over even these details—and plain food for the most part. He especially liked bread, very small fish, cheese made (pressed) by hand, and green figs. He would eat, even before dinner at whatever time and place he felt hungry (lit., at which his stomach desired). Here are his own words from his letters : " We ate dates in my carriage." And again : " While returning home in my litter from the palace, I ate an ounce of bread, and a few berries from a cluster of hard grapes." And again : " Not even a Jew, my Tiberius, observes the fast on the sabbath as carefully as I have observed it to-day; for not until after the first hour of the night, while in my bath, I chewed two mouthfuls, before I began to be anointed." Because of this carelessness, sometimes, before the banquet was begun or after it was over, he used to dine alone, since he touched nothing while the banquet was in progress.

Notes

Although it is easy to see the meaning of this passage, it has to be translated rather freely to make the meaning clear in English. Thus, in the first sentence, we must repeat " food " after the parenthesis, though in Latin the meaning is made clear by the inflections. Again, in translating the clause beginning *qui in balneo* we must change the order so as to emphasise the fact that he had not eaten before the first hour of the night. *Omiserim :* the future perfect tense, literally, " I will not have passed over . . ."

Mi Tiberi : both words are in the vocative case. *Filius* and the names of men ending in -*ius* have the ending -*i* in the vocative. The voc. masc. sing. of *meus* is always *mi*.

Tiberius was the son-in-law of Augustus, and succeeded him as Emperor.

Key to Magic Squares

	1.		2.		3.
1.	A Q U A	1.	L U N A	1.	A P E R
2.	Q U I D	2.	U X O R	2.	P O N O
3.	V I T A	3.	N O T A	3.	E N I M
4.	A D A M	4.	A R A T	4.	R O M A

KEY TO THE LATIN-INTO-ENGLISH EXERCISES AND LATIN QUOTATIONS

Exercise I (a)

1. The friendship of the inhabitants of Spain. 2. The inhabitants of Italy. 3. To (*or* with) the inhabitants of Italy (*incolis* being dative or ablative). 4. The boldness of the sailor. 5. By the wrath of the sailors. 6. To (*or* by, with or from) the islands of Italy (*insulis* may be either dative or ablative). 7. The islands of Spain (*insulas* is accusative case). 8. The shores (or, of the shore) of Spain.

Exercise 2 (a)

1. Barca is stirring up the inhabitants of Spain.
2. At first he was asking for the friendship of the inhabitants.   3. You (plur.) often overcame (or used-to-overcome) the inhabitants of this land.   4. Italy now you do not love, nor used you to love it.   5. With the inhabitants of the island you are fighting, and you are blazing with boldness and anger.   6. We were fighting in the island (of) Sicily (note the apposition, putting the two nouns in the same case where we use *of* and *genitive*), but the inhabitants refused (were refusing) their friendship.   7. You (plur.) are asking for friendship and are obtaining it.   8. Now we are hoping-for victory.

Note the different ways of translating the Present and Imperfect tense in Latin :—

Present : He loves, is loving, does love, etc.
Imperfect : He loved, was-loving, used-to-love, tried-to-love.

Note that " you " in English is sometimes singular, sometimes plural.   Latin always distinguishes them :—

Amabas : you were loving (singular), strictly *thou.*
Amabatis : you were loving (plural).

Some Roman Sayings

1. Life is not to live, but to live well.
2. I do not count the hours, unless serene.
3. He gives twice, who gives quickly.
4. While I breathe, I hope (*i.e.,* While there's life, there's hope).
5. To work is to pray.

Exercise 3 (a)

1. The boy used to love a goat. 2. The masters used to love the sons of Philip. 3. You were stirring up the horses of Philip. 4. Philip was stirring up the minds of his sons. 5. The horses of Philip (Philip's horses) are in the fields. 6. *His* sons give (*or* are giving) gifts to Philip. 7. We are giving gifts to the sons of Philip (*or* to Philip's sons). 8. Where are the sons of Philip (*or* Philip's sons) with the horses?

An Epigram from Martial

Tongilianus has a nose. I know—I don't deny it.
But now! Tongilianus has nothing but a nose.

Exercise 4 (a)

1. Thrice with the Carthaginians did ye fight, O Romans. 2. At the first we fought in Italy with the Romans. 3. By the aid of the winds you (singular) will conquer the Romans. 4. At last they have overcome (overcame) their opponents. 5. O Carthaginians, ye will no longer hope for victory and ye will refuse to renew the war. 6. We shall ask and obtain the friendship of our opponents. 7. Accordingly thereafter (after that) the Carthaginians won the friendship of the Romans. 8. A Roman fought (*or* has fought) with a Gaul.

Exercise 5 (a)

1. The leaves and boughs of the dark cypress in my garden are dear to me. 2. The cypress is full-of-shade.

3. The horse of the son of Philip was always very beautiful. **4.** Sicily is a large and beautiful island. **5.** The cypresses of Sicily are gloomy (dark) and rough. **6.** The Carthaginians were wretched while they were looking at this. **7.** Great sorrow seems to be (*or* there seems to be great sorrow) in their hearts (minds). **8.** During many years I have fought with the Romans and I shall always fight.

Revision of Vocabulary:

Ira; nauta; supero; nego; equus; auxilium; ventus; folium; specto.

Latin Phrases

1. Jealousy is blind.
2. The written word remains.
3. It is a human thing (*i.e.*, it is human) to err.

Dyed Hair

Your beard is white, your hair black. You can't dye your beard—this is the reason—and you can your hair, Olus.

Exercise 6 (*a*)

1. A great number of young men had attacked this place (*or* position). **2.** If the young men attack (will have attacked) this place the Romans will renew the war. **3.** When we have estranged (shall have estranged) Africa from the Carthaginians we shall attack Spain. **4.** After ye have extended your empire ye will preserve it with great stubbornness (*magna pertinacia,* an

ablative of manner).   5. We had preserved the Romans
when they were in great danger.   6. You (ye) had
hesitated to approve of the design of the Carthaginians.
7. After they conquer the Gauls they will extend their
empire to Spain (to the Spaniards).   8. They had
refused to attack the Romans because they had won
their friendship.   9. If I arm the inhabitants of this
island they will fight.   10. In this place the Carthaginians had fought with the Romans for many years.

Throughout this exercise note carefully the differences
in tense in Latin and English.   In sentence 1 note the
order *magnus adulescentulorum numerus*, and copy it in
similar phrases.   Latin likes to sandwich, as it were, its
genitive between the noun that governs it and the
adjective with this noun.   It sometimes also, if the
genitive has an adjective with it, puts the governing
noun between them, thus—*magnae vir sapientiae*, a
man of great wisdom.   Note that genitives in Latin are
usually governed by nouns; and when you come
across one, look for the noun which governs it.   Be on
the watch for verbs like *dubito* and *recuso*, which are
followed by a Present Infinitive in Latin; the English
Infinitive is often not translated by an Infinitive in
Latin.   A list of these verbs will be given later.   In
Sentence 7 note that often where we say *to Spain* or
some similar phrase, Latin talks of the people rather
than of the country, and says *to the Spaniards*, etc.

Exercise 7 (*a*)

1. It is the duty of the Romans to extend the bounds
of their empire.   2. Hamilcar, a man of the greatest

(utmost) boldness, was ablaze with the desire (lust) for war. 3. We were pondering in mind to renew the war (*better English* : we were pondering on (thinking of) the renewal of the war). 4. With horses, arms, men and money we shall enrich all Africa. 5. In winter there are dark clouds in the sky. 6. The Romans conquered the fleet of the Carthaginians at the islands. 7. The Roman people surpasses all-other races in valour (*virtute*, Ablative of Respect—of thing in which). 8. It is the duty of a chief (*or* it is incumbent upon a chief) to rule his people (Latin says simply " it is of "). 9. The King of the Britons, a man of great wisdom, often used to fight (was fighting) with the Romans. 10. If they make peace they will preserve their ships.

In sentence 4, note that Latin omits all the conjunctions. If you had put in any you would have required to put in all, thus : *Equis et armis et viris et pecunia.* English only puts in, as a rule, the last conjunction.

Latin Phrases

1. Art for art's sake.
2. Art is to conceal art.
3. For the sake of honour.
4. In place of a parent.
5. I am a man, and nothing human is foreign to me (*i.e.*, outside my interests).
6. (There are) as many opinions as there are men.

Live To-day !

It is not wise (lit., of a wise man), believe me, to say " I will live ". Life to-morrow is too late. Live to-day !

Exercise 8 (a)

1. Hamilcar, by surname Barca, with a large fleet sailed to Italy. 2. Both by land and by sea the Romans conquered the Carthaginians. 3. For it is not in-keeping-with his valour to ask for peace. 4. They were ratifying the alliance with a treaty. 5. The Carthaginians have broken (*or* broke) the treaties. 6. They are bringing (they bring) great gifts to Caesar *in* Rome. 7. We sailed from Malta to Rome with great difficulty. 8. Man is an animal with forethought (literally, is a prudent animal). 9. Of all animals man is the most prudent. 10. The iron from the spear was in his body (*better*, the iron head of the spear was in his body).

In sentence 1 note the order, *magna cum classe*—adjective, preposition, noun.

In sentence 6 note that English says *to Caesar in Rome*, Latin *to Rome to Caesar*, putting the place first. Watch this carefully in future sentences. You should be always parsing to yourself in doing these sentences, asking yourself what cases the nouns are in, why the verbs are plural or singular, why they are Perfect or Future tense. Soon this will keep you from making careless mistakes.

Latin Phrases

1. From words to blows.
2. What times ! what customs !
3. On the spur of the moment.
4. A healthy mind in a healthy body.

An Anonymous Epitaph

5. Bathing, drinking, love-making corrupt our bodies ; but they make life worth while—bathing, drinking, love-making.

Exercise 9 (*a*)

1. At Zama, however, Scipio conquered Hannibal. 2. At Syracuse, indeed, Cicero lived (stayed) for one year. 3. Caesar attacked a large number of the enemy. 4. At Carthage we were pondering on war. 5. Caesar surpassed (used to surpass) all men in bravery. 6. In Africa there are many large wild beasts. 7. At Athens, the city of the Athenians, there are many beautiful temples. 8. In this way Hannibal won the friendship of a large State. 9. Many men are ablaze with the desire for money. 10. It is not in accordance with my custom to stay long at Cumae.

Latin Sayings

1. Beneath one's dignity.
2. They make a wilderness and call it peace.
3. To accept a kindness is to sell (one's) freedom.
4. Truth is great and will prevail.

5. *False teeth.*

Thaïs has black teeth, Laecania snow-white ones. What is the reason ? The latter has bought ones, the former her own.

Exercise 10 (a)

1. We indeed put the enemy to flight while they were arming themselves (literally, The enemy indeed arming themselves we put to flight or have put to flight). 2. For already he had conquered all his enemies. 3. Then on the next day a huge multitude of the enemy began-to-attack Caesar. 4. For we always value the prudent man at a very great price. 5. Scipio, too, loved (was loving or used to love) his wife with a passionate (keen) love. 6. Ye will soon with your fiery steeds attack and rout the Carthaginians. 7. The Romans used-to-value Cato at a great price, Caesar at a greater. 8. For Hamilcar not only routed the enemy from the walls of Carthage, but also got together (prepared) a huge amount (supply) of money. 9. Then the soldiers were estimating very highly (at a very great price) all the plans of their leader. 10. Caesar was giving huge rewards to his brave soldiers.

Revision of Vocabulary:

Conservo ; imperium ; propago ; vir ; cupiditas ; populus ; corpus, gen. *corporis ; amor ; fama ; plus*, gen. *pluris ; omnibus*, dative plural of *omnis*, now shortened so that only the ending remains.

Note.—Omnibus is a good modern example of direct borrowing from Latin to supply a special need. It means " a conveyance for all ", as opposed to a carriage.

Latin Phrases and Extracts

1. Fortune favours the brave (literally, is favourable to).
2. A marvellous year.

3. Love conquers all things.
4. But meanwhile time flies, time the irrecoverable.
5. The quarrels of lovers are a renewal of love.
6. Art (is) long, life (is) short.

7. *You are too much a poet.*

You read to me both when-I-am-standing and you read to me when-I-am-sitting. You read to me when I run and when I lie down. I escape to the baths. You make a noise in my ear. I seek the swimming-pool. You don't let me swim. I hasten to dinner. You detain me as I go. I arrive at dinner. You drive me away as I eat. Tired I go to sleep. You wake me up as I lie down. (Though) you are a just man, good and innocent, you are a terror (literally, you are feared).

Exercise II (*a*)

1. Accordingly the Carthaginians with a large army sailed to Italy to attack the Romans (that they might attack). 2. At daybreak the cavalry put to flight a large band of the Carthaginians. 3. The citizens after that will get ready three armies *that* the enemy may *not* attack the city. 4. Meanwhile he was stirring up the Gauls to seize (that they might seize) the defile by night. 5. With all races the Romans fought (*secondary time*), *or* have fought (*primary time*). 6. The horns of the goats are very large and strong. 7. Hannibal and his officers on the next day dined at home. 8. In the third month therefore we shall sail to Rome from home.

9. Accordingly he has armed himself to preserve his house.   10. For you (*plural*) had approved of this plan that you might avoid a disaster.

Inscription Outside Theatre
Circus full,
Doors shut,
Great noise!

One Author to Another
Why do I not send you my books, Pontilianus? Lest you should send me yours, Pontilianus.

Motto
That all may be one.

Exercise 12 (*a*)
1. Then great were your hopes, sad your thoughts (literally, you were hoping great things, thinking sad things).   2. Good men and good women love virtue, wisdom and good faith.   3. Accordingly when I had overcome the first line, I attacked the second.   4. To-day without a doubt they will rout the line of battle of the enemy.   5. Since therefore the Romans were standing in line of battle we hesitated to fight.   6. When (since) the Gauls had conquered the Roman legions the city of Rome (*Latin*, the city Rome) was in great peril.   7. For we have sailed (*or* we sailed) to Rome with the greatest hope.   8. When we had made many prayers to the gods, he armed his men (literally, when he had prayed the gods many things).   9. Hannibal, on the other hand, with the greatest good faith was preserving the peace.

Note in sentence 2 the omission of all the conjunctions in Latin. You could have inserted them all—*virtutem et sapientiam et fidem*.

In sentence 6 note the apposition *urbs Roma*. Latin never says *urbs Romae*.

Two Famous Lines

1. Through its ancient customs and men stands (firm) the Roman State.
2. There are tears of (or " for ") things, and mortal (things) touch the heart.

Phrases

1. Into the midst of things.
2. Soon (it will be) night; (go) to the matter at hand.
3. The safety of the State is the supreme law.

Exercise 13 (a)

1. When however Hannibal seizes (shall have seized) that city, we shall surrender. 2. He had sailed to Rome to sacrifice a victim to Jupiter most high and holy (Jupiter best, greatest). 3. After the seizure of the city ye will explore the territory. 4. That deed at first stirred up laughter in the spectators (was stirring up laughter for those looking). 5. Then (Next) they will attack the army stationed on the shore. 6. Being about-to-attack those bands of the enemy, he has prepared large forces. 7. The Romans had suddenly routed the enemy when on-the-point-of-making a secret attack on the camp (literally, about-to-attack the camp

secretly). 8. We had sailed to Africa that we might recover the estranged towns. 9. They are about-to-behold that conquered army. 10. How many out of those large armies were about to behold their country (fatherland) again?

Phrases

1. That is.
2. Peace with you.
3. About to die, I salute you.
4. Not for me, not for you, but for us.

Latin Extracts

1. Captured Greece took captive her fierce conqueror (*i.e.*, Rome).
2. Difficult, easy, pleasant, bitter, you are at the same time (literally, the same man). I can live neither with you nor without you.

Lesson XIII : Exercise on Grammar :

Moniturus, -a, -um ; recturus, -a, -um ; auditurus, -a, -um.

Monitus, -a, -um ; rectus, -a, -um ; auditus, -a, -um.

Exercise 14 (a)

1. We have and always shall have a great supply of money. 2. Now they are conquering and always will conquer all races. 3. I shall lead a large army into Spain. 4. They will see and conquer the Romans on

the third day. 5. Before his arrival they were carrying on things (affairs) badly by land and sea. 6. When Hamilcar is waging war he never conquers the enemy. 7. But at the last they come almost to despair (or they are almost reduced to despair). 8. He holds the strongest towns of Africa beneath his sway (within his power). 9. But Hamilcar with favourable fortune (that is, with the help of fortune) carries out great exploits (things). 10. The undying hatred of Hamilcar for the Romans will stir up the second Punic war.

Latin Phrases

1. God being willing.
2. (*literally*) A change having been turned.
3. A brave man is he who conquers himself.
4. A learned man always has wealth in himself.

Exercise 15 (*a*)

1. Hamilcar thinks himself to be about to make an end of this war (*better English*, Hamilcar thinks he will make an end of this war). 2. This man thinks that man to be making an end of these wars (*better*, This man thinks that man is making an end of these wars). 3. This woman thinks that man to have done this (*better*, This woman thinks that man has done this). 4. If this man refuses (shall have refused) to make an end of this war we shall retire from Sicily. 5. We shall come to Africa to slay this man and to destroy Carthage (note the Supine after verb of motion). 6. The Vettones slew him while fighting in battle. 7. The

bystanders will say this is a brave man. 8. They say they will retire from Sicily at dawn. 9. On-the-point-of-departing from Sicily, ye are making peace with this king. 10. To-morrow they will come to Rome.

Note that in sentence 2 *eum* denotes a different person from *hic*, and that in sentence 4 *se* denotes the same person as *hic*. Always be on the look-out for this distinction.

Revision Vocabulary :

manu, abl. of *manus* (also from *scriptum*, having been written, past participle of *scribo*, write), *i.e.*, having been written by hand; *initium*; *castra*; *factum*, past participle of *facio*; *recupero*; *bellum*, *gero*; *vinco*; *deletum*, past participle of *deleo*; *male*, *factum*.

Note : The Latin *castra*, in the form, *-caster*, *-chester*, *-cester*, appears in the names of many English towns, *e.g.*, Winchester, Doncaster, Leicester, etc. Chester means simply " The Camp ". From this we can tell that a town was once occupied by the Romans, or by Britons who had adopted Roman language and culture.

I Do Not Love You

I do not love you, Sabidius, nor can I say why.
This only can I say : I do not love you.

The Primrose Way

Easy is the descent to Avernus. Night and day the door of black Dis lies open, but to recall your step and return to the upper air, this is labour.

Exercise 16 (*a*)

1. We ourselves have said they will not make an end of the war (*or*, We ourselves said they would not make an end of the war. The actual words were, " We shall not make an end of the war "). 2. Hannibal himself had said he alone had made an end of this war. (The actual words of Hannibal were, " I alone have made an end of this war ".) 3. If you say they will make an end of the war, they will sail to Carthage at daybreak. 4. You yourselves thought these had returned home with great disgrace. (The thought in the mind was, " These have returned home with great disgrace ".) 5. Those who come to Corinth look at the statues. 6. They themselves said that they alone had removed the enemy from the walls of Carthage. (The actual words were, " We alone have removed the enemy from the walls of Carthage ".) 7. Neither had said that he was slaying the captives. (The actual words of which you deny the saying were, " He is slaying the captives ".) 8. The one thought they were saying these things; the other denied it. (Note *alter . . . alter*, the one . . . the other (of two). The actual thought was, " They are saying these things ".) 9. You had seen him whom Catulus defeated at the Aegates islands. 10. Which of the two said Caesar had given provinces to them only? (The actual words were, " Caesar gave or has given provinces to them only ".)

Remember the parsing of the words in each sentence. Do not pass on till you have satisfied yourself as to the case of the nouns, number and tense of the verbs, and so on.

Latin Phrases

1. Second to none.
2. By the deed itself.
3. Those who cross the sea change their sky, not their minds.
4. *Writ on wind and water.*

My woman says that she prefers to marry no one rather than me, not if Jupiter himself were to court her. So she says. But what a woman says to her passionate lover ought to be written in wind and running water.

Exercise 17 (a)

1. We are attacking Rome with such (so great) boldness that ye have no hope of safety. 2. He had defended Eryx so boldly that Marcellus said (was saying) he (Marcellus) would never take it. 3. Ye are defending that city of yours in such a way that we have no hope of victory. 4. So bold were they that they were saying they would not hand over the city. 5. So badly are the Carthaginians waging war that they are losing the towns of all Africa. 6. The bravery of that race was so great that they always used-to-conquer their opponents. 7. So wise was he that he perceived (was perceiving) these things were false. 8. So serious (so great) an internal war has blazed out in Africa that ye are now losing, O Carthaginians, all your towns. 9. Neither is so bold as to fight with him (that man); literally, Neither is so bold that he may fight with him. 10. We said that now at last they had lost the empire of all Africa.

KEY TO THE LATIN-INTO-ENGLISH EXERCISES 259

Night

On they went darkly beneath the lonely night in the
gloom, through the empty halls of Dis and his ghostly
kingdom. Just as when under the grudging light of
an inconstant moon lies away in the forest, when
Jupiter has hidden the sky in shade and black night
has robbed the world of its colours.

Exercise 18 (a)

1. At that time so greatly were we afraid that we
sought help from the Romans and obtained it. 2.
When the Carthaginians had lost everything in Sicily
they made peace. 3. They were defending Eryx with
such great bravery that the Romans despaired of victory.
4. When (since), O Romans, you had resolved to make
an end of the war you entrusted the business to Regulus.
5. He was so fired with the desire for war (for making
war) that he refused to leave Sicily (to depart from
Sicily). 6. Some were ablaze with zeal for fighting
(with zeal of fighting), others for retreating (retiring).
7. Since (when) they knew these things useless for
living well (for a good life) they cast them away.
(There is an *esse* understood after *inutilia*.) 8. So
many mercenaries have revolted that the Carthaginians
are in despair. 9. You (plural) are imparting to others
the eagerness (desire) for warring (war). 10. By
sparing the lives of others ye will win love and friendship.

(Note Latin says " by sparing the life "; *vita* is never
used in the plural in this sense.)

Ennius

One man by delaying restored to us our fortunes (literally, " the thing ").

A Proverb

By doing nothing men learn to act wickedly.

A Sparrow

The sparrow of my lady is dead. The sparrow, my lady's pet, whom she loved more than her own eyes. For he was honey-sweet and knew his mistress as well as a girl knows her mother. Nor would he move from her lap, but hopping now here, now there, would always chirp to his mistress alone. Now he goes along the dark road to that place whence they say no one returns. O cruel deed ! Ah, poor little bird ! It's all because of you that my lady's eyes are swollen and red with weeping. (*Tua opera*—lit., " by your doing ".)

Exercise 19 (a)

1. When (since) we were in Sicily he departed from the city. 2. They were a long time at Athens for the purpose of seeing the statues. 3. When Caesar is at Rome he will preserve the laws (the future *erit* is used because the principal verb is future). 4. Then they were making haste that they might be at Rome on that day. 5. He, while fighting, was slain by a Gaul of

huge frame. 6. Those captives after the battle of Cannae had been slain by Hannibal. 7. Then indeed we shall retire from Greece, when we have been conquered (shall have been conquered) by the Romans. 8. If the Carthaginians are conquered in this battle, they will be in great danger (note the tense, shall have been conquered). 9. After subduing the most warlike nations he was slain on a journey by a slave (literally, after the most warlike nations having been subdued). 10. The woman was betrayed by a slave to whom she had given many gifts.

Exercise 20 (a)

1. We so defended Eryx that the war seemed not to have been waged in that place (*esse* could have been omitted). 2. Such great wars then blazed forth that these cities were almost being destroyed. 3. When a hundred thousand of mercenaries had been formed (made) he removed them from the walls of Carthage. 4. That city was being besieged by a very large number of barbarians. 5. So bravely did they fight that the enemy were being driven out. 6. Shut in by the narrowness of the place (places) the women were being slain (were perishing) by hunger and disease. 7. Hannibal was at Rome, not the Romans at Carthage. 8. Before the siege of the city by the Spaniards a great number of the Carthaginians were slain. 9. They had been wise, brave and warlike, sufficiently skilled in all things. 10. By those woes the women were so terrified that they sought help.

A Night Scene from Virgil

It was night, and over the earth weary creatures were
enjoying peaceful sleep. The woods and the wild
seas had sunk to rest. It was the time when the stars
roll midway in their gliding path, when all the land is
silent, and beasts and gay birds, both those that haunt
far and wide the liquid lakes, and those that dwell in
the thorny country bushes (literally, country, rough
with thickets) are couched in sleep under the silent
night. These smooth their cares and hearts that forgot
their labours.

Revision of Vocabulary :

inspectum, past participle of *inspicio ; patria ; provincia ; ferox ; intellectus,* past participle of *intellego ;
abjectus,* past participle of *abjicio ; perditus,* past
participle of *perdo ; itineris,* gen. of *iter ; expulsus,* past
participle of *expello ; vexo.*

Exercise 21 (a)

1. Urbs a militibus obsidetur. 2. Rosae servis a
femina datae sunt. 3. Antonius a Cleopatra maxime
amabatur. 4. Castra aggeribus contra hostes munien-
tur. 5. Barbari puellas ceperunt. 6. Iste imperator
omnia in Hispania iam amisit.

Latin Phrases

1. There is no arguing about taste (lit., " It must
not be argued about tastes ".)
2. That which had to be proved.

3. That which had to be done.

4. Carthage must be destroyed.

5. Never despair !

6. Now we must drink, now the earth must be trodden with a free foot.

7. Whatever shall be, every fortune must be overcome by bearing it.

Tacitus

A climate most foul with rain and cloud.

A Female Bluebeard

Wicked Chloe inscribed on the tombs of her seven husbands " Chloe did this ". What could be plainer ? (*Chloe fecit* is deliberately ambiguous. It means "built this tomb" as well as "caused the death of her husbands ".)

Catullus on Cicero

Most eloquent of the descendants of Romulus, all who are and all who have been, Marcus Tullius, and all who shall be hereafter in other years—to you, Catullus pays his greatest thanks, Catullus the worst of all poets, as much the worst poet of all as you are of all the best advocate.

Books

You demand that I present you, Tucca, with my books. I will not do it. For you wish to sell them, not to read them.

Quotations

1. A wise man will rule his mind, a fool will be a slave to it.
2. Time must be obeyed.
3. The conquering cause pleased the gods, but the conquered cause pleased Cato.

From the Prayer Book

1. Sing to the Lord.
2. Bless-ye, all ye works.
3. Come let us sing unto the Lord.

Wren's Epitaph

If you want my memorial, look around.

A Drunkard's Promises

You promise everything, when you have drunk the whole night long. In the morning you make good no promise. Pollio, drink in the morning!

A Humble Invitation

Dare, my guest, to despise wealth, count yourself worthy of a god, and come not harsh to my poverty.

May She Meet the Wife!

Lycoris buried all the women friends she had, Fabianus.

May she become a friend of my wife!

Latin Phrases

2. Let the buyer beware.
3. Let him either drink or depart.
4. Though the heavens fall, let justice be done.
5. May there be no ill-omen.
6. Let arms yield to the toga.
7. While we live, let us live.
8. May he rest in peace.

On a Rival

A certain man, dearest Julius, is bursting with envy; because Rome reads me he is bursting with envy. He is bursting with envy because in every crowd I am always pointed out with the finger; he is bursting with envy. He is bursting with envy because both Caesars gave me the right (of a father) of three sons; he is bursting with envy. He is bursting with envy because I have a pleasant bit of country near the city and a small house in town. He is bursting with envy. He is bursting with envy because I am delightful to my friends, because I am a frequent guest; he is bursting with envy. He is bursting with envy because I am loved and approved of. Let anyone whoever he is, who is bursting with envy, burst!

Two Famous Lines

1. So many evils could superstition persuade (men to commit).
2. They can because they believe they can (*lit.*, seem to themselves to be able).

Paula

Paula wishes to marry me; I refuse to marry Paula; She is an old woman. I might be willing if she were an older woman.

Come, Live with Me and be My Love

Let us live, my Lesbia, and love, and value at one farthing all the talk of crabbed old men. Suns may set and rise again. For us when once brief light has set there remains to be slept one continuous night. Give me a thousand kisses, then a hundred, then another thousand, then a second hundred, then yet another thousand, then a hundred. Then when we have made up many thousands, we will confuse the reckoning lest we know it or lest any malicious person should be able to cast an evil eye upon us, since he knows that our kisses are so many.

Shepherds in the Fields

There were in the same region shepherds sleeping in the fields and guarding their sheep by night. And the messenger of the Lord stood by them and the glory of the Lord shone round them and they feared with a great fear. And the messenger said to them, " Be not afraid for behold I announce to you a great joy which shall be to the whole people, because to you to-day is born a Saviour who is Christ the Lord in the city of David. And this shall be a sign to you, you shall find the infant clothed in swaddling clothes and lying in a stable." And suddenly there was with the messenger a multitude from the heavenly host praising God and saying " Glory in the highest to God and on earth peace among men of good-will ".

Indifference

I have no great desire to wish to please you, Caesar.
Nor to know whether you are a dark or fair man.

To be Wroth with One we Love

I hate and I love; why I do that, perhaps you ask.
I know not, but I feel that it is happening, and I am
    in a torment.

A Christmas Hymn

Come, ye faithful, joyful, triumphant, come, come to Bethlehem. See him that is born King of angels. Come ye, let us adore the Lord.

The Virgin Mother brings forth God of God, light of light. True God born not made. Come ye, let us adore the Lord.

Lo ! leaving their flocks, shepherds hasten summoned to the humble cradle. Let us hurry with glad step. Come ye, let us adore the Lord.

While the star leads the way the Magi, adoring Christ, give gold, incense, myrrh as presents. Let us offer our hearts to the infant Jesus. Come ye, let us adore the Lord.

We shall see the eternal splendour of the eternal father hidden in flesh. The infant God wrapped in rags. Come ye, let us adore the Lord.

Lo ! the choir of angels now sing hymns. Let the palace of the heavenly ones now sing. Glory to God in the highest. Come ye, let us adore the Lord.

St. Augustine

Thou hast made us for thyself, O Lord, and our heart is restless until it rests in thee.

'Arry

If ever 'Arry wanted to say " extras " he would say " hextras " and " hambush " for " ambush " and he hoped that he had spoken wonderfully whenever he said " hambush " with all his power. So, I expect, his mother had said, Liber, his uncle, so his grandfather and grandmother on his mother's side. When he was sent to Syria the ears of all of us had a rest. They heard the same words pronounced softly and lightly and they had no fear of such words for the future; when suddenly there arrives a horrible message that the Ionian waves ever since 'Arry went there were henceforward not Ionian but Hionian.

KEY TO THE ENGLISH-INTO-LATIN EXERCISES

Exercise I (b)

1. Amicitia Italiae nautarum. 2. Incolae Hispaniae. 3. Incolarum Italiae. 4. Ira nautae. 5. Victoria poetarum. 6. Insulis. 7. Nautis Hispaniae et Italiae. 8. Ora Italiae.

Remember in Latin prose the quantity of the -a in the ablative singular (that is, whether it is long or short) would not be marked, and only the sense would tell you which case it was.

If you wish a little more practice before going on, take the

Key now and re-translate the sentences, comparing them with the Exercises. This will give facility in recognising the cases.

You should now make sure of the vocabulary : learn it off by heart. No words in it will be repeated in the succeeding vocabularies. If you forget any you must consult the general Vocabulary at the end.

Exercise 2 (b)

1. Hispaniae incolas armat Barca. 2. Primo incolarum amicitiam conciliabat. 3. Hujus incolas terrae superabat. 4. Italiam nunc non amat neque amabat. 5. Cum Italiae incolis bellabat atque ferocia et ira flagrabat. 6. In insula Sicilia pugnabat. 7. Italiae autem incolae Barcam superabant. 8. Tum amicitiam rogat atque impetrat. 9. Nunc iram in Italiam renovat. 10. Victoriam, O Barca, speras.

Again we should advise you to take this translation and re-translate it, comparing it with the Exercises.

Exercise 3 (b)

1. Filios Philippi amamus. 2. Filii Philippi equos amabant. 3. Philippus filiis equos dat. 4. Ubi nunc sunt equi Philippi? 5. Sunt in agris. 6. Capri et equi sunt filiorum Philippi. 7. Cum equis et capris et filiis Philippus est in agris.

You will have noticed now that the Latin verb is almost always at the end of the sentence. An emphatic word is sometimes put there instead of it : watch carefully when this occurs. *Est* and *sunt* are rather weak words, and need not be put at the end.

The usual order is nominative, dative, accusative, verb, but of course this may be varied. You might have an adverb before the nominative or a conjunction, and you might have an adverb between the accusative and its verb. Re-translate this exercise now for further practice.

Exercise 4 (b)

Poeni cum Romanis ter pugnaverunt. Primo in Sicilia pugnaverunt, atque ventorum auxilio Poeni Romanorum nautas saepe superaverunt. Sed tandem apud Siciliam adversarios superaverunt Romani nautae. Poeni postea non jam victoriam speraverunt atque bellum renovare recusaverunt. Tum adversariorum amicitiam rogaverunt atque impetraverunt. Itaque Poeni et Romani non jam erant adversarii.

Exercise 5 (b)

Cara mihi est cupressus in horto meo. Folia enim sunt umbrosa. Magna et vetusta est, sed semper erat pulchra. Auctumno est pulcherrima. Postea videtur aspera et atra. Tum miser sum ubi specto; magna enim maestitia in animo mihi (or meo) videtur esse. Multos annos cupressum meam amavi et semper amabo.

Exercise 6 (b)

1. Magnum Poenorum numerum in hoc loco oppugnaverant. 2. Si hunc locum oppugnaverimus, bellum renovabunt Hispani. 3. Cum Hispaniam a Poenis abalienaveritis, Africam oppugnabitis. 4. Postquam imperium propagaverimus magna pertinacia conservabimus. 5. Romanos conservare dubitaveramus ubi magno in periculo erant. (Note the order *magno in periculo*.) 6. Consilium Barcae comprobare dubitaveram. 7. Postquam Africam superaverimus imperium *ad Hispanos* propagabimus. 8. Romanos oppugnare recusabimus, quod amicatiam conciliaverunt. 9. Ubi Hispanos armavero cum Gallis pugnabo. 10. Hoc in loco, multos (per) annos cum Philippo pugnaveramus.

Exercise 7 (b)

1. Est imperatoris fines imperii conservare. 2. Mente agitabatis pacem renovare. 3. Africam, O Hannibal, equis et pecunia locupletavisti. 4. Auctumno coelum est pulchrum.

5. Romanorum naves Poenos apud insulas oppugnaverunt.
6. Romani, magna populus virtute, ceteras gentes gubernabant.
7. Est principis hostes superare. 8. Pacem conciliare est
imperatoris. 9. Non iam navibus cum Romanis pugnabimus.
10. Ubi classem Poenorum superaverimus, pacem conciliabimus.

Exercise 8 (b)

1. Caius, cognomine Caesar, magnis cum copiis Melitam
navigavit. 2. Et mari et terra classes Romanorum (or
Romanas) superavimus. 3. Non meae est virtutis pacem
conciliare. 4. Pacem foedere confirmavimus. 5. Foedus, O
Carthaginienses, violavistis. 6. Romam ad Caesarem magnis
cum donis navigamus. 7. Roma Londinium est longa navigatio
(*literally* is a long sailing). 8. Animalia maris sunt maxima.
9. Homo animalia cetera virtute superat. 10. Ferrum hastilis
renovabat.

Note *all animals* means *all other animals*, therefore use *ceteri*.
Do not forget the extra practice to be got from re-translating
these exercises in the Key. You are supposed to be doing this
each time.

Exercise 9 (b)

1. Zamae autem adversarios Romani superaverunt. 2.
Multos quidem annos Pompeius Romae habitavit. 3. Prima
luce magna hostium multitudo Romanos oppugnavit. 4.
Carthagine Poeni bellum mente agitabant. 5. Caesar et
Pompeius famae cupiditate ceteros Romanos superaverunt (*or*
superabant, *denoting a state, not a single act*). 6. Athenis
multae et pulchrae statuae sunt. 7. Hac ratione Hannibal
civitatum amicitiam Italiae conciliaverat. 8. Annum unum
parva cum natione in Africa pugnabamus. 9. Cupiditatem
pecuniae virtutis amore homines superant. 10. Non est meae
consuetudinis nationes bellicosas oppugnare.

Exercise 10 (b)

1. Romani Poenos fines explorantes oppugnaverunt. 2. Jam enim omnes civitates abalienaverant. 3. Tum magna hominum multitudine hostes Caesarem oppugnaverunt. 4. Fortem autem semper pluris aestimabimus. 5. Uxores quidem amore acri amamus. 6. Acres Carthaginiensium equi mox hostes oppugnabunt et fugabunt. 7. Virtutem magni, pluris etiam pecuniam aestimavistis. 8. Non solum a muris hostes fugabimus sed etiam urbem oppugnabimus. 9. Milites fortis consilia ducis parvi aestimaverunt (*or* aestimabant). 10. Duces praemia magna fortibus militibus dant.

Exercise 11 (b)

1. Itaque Caesar magno cum exercitu ad Britanniam navigavit ut hostes oppugnaret. 2. Prima luce equitatu hostium manum fugavimus. 3. Magistratus postea exercitum comparaverunt ne hostes urbem oppugnarent. 4. Hostes Gallos concitant ut saltum noctu occupent. 5. Exercitibus Romani gentes omnes superaverunt. 6. Cornibus capri inimicos oppugnant. 7. Postero die magistratus domi cenaverunt. 8. Caius enim Roma tertio mense navigaverat. 9. Itaque sese armant ut domos conservent. 10. Hoc consilium comprobavimus ut casum vitaremus.

Exercise 12 (b)

1. Tum magna sperabat, cogitabat maesta. 2. Itaque cum aciem primam fugavisset, secundam oppugnavit. 3. Hodie enim haud dubie hostium aciem fugabimus. 4. Hostes in acie stabant. 5. Respublica autem magno in periculo erat cum legiones Galli fugavissent. 6. Legiones enim Romanas summa spe oppugnaverant. 7. Cum deos multa oravissent proelium renovaverunt. 8. Multa cogitabat ubi aciem Romanam spectabat. 9. Summa enim fide pacem Hannibal conciliaverat.

Be sure you are careful never to put *enim* and *autem* first in the sentence.

Exercise 13 (b)

1. Sed cum eas gentes Romani superaverint manus dabunt.
2. Jovi optimo maximo hostias immolatum ad eam insulam noctu navigavit. 3. Post occupatum saltum agros exploraverunt. 4. Ea facta initio risum pugnantibus concitaverunt. 5. Deinde legiones in litore collocatas fugavit. 6. Itaque Romam oppugnaturus magnum exercitum comparavit. 7. Hostes castra clam oppugnaturos subito fugavit. 8. Navigavimus enim ad Africam ut urbes abalienatas recuperaremus. 9. Ubi sunt copiae superatae? Pacem rogaturae sunt. 10. Quot ex eo exercitu magno patriam rursus spectaturi sunt?

Exercise 14 (b)

1. Multos per annos cum Romanis bellum gerebamus. 2. Tertio die hostium aciem videbimus. 3. Omnes gentes vincent et imperio suo tenebunt. 4. Copias magnas in Romanos ducitis. 5. Ante Romanorum adventum et mari et terra bellum male gerebamus. 6. Ubi bellum gerebamus semper hostes vincebamus. 7. Sed tandem prope ad desperationem pervenimus (*perveniebamus* would mean " we were coming "). 8. Romam, urbem Italiae valentissimam, veniebant. 9. Magnas res secunda fortuna geremus. 10. Hannibal perpetuo odio erga Romanos exercitum in Italiam ducit.

Exercise 15 (b)

1. Dicit hunc hujus belli finem facturum esse. 2. Dicit hos hujus belli finem facere. 3. Hi eos dicunt horum bellorum finem fecisse. 4. Si Catulus negaverit hoc bellum se compositurum esse ex Sicilia decedemus. 5. Hic bellum compositum et Carthaginem deletum ad Africam venit. 6. Vetonnes eum in proelio pugnantem interficient. 7. Adstantes dicunt hanc esse fortem. 8. Dicit se Roma cras decessurum esse. 9. Decessurus Sicilia pacem cum Catulo conciliavit. 10. Prima luce Romam adveniemus.

Exercise 16 (b)

1. Catulus ipse negaverat se bellum compositurum esse (said . . . not = deny. The actual words were, " I shall not end the war "). 2. Catulus solus dixerat se ipsum bellum composuisse. (The actual words were, " I myself ended *or* have ended the war ".) 3. Si Catulus dixerit se bellum compositurum esse Romam statim navigabimus. 4. Ipsi putaveramus eos solos magno cum dedecore domum redituros esse. (The thought was, " They are about-to-return ".) 5. Qui Romam veniunt, aedificia pulchra inspiciunt. 6. Hannibal ipse dixit se solum hostes a muris Carthaginis removisse. (The actual words were, " I alone removed *or* have removed the enemy from the walls ".) 7. Uter dixit Romanos captivos interficere ? 8. Alter dixit haec ita esse; alter negavit. 9. Eum videramus qui urbes Africae (*or* in Africa) valentissimas patriae restituerat. (Note " the man who " always *eum qui* : avoid *hominem qui* in such a phrase.) 10. Neuter dixit Caesarem hanc provinciam sibi soli dedisse. (*Sibi* is used because it refers to the subject of *dixit*, the main verb. The actual words were, " Caesar gave this province to me alone ".)

Exercise 17 (b)

1. Ille Erycem ita ferociter (tanta ferocia) defendebat ut Romani nullam victoriae spem haberent. 2. Ille Erycem tanta fortitudine defendit ut Romani non putent se eum capturos esse. 3. Urbem tuam sic defendebat ut Romani nullam victoriae spem haberent. 4. Tam ferox erat (not *fuit*, because " was " denotes a state) ut negaret se urbem vestram traditurum esse. 5. Romani ita male bellum gerebant ut omnia oppida amitterent. 6. Illius fortitudo viri tanta erat ut omnes adversarios vinceret. 7. Adeo sapiens est ut intellegat haec esse falsa. 8. Tantum bellum exarsit ut Poeni oppida Africae amitterent. 9. Uter tam ferox est ut cum illo pugnet ? 10. Dixit se ipsos imperium totius Africae amisisse.

In sentence 10 *eos* or *illos* might be used for *se*, if you meant that *they* did not include *He*.

Exercise 18 (b)

1. Poeni adeo timebant ut a Romanis auxilium etiam petiverint atque impetraverint. 2. Cum, O Carthaginienses, omnia in Sicilia amisissetis pacem conciliavistis. 3. Tam ferociter (Tanta fortitudine) Erycem defendistis ut decesserimus. 4. Cum belli finem facere constituissent rem Hamilcari permiserunt. 5. Adeo bellandi studio flagrabat ut Sicilia decedere recusaverit. 6. Alii regendi studio flagrabant, alii cupiditate pecuniae. 7. Cum haec ad pugnandum inutilia cognovisset perdidit. 8. Tot mercenarii milites desciverant ut Poeni desperarent. 9. Aliis bellandi studium permittamus. 10. Parcendo aliorum bonis amorem conciliabimus.

Exercise 19 (b)

1. Nunc quidem in Sicilia sunt multi Carthaginienses. 2. Diu Romae eramus. 3. Si Romae ero, te visum veniam. 4. Cum Romae eris (-tis) Capitolium videbis (-tis) (spectabis, -tis). 5. Festinat ut Romae illo die sit. 6. Cassius post pugnam a servo pugione interfectus est (occisus est). 7. Antonius a Cleopatra amatus erat. 8. Cum a Romanis victi erunt, ex Sicilia profecto decedent. 9. Si hoc proelio a Scipione victi erimus magno in periculo profecto erimus. 10. Cum mercenarii milites descivissent, Carthago magno in periculo erat.

Exercise 20 (b)

1. Sic Erycem defendit ut eo loco finem belli fecerit. 2. Tantum bellum exarserat ut Carthago nunquam simili in periculo fuerit. 3. Cum centum milia armatorum facta essent, hostes oppugnare constituit. 4. Magno hostium numero Italia vexabatur. 5. Tam ferociter pugnaverunt ut urbs conservaretur (*or* conservata sit). 6. Locorum angustiis clausi plures fame interfecti sunt quam ferro. 7. Vos Romae fuistis, nos non in Graecia fuimus. 8. Ante urbem ab hostibus captam magnus eorum numerus interfectus est. 9. Multos

annos Corinthi fueram statuas videndi (spectandi) causa.
10. Adeo his malis perterriti sunt (timebant, timuerunt) ut
manus dederint.

Exercise 21 (b)

1. Res in Sicilia et mari et terra male geruntur. 2. Nullus
nocendi locus hostibus dabitur. 3. E contrario, occasione
data, hostes lacessentur. 4. Res in Sicilia bene gerebantur.
5. Bellum eo loco nobis gerendum est (*gerendum* is gerundive.
Note the absence of the preposition *in* with *eo loco*. Remember
nobis is Dative). 6. Ab hominibus amicis non nocendum est
(*nocendum* is gerund). 7. A Sicilia nobis intra paucos dies
discendum est. (Note preposition, *intra*, within, takes
Accusative case.) 8. A Romanis nunquam hostibus cedendum
est. 9. Eryx Carthaginiensibus (Poenis) defendendus est. 10.
Si res in Sicilia male gerentur ex ea insula decedemus. (*Gerentur*
is Future, not Future Perfect, because the meaning is, " If
affairs shall be going on badly ", not " shall have gone ".)
11. Statuemus hujus belli finem facere. 12. Si classis nostra
a Romanorum consule superata erit pacem conciliabimus.

Exercise 22

1. Ego bellandi (belli) cupiditate flagrabam, tu paci serviendum esse putabas. 2. Nobis haec dona dedit, illa vobis (tibi).
3. Omnium nostrum sapientissimus (es) tu, ego fortissimus.
4. Victi nobis manus dederunt. 5. Patria mea belli calami-
tatibus exhausta mihi carissima est. 6. Ille te sapientior est.
7. Ad sapientissimum Romanorum haec dona mittit. 8.
Bellandi (belli) cupiditate acriore quam tu ego flagrabam.
9. Hoc opus omnium facillimum est, illud difficillimum. 10.
Patris simillimus est; frater (ejus) matris est similior. 11.
Potius, patria succumbente, peribo. 12. Dixit se maximo cum
flagitio domum rediturum. 13. Postea hoc consilo pacem
conciliaveramus. 14. Relictis armis ille cum suis Sicilia
decessit.

Note in 12 the omission of *esse*. It might be inserted.

Exercise 23

1. Ab eis petebat ut haec facerent (*Substantival*). 2. Ab eis petii (petivi) ut haec faciant (*Substantival*). 3. Id egerunt (egere) ut exercitum in Hispaniam mitterent (*Substantival*). 4. Id efficiemus ut duces in Hispaniam mittamur (*Substantival*). 5. Patriam multo aliter se habentem ac sperabamus cognovimus. 6. Mercenarios milites coegit ut eis in Romanos uteretur (*Final*). 7. Carthaginem ipsam oppugnavimus ut tota Africa abalienetur (*Final*). 8. Eos eo compellet ut plures fame quam ferro interituri sint (*Consecutive*). 9. Senatus decrevit ut Carthago oppugnaretur et deleretur (*Substantival*). 10. Senatus decernit ut Carthago oppugnetur et deleatur (*Substantival*). 11. Senatus decernet ut Carthago deleatur (*Substantival*). 12. Carthaginem oppugnavit ut eam deleret (*Final*). 13. Ab eo petivit ne se Romam mitteret (*Substantival*) (*se* referring to the subject of *petivit*. If not, *eum* or *illum*). 14. Militibus imperavit ut hostes a muris removerent (*Substantival*). 15. Militibus imperavit ut ab Italia statim decedant (*Substantival*).

Exercise 24

1. Catulus Carthaginiensibus (Poenis) imperavit ut Sicilia decederent. 2. Oppidis abalienatis subvenit. 3. Hannibali exercitus imperium invidebam. 4. Princeps largitione Carthaginiensibus multa profuit. 5. Valentissima totius Africae oppida patriae restituemus. 6. Nunquam Hannibali atque Carthaginiensibus serviemus. 7. Negavit se unquam Romanis serviturum esse. 8. Tantum otium in Africa (Africae) reddidit ille ut nullum bellum multis annis fuisse videatur. 9. Missus est in Hispaniam cum exercitu quo facilius causam bellandi reperiret. 10. Tecum filium novem annorum ducis. 11. Hujus viri mentionem fecit quod multa et magna gessit. 12. Terra marique hostibus resistemus. 13. Hannibal Romanis bellum perpetuum minatur. 14. In Hispaniam cum exercitu venit quo melius haec perageret. 15. Cum haec ex sententia peregisset domum profectus est.

Exercise 25

1. Si res refectae essent bellum renovavisset. 2. Si eos virtute vicisset, manus dedissent. 3. Si Catulus se negavisset bellum compositurum, Sicilia Romani decessissent. 4. Si res reficiantur, bellum renovet. 5. Si eos virtute vicerit, manus dabunt. 6. Si eos virtute vincat manus dent. 7. Si Catulus se neget bellum esse compositurum Sicilia decedant. 8. Si Catulus negaverit se bellum compositurum Sicilia decedent. 9. Secundum bellum Poenicum perpetuo hujus odio erga Romanos maxime concitatum esse videtur. 10. Magnas res gerite, gentes bellicosissimas subigite, Africam viris et pecunia locupletate. 11. Dixit Africam equis et viris locupletatum iri. 12. Dixit se meditari bellum in Italiam inferre. 13. Dicit Africam viris pecuniaque locupletari. 14. Nono anno postquam in Hispaniam venerunt occisi sunt. 15. Inimicos vestros amate.

Note *vestros* not *tuos*, because the *your* is plural.

Exercise 26

1. Romanos vincere (superare) poterimus. 2. Omnes gentes vincere (superare) poterant. 3. Omnes gentes virtute antecedere poteratis. 4. Inimicum tuum non potes interficere (occidere). 5. Unius virtutem devincere potueramus (devincere = *utterly subdue*). 6. Odium tuum erga Romanos deponere potueris. 7. Dicit se inimicos interficere posse. 8. Dicit se gentes cunctas (omnes) virtute antecedere posse. 9. Dicit Hannibalem omnes (or ceteros = *all other*) imperatores prudentia antecedere potuisse. 10. Si Hannibal hic nunc esset Italiam superaret. 11. Si Hannibal in eo proelio esset (*or* fuisset, *state or act*) hostes vicisset. 12. Nisi Hannibal omnes imperatores (*or* duces) prudentia antecessisset (antecederet, *had been surpassing*) non esset (*or* fuisset) omnium maximus dux. 13. Si hoc faceremus poenas gravissimas dedissemus. 14. Si hoc fecisses (fecissetis) poenas gravissimas dares (daretis). 15. Si sapiens esset non illud faceret (a state and a continuous action in the past, hence Imperfect).

Exercise 27

1. Non dubium est quin redeat. 2. Non dubium erat quin rediret (note the Imperfect in secondary time). 3. Non fieri potest quin abeat. 4. Non fieri poterat quin abires (note the Imperfect again). 5. Nemo erat quin (putaret, crederet, existimaret) hostes abire. 6. Nemo est quin nunc urbem ineat. 7. Si Romam adibat errabat. 8. Si domum init stultus est. 9. Ego Romam ibo si Carthaginem ibit ille. (Insert pronouns because they are emphatic, signifying contrast.) 10. Si hoc facit nil boni inest (*insum, inesse,* to be in).

Exercise 28

1. Ab eo petunt (quaerunt) num ad se libros is laturus sit. 2. Ab eo quaerunt pecuniamne magnam secum ferat. 3. Ab eo quaerunt num secum pecuniam magnam tulerit. 4. Ab eis quaesivimus num quid pecuniae secum tulissent. 5. Ab eis quaesivimus num quid pecuniae secum ferrent. 6. Ab eis quaesivimus pecuniamne magnam secum laturi essent (note the *cum* after *se*; so with *me, te, vobis,* etc.). 7. Si equitatum omnem tecum duxeris vinces. 8. A me quaesivit num secum ad castra ire vellem ("would go" here means "I was willing to go"). 9. Hamilcar ab Hannibale quaerit velitne ad castra secum ire (*or* num ad castra iturus sit. The first sentence asks if Hannibal is willing, the second asks if he is about to go). 10. Abiit equitatum ductum (Supine after verb of motion). 11. Ab eo quaesivimus quando Romam rediturus esset. 12. Nescio quos libros secum ab Italia ferat. 13. Milites nesciebant num id publice comprobaretur. 14. Proximo triennio omnes Hispaniae gentes subegerunt Poeni (*proximus* is an irregular superlative, whose comparative is *propior,* nearer. There is no positive adjective. See Lesson XXII).

Exercise 29

1. Tandem Pyrenaeum saltum transire inceperunt. 2. Unum ex his exercitibus in Africam mittere malebat (*ex* and ablative is more common than the genitive after an adjective

of number). 3. Hannibal effecit ut elephantus ornatus ea
transire possit (*ut* consecutive). 4. Apud flumen Padum cum
P. Cornelio Scipione manum conserere conatus est (*manum
conserere*, to knit the hands together as in wrestling). 5.
Alterum exercitum in Hispania linquere debent, alterum in
Italiam ducere. 6. Alterum exercitum in Hispania debebant
linquere, alterum in Italiam ducere. 7. Scimus loca pate-
facere, itinera munire (you can omit the conjunction *et* if you
please). 8. Hannibal Alpes saltu Graio transiisse videtur.
9. Alpicos transitu prohibere conantes Hannibal profligavisse
dicitur. 10. Hoc itinere adeo gravi morbo adfecti sunt ut
dimidium exercitus interierit (*may have perished*). 11. Nesciunt
utrum Hannibal Etruriam petierit necne. 12. Non possum
dicere utrum Hannibal hoc velit necne. 13. Quaesivit num
nollet in Hispaniam ire atque Carthagine manere mallet.
14. Ab eis quaeremus quando hoc facere malint. 15. Nobis
dixisti (*or* dixistis) quae hostes voluerint.

Exercise 30

1. In propinquis urbi montibus castra ibi habendi causa
moratus est (*avoid* castrorum habendorum). 2. Romam hoc
proelium pugnandi causa profectus est (*better*, causa hujus
proelii pugnandi, *or* ad hoc proelium pugnandum, *Gerundive*).
3. Caium Centenium praetorem praemittere voluit ad saltum
occupandum (*or* causa saltum occupandi, *or* causa saltus
occupandi). 4. Magnam gloriam sibi comparavit hostes uno
proelio fugando (*or* hostibus uno proelio fugandis). 5. Decemviros legibus scribendis creare maluissemus. 6. Hoc fecit ut
Hannibal bellum componere velit. 7. Causa hostium circum-
veniendorum (*or* causa hostes circumveniendi) celeriter iter
facere volebat. 8. Cum valetudine gravi premeretur lectica
ferri maluit (*or* malebat). 9. In Apuliam ad consulibus
obviam veniendum iter fecit (*or* causa consulibus obviam
veniendi, *or* consulibus obviam ventum). 10. Nullo resistente
causa urbis expugnandae (*or* causa urbis vi capiendae, *or* causa
urbem expugnandi, *or* ad urbem expugnandam) Romam
profectus est. 11. Quintus Fabius Maximus se ei obiicere

voluit. 12. Urbis oppugnandae causa Romam proficisci
nolebant (variations are possible as in sentence 10). 13. Hoc
fecit ne consul urbem relinquere vellet (*or* urbe exire, decedere,
discedere). 14. Romanos oppugnandi causa Capuam reversus
est. 15. Consulem cum exercitu circumventum occidit.

Exercise 31

1. Vereor ut Caesar rex fiat. 2. Verebar ut Caesar rex
fieret. 3. Verebantur ne Caesar flumen transiret. 4. Veren-
tur ne Caesar flumen transeat. 5. Caesar verebatur rex fieri.
6. Caesar veretur rex fieri. 7. Caesar veretur flumen transire.
8. Caesar verebatur flumen transire. 9. Virtutem colendo
beati fiemus. 10. Non ita multis diebus hi fient consules.
11. Hanc post rem gestam callidissimus dux fiam. 12. Caesar
dixit eum (illum) dolo consulem factum esse. 13. Caesar dicit
se nihil (non) timere (vereri) ne Cicero consul fiat. 14.
Homines fiunt callidi (*or* boni) duces militares res exercendo.
15. Ex hoc intellegi potest quantus ille dux factus sit. (Latin
says " it is able to be understood ", not *intellegere*.)

Exercise 32

1. Eum miseruit (*or* miserebat), filii ducis quem apud
Rhodanum fugaverat. 2. Me oportet patriam defendere
domum revocatum. 3. Eum oportuit (*or* oportebat) patriam
defendere domum revocatum. 4. Me iuvat tantum bellum
composuisse (quod tantum bellum composui). 5. Eos iuvat
quod reliquos e fuga collegerunt. 6. Romanos puduit
(pudebat) quod apud Trebiam ab Hannibale superati erant (*or*
superatos esse *without* quod). 7. Scio Romanos puduisse quod
apud Trebiam superati sint (Subjunctive because of Oratio
Obliqua). 8. Scivit Romanos poenituisse quod Carthaginem
delevissent. (In the last two sentences the accusative and
infinitive was also possible.) 9. Tibi licet esse consuli Romae
neque exercitui praeesse. 10. Ei licuisset esse regi Carthagine
si vellet. 11. Ei libebat Hadrumeti permanere (morari)
reliquos ex exercitu colligenti. 12. Intererat militum jussis

Hannibalis fideliter parere : nostra (interest) Hannibalem ipsum superare. 13. Omnium interest facere ea quae recta sunt (those things which are right). 14. Dixit sibi licuisse novis dilectibus exercitum comparare. 15. Numidas poenituit Hannibali insidiatos esse (*or* quod insidiati erant). 16. Eis persuasum est ut hoc faciant. 17. Agris a Poenis nocebitur (*or* Poeni agris nocebunt). 18. Si agris a Poenis nocitum erit, Romam legatos mittemus. 19. Regi ab optimo quoque parebitur. 20. Militibus imperatum est ut ex urbe tribus diebus decederent.

Exercise 33

1. Legati Romam veniunt qui senatui populoque Romano gratias agant (*you could say also* ut . . . agant). 2. Legati Romam venerunt qui (*or* ut) senatui populoque Romano gratias agant. 3. Legati Romam ierunt qui (*or* ut) pacem a Romanis peterent. 4. Legati Romam ibunt qui (*or* ut) pacem a Romanis petant. 5. Carthaginienses non ii sunt qui pacem faciant (*qui* Consecutive). 6. Romani non ii erant qui pacem peterent (*qui* Consecutive). 7. Ego, qui serius advenissem, non patrem meum vidi (*qui* Causal). 8. Te, cujus opera hoc bellum susceptum sit, cum imperio apud exercitum habebimus (*qui* Concessive). 9. Ii qui (*or* cum) revocati essent, domum redierunt (*qui* Causal). 10. Ii qui revocati sint domum redibunt (*qui* Causal). 11. Ab eis petierunt ut captivi Fregellis essent (*ut* Substantival). 12. Eis qui pacem secum fecissent coronam auream dederunt (*qui* Causal).

Exercise 34

1. Cum naves solvisset et vela ventis dedisset duae naves missae sunt quae eum comprehenderent. 2. Cum naves solverit et vela ventis dederit duas naves mittemus quae eum comprehendant. 3. A servulo interfectus est priusquam epistolam (litteras) scriberet (Subjunctive because the result is prevented). 4. Servus eum interficere jussus est priusquam epistolam scribat (Subjunctive of the intention). 5. Antiocho fugato, fugit ille priusquam Romani eum comprehendere

possent (or potuerunt. The Subjunctive denotes that he fled to prevent the seizure; the Indicative simply connects the clauses by time). 6. Dum epistolam Romam ad matrem scribit eum servulus interfecit. (Note " to Rome to his mother ", or Eum epistolam Romam, etc., scribentem servulus interfecit.) 7. Dum sui multitudine adversariorum superabantur Hannibal eos quibuscum conflixerat fugabat. 8. Dum Carthagine Cretam iter facit eum latrones oppugnaverunt (or Carthagine eum Cretam iter facientem latrones oppugnaverunt). 9. Hannibal mansit donec Rhodiorum classis conflixit (or configeret. The Subjunctive denotes that he waited intentionally, the Indicative simply that he waited, without any idea of intentional waiting or expectation of joining battle being expressed). 10. Consistere nolebat donec Cretam ad Gortynios veniret. 11. Dum Hannibal cum Antiocho erat, ille omnibus in proeliis superior erat. 12. Hoc sine dubio accidisset, si Romanis sui potestatem fecisset. 13. Abire constituit priusquam in magnum periculum propter avaritiam Cretensium veniret. 14. Dum Antiochus Hannibalis consiliis parere volebat in bello felix (or superior) erat. 15. Desperatis rebus Hannibal in Syriam ad Antiochum venit.

Exercise 35

1. Trecentas sexaginta quinque amphoras plumbo impleverant. 2. Ducentae viginti novem amphorae auro et argento impletae erant. 3. Puero tria poma dedit. 4. Dixit se ducentas naves Hannibali daturum fuisse. 5. Roma anno septingentesimo quinquagesimo tertio ante Christum natum condita est. 6. Pugna Cannensis anno ducentesimo sexto decimo ante Christum natum facta est. 7. Hannibal septuaginta annos vixit. 8. Caesar ducibus binas naves dederat. 9. Eis ducenos sestertios dabimus. 10. Darius in Europam amplius mille navibus navigavit (amplius has no effect on the case). 11. Ter Romani in hostes impetum fecerunt; tandem fugati sunt. 12. Vicies antehac urbem Romam vidi. 13. Hannibal ex Alpibus in Italiam cum quinque et viginta milibus hominum descendit. 14. Sedecim annos, Hannibale duce

Carthaginienses cum Romanis bellaverunt. 15. Anno ducentesimo secundo ante Christum natum apud Zamam Poenos
devicerunt Romani.

Exercise 36

1. Dixit Eumenem propter Romanorum societatem plus
valere. (He said, " Eumenes has more power ", *plus valet*).
2. Dixit eos conventuros esse eo die quo navale proelium
facturus esset (he might be about to fight). 3. Dixit se eos
vidisse qui in hoc navali prolio pugnarent (Latin says " who
might be fighting "). 4. Dixit se eos vidisse qui in hoc navali
proelio pugnarent (the same as sentence 3 exactly). 5. Dixit
se facturum ut scirent in qua nave aurum veheretur. 6. Arbitrabatur si hunc removisset omnia sibi facilia fore. 7. Dixit
se ducem vidisse qui tamdiu cum Romanis pugnavisset. 8.
Dicit se nuntium (tabellarium) vidisse qui cum caduceo ad
Eumenem missus sit. 9. Dicit eos, qui navem Eumenis
oppugnent, fugari. 10. Dicit eos qui navem Eumenis oppug-
naverint fugatum iri (direct form : Those who attack will be
routed, *Ei qui oppugnaverint fugabuntur*). 11. Hannibal nuntium mittit priusquam signum proelii dari possit. 12. Dixit
Hannibalem nuntium misisse priusquam signum proelii dari
posset. 13. Dixit Hannibalem nuntium misisse priusquam
signum proelii datum esset. 14. Dixit Hannibalem tabellarium
misisse ut palam faceret suis quo loco rex esset. 15. Dixit se
omnibus eis praecepisse ut in navem Eumenis unam con-
currerent.

Exercise 37

1. Negavit se id consecuturum esse nisi intra sua praesidia
se recepisset. 2. Negavit se id consecuturum esse nisi intra
praesidia sua se reciperet. 3. Negavit se id consecuturum
fuisse nisi intra praesidia sua se recepisset. 4. Negavit se
stultum futurum esse si id faceret. 5. Pollicitus est si illum
cepissent aut interfecissent magnum eis praemium fore (*or
magno eis praemio fore*). 6. Affirmavit (Dixit) si illum
cepissent aut interfecissent magnum eis praemium futurum

fuisse.   7. Dixit si illum interficerent, magnum eis praemium
fore.   8. Dixit nisi fuga salutem petiisset futurum fuisse ut
interficeretur (this construction is used because the Latin verb
has no Future Perfect Infinitive Passive).   9. Dixit eos nisi
fuga salutem peterent interfectum iri.   10. Dicit nisi fuga
salutem petierint eos interfectum iri (or fore ut ei interficiantur
" it-to-be-about-to-be that they may be slain ").   11. Dicit
nisi fuga salutem petiissent futurum fuisse ut interficerentur.
12. Negat eos nisi stulti fuissent illud facturos esse.   13. Etsi
hujus causam mirabatur tamen proelium committere non
dubitavit (or quominus proelium committeret).   14. Nemo
dubitabat quin aliquid de pace scriptum esset (or, *more literally*,
quin aliquid de pace scriptum attulisset).   15. Nave hunc in
modum (or ita) suis declarata eodem unde egressus erat se
recepit.

Exercise 38

1. Quae jacta subito risum pugnantibus concitarunt (concitarunt *contracted for* concitaverunt).   2. Adeo nova re
perterriti sunt ut non videre possent quid potissimum vitarent.
3. Bellum male gerere est mali ducis.   4. Etsi Antiochum
multa stultissime conari videbant nulla in re eum deseruerunt.
5. Cum se minus robustum domesticis opibus esse videret
ceteros reges conciliavit.   6. Bellum acriter inter eos terra
marique gerebatur : quo magis Hannibal cupiebat eum opprimi.
7. Dixit se facillime inventurum esse locum ubi ille esset.
8. Militibus imperavit ut propere ad se nuntiarent num undique
obsessus esset (or obsideretur, " was being beset ").   9. Puer
celerrime nuntiavit omnes exitus occupatos esse.   10. Poeni
senserunt id non fortuito factum neque imperium diutius
retinendum.   11. Ad te celeriter nuntiabo quid sit.   12. Si
nobis imperavisses facile invenissemus ubi ille esset.   13. Vidit
eos non fortuito venisse sed se petere.   14. Memor virtutis
pristinae venenum sumpsit ne vitam alieno arbitrio dimitteret.
15. Nuntii nuntiaverunt plures praeter consuetudinem armatos
apparere.

NUMERALS

	CARDINAL.	ORDINAL.
1	Un-us, -a, -um, *one*	Prīm-us, -a, -um, *first*
2	Du-o, -ae, -o, *two*	Secund-us, -a, -um (alter), *second*
3	Trēs, tria, *three*	Terti-us, -a, -um, *third*
4	Quattuor, *four*, etc.	Quart-us, -a, -um, *fourth*, etc.
5	Quinque	Quint-us, -a, -um
6	Sex	Sext-us, -a, -um
7	Septem	Septim-us, -a, -um
8	Octō	Octāv-us, -a, -um
9	Novem	Nōn-us, -a, -um
10	Decem	Decim-us, -a, -um
11	Undecim	Undecim-us, -a, -um
12	Duodecim	Duodecim-us, -a, -um
13	Trēdecim	Terti-us decim-us, etc.
14	Quattuordecim	Quart-us decim-us, etc.
15	Quindecim	Quint-us decim-us, etc.
16	Sēdecim	Sext-us decim-us, etc.
17	Septendecim	Septim-us decim-us, etc.
18	Duodēvigintī	Duodēvicēsim-us, etc.
19	Undēvigintī	Undēvicēsim-us, etc.
20	Vigintī	Vicēsim-us, etc.
30	Trigintā	Tricēsim-us, etc.
40	Quadrāgintā	Quadrāgēsim-us, etc.
50	Quinquāgintā	Quinquāgēsim-us, etc.
60	Sexāgintā	Sexāgēsim-us, etc.
70	Septuāgintā	Septuāgēsim-us, etc.
80	Octōgintā	Octōgēsim-us, etc.
90	Nōnāgintā	Nōnāgēsim-us, etc.
100	Centum	Centēsim-us, etc.
200	Ducent-ī, -ae, -a	Ducentēsim-us, etc.
300	Trecent-ī, -ae, -a	Trecentēsim-us, etc.
400	Quadringent-ī, -ae, -a	Quadringentēsim-us, etc.
500	Quingent-ī, -ae, -a	Quingentēsim-us, etc.
600	Sescent-ī, -ae, -a	Sexcentēsim-us, etc.
700	Septingent-ī, -ae, -a	Septingentēsim-us, etc.
800	Octingent-ī, -ae, -a	Octingentēsim-us, etc.
900	Nongent-ī, -ae, -a	Nongentēsim-us, etc.
1,000	Mille	Millēsim-us, etc.
2,000	Duo mīlia	Bis millēsim-us, etc.
100,000	Centum mīlia	Centiēs millēsim-us, etc.
1,000,000	Deciēs centēna mīlia	Deciēs centiēs millēsim-us, etc.

DISTRIBUTIVE.	NUMERAL ADVERBS.
Singul-ī, -ae, -a, *one each*	Semel, *once*
Bīn-ī, -ae, -a, *two each*	Bis, *twice*
Tern-ī (trīn-ī), -ae, -a, *three each*	Ter, *thrice*
Quatern-ī, -ae, -a, *four each*, etc.	Quater, *four times*, etc.
Quīn-ī, -ae, -a	Quinquiēs
Sēn-ī, -ae, -a	Sexiēs
Septēn-ī, -ae, -a	Septiēs
Octōn-ī, -ae, -a	Octiēs
Novēn-ī, -ae, -a	Noviēs
Dēn-ī, -ae, -a	Deciēs
Undēn-ī, -ae, -a	Undeciēs
Duodēn-ī, -ae, -a	Duodeciēs
Tern-ī dēn-ī, -ae, -a	Ter deciēs
Quatern-ī dēn-ī, -ae, -a	Quater deciēs
Quīn-ī dēn-ī, -ae, -a	Quinquiēs deciēs
Sēn-ī dēn-ī, -ae, -a	Sexiēs deciēs
Septēn-ī dēn-ī, -ae, -a	Septiēs deciēs
Duodēvīcēn-ī, -ae, -a	Duodēvīciēs
Undēvīcēn-ī, -ae, -a	Undēvīciēs
Vīcēn-ī, -ae, -a	Vīciēs
Trīcēn-ī, -ae, -a	Trīciēs
Quadrāgēn-ī, -ae, -a	Quadrāgiēs
Quinquāgēn-ī, -ae, -a	Quinquāgiēs
Sexāgēn-ī, -ae, -a	Sexāgiēs
Septuāgēn-ī, -ae, -a	Septuāgiēs
Octōgēn-ī, -ae, -a	Octōgiēs
Nōnāgēn-ī, -ae, -a	Nōnāgiēs
Centēn-ī, -ae, -a	Centiēs
Ducēn-ī, -ae, -a	Ducentiēs
Trecēn-ī, -ae, -a	Trecentiēs
Quadringēn-ī, -ae, -a	Quadringentiēs
Quingēn-ī, -ae, -a	Quingentiēs
Sescēn-ī, -ae, -a	Sexcentiēs
Septingēn-ī, -ae, -a	Septingentiēs
Octingēn-ī, -ae, -a	Octingentiēs
Nongēn-ī, -ae, -a	Nongentiēs
Singula mīlia	Mīliēs
Bīna mīlia	Bis mīliēs
Centēna mīlia	Centiēs mīliēs
Deciēs centēna mīlia	Deciēs centiēs mīliēs

TABLES OF VERBS

The quantity or length of syllables in these tables is marked on this plan : short vowels are not marked at all; vowels which are long because they stand before two consonants are not marked; other long vowels are marked long.

Verb *Sum*, I am.

(Tenses from the Present Stems.)

INDICATIVE.   SUBJUNCTIVE.

Present.   *Present.*

Sum,	I am.	Sumus,	we are.	Sim	Sīmus
Es,	thou art.	Estis,	you are.	Sīs	Sītus
Est,	he is.	Sunt,	they are.	Sit	Sint

Imperfect.   *Imperfect.*

Eram,	I was.	Erāmus,	we were.	Es-sem	Essēmus
Erās,	thou wert.	Erātis,	you were.	Es-sēs	Essētis
Erat,	he was.	Erant,	they were.	Es-set	Essent

Future.

Erō,	I shall be.	Erimus,	we shall be.
Eris,	thou wilt be.	Eritis,	you will be.
Erit,	he will be.	Erunt,	they will be.

INFINITIVE PRESENT.
Esse.

IMPERATIVE.

Es,	be (thou).	Estō,	thou shalt be.
Este,	be (ye).	Estōte,	ye shall be.
		Estō,	he shall be.
		Suntō,	they shall be.

(From Perfect Stem *Fu-*.)

INDICATIVE.   SUBJUNCTIVE.

Perfect.   *Perfect.*

Fu-ī,	I have been *or* I was.	Fu-erim
Fu-istī,	thou hast been *or* thou wert.	Fu-eris
Fu-it,	he has been *or* he was.	Fu-erit
Fu-imus,	we have been *or* we were.	Fu-erimus
Fu-istis,	you have been *or* you were.	Fu-eritis
Fu-ērunt, or -ēre,	they have been *or* they were.	Fu-erint

INDICATIVE.	SUBJUNCTIVE.
Pluperfect.	*Pluperfect.*

Fu-eram, I had been.	*Fu-issem*
Fu-erās, thou hadst been.	*Fu-issēs*
Fu-erat, he had been.	*Fu-isset*
Fu-erāmus, we had been.	*Fu-issēmus*
Fu-erātis, you had been.	*Fu-issētis*
Fu-erant, they had been.	*Fu-issent*

Future Perfect.	PRESENT INFINITIVE.
Fu-erō, I shall have been.	*Fu-isse.*
Fu-eris, thou wilt have been.	
Fu-erit, he will have been.	
Fu-erimus, we shall have been.	
Fu-eritis, you will have been.	
Fu-erint, they will have been.	

(From Supine Stem *Fut-*.)

First Supine wanting.
Second Supine wanting.
Future Participle.   *Futūrus, -a, -um.*
Future Infinitive.   *Futūrus esse.*

TABLES OF THE REGULAR VERBS

Active Voice

First Conjugation.   Example, *Amo,* I love.

(From Present Stem *Am-*.)

INDICATIVE MOOD.		SUBJUNCTIVE MOOD.	
Present.		*Present.*	
Am-ō	*-āmus*	*Am-em*	*-ēmus*
-ās	*-ātis*	*-ēs*	*-ētis*
-at	*-ant*	*-et*	*-ent*
Imperfect.		*Imperfect.*	
Am-ābam	*-ābāmus*	*Am-ārem*	*-ārēmus*
-ābās	*-ābātis*	*-ārēs*	*-ārētis*
-ābat	*-ābant*	*-āret*	*-ārent*

INDICATIVE		Present Participle. *Am-ans*
Future		Present Infinitive. *Am-āre*
Am-ābo	*-ābimus*	Gerund. *Am-andum*, etc.
-ābis	*-ābitis*	
-ābit	*-ābunt*	

IMPERATIVE MOOD.

Am-ā	*-āte*	*Am-ātō*	*-ātōte*
Love thou.	Love ye.	Thou shalt love.	Ye shall love.
		-ātō	*-antō*
		He shall love.	They shall love.

(From Perfect Stem *Amav-*.)

INDICATIVE MOOD.		SUBJUNCTIVE MOOD.	
Perfect.		*Perfect.*	
Amāv-ī	*-imus*	*Amāv-erim*	*-erimus*
-istī	*-istis*	*-erīs*	*-eritis*
-it	*-ērunt* or *ēre*	*-erit*	*-erint*
Pluperfect.		*Pluperfect.*	
Amāv-eram	*-erāmus*	*Amāv-issem*	*-issēmus*
-erās	*-erātis*	*-issēs*	*-issētis*
-erat	*-erant*	*-isset*	*-issent*
Future Perfect.		PERFECT INFINITIVE.	
Amāv-erō	*-erimus*	*Amāv-isse*	
-eris	*-eritis*		
-erit	*-erint*		

(From Supine Stem *Amat-*.)

First Supine.   *Amāt-um.*
Second Supine.   *Amāt-ū.*
Future Participle.   *Amāt-ūrus, -a, -um.*

Future Infinitive = Future Participle + *esse* = *Amātūrus esse,* to be about to love.

Second Conjugation.   Example, *Moneo,* I warn.

(From Present Stem *Mon-*.)

INDICATIVE MOOD.		SUBJUNCTIVE MOOD.	
Present.		*Present.*	
Mon-eō	*-ēmus*	*Mon-eam*	*-eāmus*
-ēs	*-ētis*	*-eās*	*-eātis*
-et	*-ent*	*-eat*	*-eant*

Imperfect.

Mon-*ēbam*	-*ēbāmus*		
-*ēbās*	-*ēbātis*		
-*ēbat*	-*ēbant*		

Imperfect.

Mon-*ērem*	-*ērēmus*
-*ērēs*	-*ērētis*
-*ēret*	-*ērent*

Future.

Mon-*ēbō*	-*ēbimus*
-*ēbis*	-*ēbitis*
-*ēbit*	-*ēbunt*

Present Participle.   Mon-*ens*
Present Infinitive.   Mon-*ēre*
Gerund.   Mon-*endum*, etc.

IMPERATIVE MOOD.

Mon-*ē*	-*ēte*	Mon-*ētō*	-*ētōte*
Warn thou.	Warn ye.	Thou shalt warn.	Ye shall warn.
		-*ētō*	-*ento*
		He shall warn.	They shall warn.

(From Perfect Stem *Monu-*.)

INDICATIVE MOOD.   SUBJUNCTIVE MOOD.

Perfect.

Monu-*ī*	-*imus*
-*istī*	-*istis*
-*it*	-*ērunt* or -*ēre*

Perfect.

Monu-*erim*	-*erimus*
-*eris*	-*eritis*
-*erit*	-*erint*

Pluperfect.

Monu-*eram*	-*erāmus*
-*erās*	-*erātis*
-*erat*	-*erant*

Pluperfect.

Monu-*issem*	-*issēmus*
-*issēs*	-*issētis*
-*isset*	-*issent*

Future Perfect.

Monu-*erō*	-*erimus*
-*eris*	-*eritis*
-*erit*	-*erint*

PERFECT INFINITIVE.

Monu-isse

(From Supine Stem *Monit-*.)

First Supine.   *Monit-um.*
Second Supine.   *Monit-ū.*
Future Participle.   *Monit-ūrus, -a, -um.*

Future Infinitive = Future Participle + *esse* = *Monitūrus esse,* be about to advise.

Third Conjugation. Example, *Rego*, I rule.
(From Present Stem *Reg-*.)

INDICATIVE MOOD.		SUBJUNCTIVE MOOD.	
Present.		*Present.*	
Reg-ō	-imus	Reg-am	-āmus
-is	-itis	-ās	-ātis
-it	-unt	-at	-ant
Imperfect.		*Imperfect.*	
Reg-ēbam	-ēbāmus	Reg-erem	-erēmus
-ēbas	-ēbātis	-erēs	-erētis
-ēbat	-ēbant	-eret	-erent
Future.		Present Participle. *Reg-ens*	
Reg-am	-ēmus	Present Infinitive. *Reg-ere*	
-ēs	-ētis	Gerund. *Reg-endum,* etc.	
-et	-ent		

IMPERATIVE MOOD.

Reg-e	-ite	Reg-itō	-itōte
Rule thou.	Rule ye.	Thou shalt rule.	Ye shall rule.
		-itō	-untō
		He shall rule.	They shall rule.

(From Perfect Stem *Rex-*.)

INDICATIVE.		SUBJUNCTIVE.	
Perfect.		*Perfect.*	
Rex-ī	-imus	Rex-erim	-erimus
-istī	-istis	-eris	-eritis
-it	-ērunt or -ēre	-erit	-erint

INDICATIVE.		SUBJUNCTIVE.	
Pluperfect.		*Pluperfect.*	
Rex-eram	-erāmus	Rex-issem	-issēmus
-erās	-erātis	-issēs	-issētis
-erat	-erant	-isset	-issent

Future Perfect.		PERFECT INFINITIVE.
Rex-erō	-erimus	*Rex-isse*
-eris	-eritis	
-erit	-erint	

(From Supine Stem *Rect-*.)

First Supine.   *Rect-um.*
Second Supine.   *Rect-ū.*
Future Participle.   *Rect-ūrus, -a, -um.*

Future Infinitive = Future Participle + *esse* = *Rectūrus esse*, to be about to rule.

Fourth Conjugation.   Example, *Audio*, I hear.

(From Present Stem *Aud-*.)

INDICATIVE MOOD.		SUBJUNCTIVE MOOD.	
Present.		*Present.*	
Aud-iō	*-īmus*	*Aud-iam*	*-iāmus*
-īs	*-ītis*	*-iās*	*-iātis*
-it	*-iunt*	*-iat*	*-iant*
Imperfect.		*Imperfect.*	
Aud-iēbam	*-iēbāmus*	*Aud-īrem*	*-īrēmus*
-iēbās	*-iēbātis*	*-īrēs*	*-īrētis*
-iēbat	*-iēbant*	*-īret*	*-īrent*

Future.		
Aud-iam	*-iēmus*	Present Participle. *Aud-iens*
-iēs	*-iētis*	Present Infinitive. *Aud-īre*
-iet	*-ient*	Gerund. *Aud-iendum*, etc.

IMPERATIVE MOOD.

Aud-ī	*-īte*	*Aud-ītō*	*-ītōte*
Hear thou.	Hear ye.	Thou shalt hear.	Ye shall hear.
		-ītō	*-iuntō*
		He shall hear.	They shall hear.

(From Perfect Stem *Audiv-*.)

INDICATIVE MOOD.		SUBJUNCTIVE MOOD.	
Perfect.		*Perfect.*	
Audīv-ī	*-imus*	*Audīv-erim*	*-erimus*
-istī	*-istis*	*-eris*	*-eritis*
-it	*-ērunt* or *-ēre*	*-erit*	*-erint*

Pluperfect.		*Pluperfect.*	
Audīv-eram	-erāmus	Audīv-issem	-issēmus
-erās	-erātis	-issēs	-issētis
-erat	-erant	-isset	-issent

Future Perfect.		Perfect Infinitive.
Audīv-erō	-erimus	Audīv-issĕ
-eris	-eritis	
-erit	-erint	

(From Supine Stem *Audīt-*.)

First Supine.	*Audīt-um.*
Second Supine.	*Audīt-ū.*
Future Participle.	*Audīt-ūrus, -a, -um.*

Future Infinitive = Future Participle + *esse* = *Audītūrus esse*, to be about to hear.

Passive Voice

First Conjugation. *Amor*, I am loved.

(From Present Stem *Am-*.)

Indicative Mood.		Subjunctive Mood.	
Present.		*Present.*	
Am-or : I am being loved.		Am-er	Am-ēmur
Am-āmur : We are being loved.			
Am-āris (-are) : You are being loved		-ēris (-ēre)	-ēminī
Am-āmini : Ye are being loved.			
Am-ātur : He is being loved.		-ētur	-entur
Am-antur : They are being loved.			
Imperfect.		*Imperfect.*	
Am-ābar : I was being loved.		Am-ārer	-ārēmur
Am-ābāmur : We were being loved			
Am-ābāris (-ābāre) : You were being loved.		-ārēris (-ārēre)	-ārēminī
Am-ābāminī : Ye were being loved.			
Am-ābātur : He was being loved.		-ārētur	-ārentur
Am-ābantur : They were being loved.			
Future.		Present Participle.
Am-ābor : I shall be loved.		——
Am-ābimur : We shall be loved.		Present Infinitive.
Am-āberis (-ābere) : You shall be loved.		Amārī : To be loved.
Am-ābiminī : Ye shall be loved.		
Am-ābitur : He shall be loved.		Gerundive. *Amandus, -a,*
Am-ābuntur : They shall be loved.		*-um.*

IMPERATIVE MOOD.

Am-āre : Be thou loved.   *Am-āmini* : Be ye loved.
   Am-ātor : You shall be loved.   *Am-ātor* : He shall be loved.
   Am-antor : They shall be loved.

Perfect Tenses

INDICATIVE MOOD.		SUBJUNCTIVE MOOD.	
Perfect.		*Perfect.*	
Amātus, etc., *sum*	*Amātī*, etc., *sumus*	*Amātus*, etc., *sim*	*Amātī*, etc., *sīmus*
„ es	„ estis	„ sīs	„ sītis
„ est	„ sunt	„ sit	„ sint
Pluperfect.		*Pluperfect.*	
Amātus eram	*Amātī erāmus*	*Amātus essem*	*Amātī essēmus*
„ erās	„ erātis	„ essēs	„ essētis
„ erat	„ erant	„ esset	„ essent
Future Perfect.			
Amātus ero	*Amātī erimus*	PERFECT INFINITIVE.	
„ eris	„ eritis	*Amātus esse*	
„ erit	„ erunt		

(From Supine Stem *Amāt-*.)

Past Participle Passive.   *Amātus, -a, -um.*
Future Infinitive Passive. *Amātum īrī.*

Second Conjugation. *Moneor*, I am warned.
(From Present Stem *Mon-*.)

INDICATIVE MOOD.		SUBJUNCTIVE MOOD.	
Present.		*Present.*	
Mon-eor	-ēmur	*Mon-ear*	-eāmur
-ēris (or -ēre)	-ēminī	-eāris (or -eāre)	-eāminī
-ētur	-entur	-eātur	-eantur
INDICATIVE.		SUBJUNCTIVE.	
Imperfect.		*Imperfect.*	
Mon-ēbar	-ēbāmur	*Mon-ērer*	-ērēmur
-ēbāris (or -ēbāre)	-ēbāminī	-ērēris (or -ērēre)	-ērēminī
-ēbātur	-ēbantur	-ērētur	-ērentur

	Future.		**Present Participle.**
Mon-ēbor		*-ēbimur*	———
	-ēberis (or *-ēbere*)	*-ēbiminī*	**Present Infinitive.**
	-ēbitur	*-ēbuntur*	*Monērī*

Gerundive.
Monendus, -a, -um

IMPERATIVE MOOD.

Mon-ēre	*-ēminī*	*Mon-ētor*	
		-ētor	*-entor*

Perfect Tenses

INDICATIVE MOOD.		SUBJUNCTIVE MOOD.	
Perfect.		*Perfect.*	
Monitus sum	*Monitī sumus*	*Monitus sim*	*Monitī sīmus*
,, es	,, estis	,, sīs	,, sītis
,, est	,, sunt	,, sit	,, sint
Pluperfect.		*Pluperfect.*	
Monitus eram	*Monitī erāmus*	*Monitus essem*	*Monitī essēmus*
,, erās	,, erātis	,, essēs	,, essētis
,, erat	,, erant	,, esset	,, essent
Future Perfect.			
Monitus erō	*Monitī erimus*	PERFECT INFINITIVE	
,, eris	,, eritis	*Monitus esse*	
,, erit	,, erint		

(From Supine Stem.)

Past Participle Passive.   *Monitus, -a, -um.*
Future Infinitive Passive.   *Monitum īrī.*

Third Conjugation.   *Regor*, I am ruled.
(From Present Stem *Reg-*.)

INDICATIVE MOOD.		SUBJUNCTIVE MOOD.	
Present.		*Present.*	
Reg-or	*-imur*	*Reg-ar*	*-āmur*
-eris (-ere)	*-iminī*	*-āris (-āre)*	*-āminī*
-itur	*-untur*	*-ātur*	*-antur*

Imperfect.		*Imperfect.*	
Reg-*ēbar*	-*ēbāmur*	Reg-*erer*	-*erēmur*
-*ebaris* (-*ēbāre*)	-*ēbāminī*	-*erēris* (-*erēre*)	-*erēminī*
-*ēbātur*	-*ēbantur*	-*erētur*	-*erentur*

Future.		Present Participle.	
Reg-*ar*	-*ēmur*		
-*ēris* (-*ēre*)	-*ēminī*	Present Infinitive.	
-*ētur*	-*entur*	Reg-*ī*	

Gerundive.
Reg-*endus, -a, -um.*

IMPERATIVE MOOD.

Reg-*ere*	-*iminī*	Reg-*itor*	
		-*itor*	-*untor*

Perfect Tenses

INDICATIVE MOOD.		SUBJUNCTIVE MOOD.	
Perfect.		*Perfect.*	
Rectus sum	Rectī sumus	Rectī sim	Rectī sīmus
,, es	,, estis	,, sīs	,, sītis
,, est	,, sunt	,, sit	,, sint
Pluperfect.		*Pluperfect.*	
Rectus eram	Rectī erāmus	Rectus essem	Rectī essēmus
,, erās	,, erātis	,, essēs	,, essētis
,, erat	,, erant	,, esset	,, essent
Future Perfect.			
Rectus erō	Rectī erimus	PERFECT INFINITIVE.	
,, eris	,, eritis	Rectus esse	
,, erit	,, erunt		

(From Supine Stem *Rect-*.)

Past Participle Passive. Rectus, -a, -um.
Future Infinitive Passive. Rectum īrī.

Fourth Conjugation. *Audior*, I am heard.
(From Present Stem *Aud-*.)

INDICATIVE MOOD.		SUBJUNCTIVE MOOD.	
Present.		*Present.*	
Aud-*ior*	-*īmur*	Aud-*iar*	-*iāmur*
-*īris* (-*īre*)	-*īminī*	-*iāris* (-*iāre*)	-*iāminī*
-*ītur*	-*iuntur*	-*iātur*	-*iantur*

Imperfect.		*Imperfect.*	
Aud-iēbar	-iēbāmur	Aud-īrer	-īrēmur
-iēbaris (-iēbāre)	-iēbāminī	-īrēris (-īrēre)	-īrēminī
-iēbātur	-iēbantur	-īrētur	-īrentur

Future.		Present Participle.
Aud-iar	-iēmur	———
-iēris (-iēre)	-iēminī	Present Infinitive.
-iētur	-ientur	Aud-īrī
		Gerundive.
		Audiendus, -a, -um.

IMPERATIVE MOOD.

Aud-īre	-īminī	Aud-ītor	-iuntor
		-ītor	

Perfect Tenses

INDICATIVE MOOD.		SUBJUNCTIVE MOOD.	
Perfect.		*Perfect.*	
Audītus sum	Audītī sumus	Audītus sim	Audītī simus
„ es	„ estis	„ sīs	„ sītis
„ est	„ sunt	„ sit	„ sint

INDICATIVE.		SUBJUNCTIVE.	
Pluperfect.		*Pluperfect.*	
Audītus eram	Audītī erāmus	Audītus essem	Audītī essēmus
„ erās	„ erātis	„ essēs	„ essētis
„ erat	„ erant	„ esset	„ essent

Future Perfect.		
Audītus erō	Audītī erimus	PERFECT INFINITIVE.
„ eris	„ eritis	Audītus esse
„ erit	„ erunt	

(From Supine Stem   *it-*.)

Past Participle Passive.   *Audītus, -a, -um.*
Future Infinitive Passive.   *Audītum īrī.*

TABLES OF THE IRREGULAR VERBS

	INDICATIVE.					
	Singular.				*Plural.*	
PRESENT.	Pos-sum	pot-es	pot-est	pos-sumus	pot-estis	pos-sunt
	Volo	vīs	vult	volumus	vultis	volunt
	Nōlo	nōnvīs	nōnvult	nōlumus	nōnvultis	nōlunt
	Mālo	māvīs	māvult	mālumus	māvultis	mālunt
	Fero	fers	fert	ferimus	fertis	ferunt
	Fīo	fis	fit	——	——	fīunt
	Eo	īs	it	īmus	ītis	eunt
IMPERFECT.	Pot-eram	-erās	-erat	-erāmus	-erātis	-erant
	Volē- Nōlē- Mālē- Ferē- Fīē- I- } bam	-bās	-bāt	-bāmus	-bātis	-bant
FUTURE.	Pot-erō	-eris	-erit	-erimus	-eritis	-erunt
	Vol- Nōl- Māl- Fer- Fī- } am	-ēs	-et	-ēmus	-ētis	-ent
	Ib-o	-is	-it	-imus	-itis	-unt

PARTICIPLE.		INFINITIVE.	GERUND.
Vol- Nōl- Māl- Fer- } ens		—— posse velle nolle malle ferre fieri ire	—— vol- nol- māl- fer- } endum
Gen. euntis			—— e-undum *Gen.* volendi, etc.

SUBJUNCTIVE.

		Singular.			Plural.	
Present.	Pos-sim Vel- Nōl- }im Māl- Fer- Fī- }am E-	pos-sis -īs -ās	pos-sit -it -at	pos-sīmus -īmus -āmus	pos-sītis -ītis -ātis	pos-sint -int -ant
Imperfect.	Poss- Vell- Noll- Mall- }em Ferr- Fier- Ir-	-ēs	-et	-ēmus	-ētis	-ent

IMPERATIVE.

	Singular.		Plural.	
	——	——	——	——
Nōl-ī, nōl-ītō	nōl-ītō	nōl-īte, nōl-ītōte	nōl-untō
Fer, fer-tō	fer-tō	fer-te, fer-tōte	fer-untō
Fī	—	fī-te	
I, ī-tō	ī-tō	ī-te, ī-tōte	e-untō

INDICATIVE					
Singular.				*Plural.*	
Fer-or	fer-ris	fer-tur	fer-imur	fer-iminī	fer-untur
Fer-ēbar	fer-ēbāris	fer-ēbātur	fer-ēbāmur	fer-ēbāminī	fer-ēbāntur
Fer-ar	fer-ēris	fer-ētur	fer-ēmur	fer-ēminī	fer-entur

SUBJUNCTIVE.					
Fer-ar	fer-āris	fer-ātur	fer-āmur	fer-āminī	fer-antur
Ferr-er	ferr-ēris	ferr-ētur	ferr-ēmur	ferr-ēminī	ferr-entur

IMPERATIVE.			
Fer-re, fer-tor	fer-tor	fer-iminī	fer-untor

GERUNDIVE	Fer-endus	PRESENT INFINITIVE	Ferr-ī

ALPHABETICAL LIST OF LATIN VERBS

This list is meant to supplement the Vocabulary. It will probably be easier to find a verb in it than in the other. You should work about in this as much as possible in going over the book the first time, and learn the list off by heart when going over the book the second time. The second column gives the ending of the Present Infinitive, which determines to which conjugation the verb belongs.

A

	Inf.	Perfect	Supine	
Abd-ō	abd-ere	abdid-ī	abdit-um	hide
Abig-ō	abig-ere	abēg-ī	abact-um	drive away
Abol-eō	abol-ēre	abolēv-ī	abolit-um	abolish
Accend-ō	accend-ere	accend-ī	accens-um	kindle, set on fire
Accumb-ō	accumb-ere	accubu-ī	accubit-um	recline at table
Acu-ō	acu-ere	acu-ī	acūt-um	sharpen
Add-ō	add-ere	addid-ī	addit-um	put to, add
Adim-ō	adim-ere	adem-ī	adempt-um	take away
Adipisc-or	adipisc-ī	adept-us sum		obtain
Adolesc-ō	adolesc-ere	adolēv-ī	adult-um	grow up
Adst-ō	adst-āre	adstit-ī		stand by
Afflig-ō	afflig-ere	afflix-ī	afflict-um	dash down
Agnosc-ō	agnosc-ere	agnōv-ī	agnit-um	recognise
Ag-ō	ag-ere	ēg-ī	act-um	drive
Alg-eō	alg-ēre	als-ī		be cold
Al-ō	al-ere	alu-ī	alt-um, alit-um	nourish
Amic-iō	amic-īre	amicu-ī, amix-ī	amict-um	clothe
Amplect-or	amplect-ī	amplex-us sum		embrace
Aper-iō	aper-īre	aperu-ī	apert-um	open
Arc-eō	arc-ēre	arcu-ī		ward off
Arcess-ō	arcess-ere	arcessīv-ī	arcessīt-um	summon

Ard-eō	ard-ēre	ars-ī	ars-um	*be on fire, (intrs.) blaze*
Ascend-ō	ascend-ere	ascend-ī	ascens-um	*climb*
Assent-ior	assent-īrī	assens-us sum	——	*agree to*
Argu-ō	argu-ere	argu-ī	——	*show*
Aud-eō	aud-ēre	aus-us sum	——	*dare*
Aug-eō	aug-ēre	aux-ī	auct-um	*increase, (trs.) make grow*

B

Bib-ō	bib-ere	bib-ī	——	*drink*

C

Cad-ō	cad-ere	cecid-ī	cās-um	*fall*
Caed-ō	caed-ere	cecīd-ī	caes-um	*cut, fell*
Can-ō	can-ere	cecin-ī	cant-um	*sing*
Capess-ō	capess-ere	capessīv-ī	capessīt-um	*seize eagerly*
Cap-iō	cap-ere	cēp-ī	capt-um	*take*
Carp-ō	carp-ere	carps-ī	carpt-um	*pluck*
Cav-eō	cav-ēre	cāv-ī	caut-um	*beware*
Cēd-ō	ced-ere	cess-ī	cess-um	*yield*
Cens-eō	cens-ēre	censu-ī	cens-um	*think, vote*
Cern-ō	cern-ere	crēv-ī	crēt-um	*distinguish*
Ci-eō	ci-ēre	cīv-ī	cit-um	*rouse*
Cing-ō	cing-ere	cinx-ī	cinct-um	*surround*
Circumd-ō	circumd-are	circumded-ī	circumdat-um	*put round*
Claud-ō	claud-ere	claus-ī	claus-um	*shut*
Cognosc-ō	cognosc-ere	cognōv-ī	cognit-um	*recognise*
Cōg-ō	cog-ere	coēg-ī	coact-um	*compel*
Collig-ō	collig-ere	collēg-ī	collect-um	*collect*
Col-ō	col-ere	colu-ī	cult-um	*till, cultivate*
Cōm-ō	com-ere	comps-ī	compt-um	*deck*
Comper-iō	comper-īre	comper-ī	compert-um	*learn*
Comping-ō	comping-ere	compēg-ī	compact-um	*fix together*
Compl-eō	compl-ēre	complēv-ī	complēt-um	*fill up*
Conc-iō	conc-īre	concīv-ī	concīt-um	*call together*
Concut-iō	concut-ere	concuss-ī	concuss-um	*shake violently*
Cond-ō	cond-ere	condid-ī	condit-um	*to found, hide*
Confic-iō	confic-ere	confēc-ī	confect-um	*finish*
Confit-eor	confit-ērī	confess-us sum	——	*confess*
Congru-ō	congru-ere	congru-ī	——	*agree*
Conser-ō	conser-ere	consēv-ī	consit-um	*plant (with something)*

Conser-ō	conser-ere	conseru-ī	consert-um	*to knit together*
Conspic-iō	conspic-ere	conspex-ī	conspect-um	*behold*
Constitu-ō	constitu-ere	constitu-ī	constitūt-um	*resolve*
Const-ō	const-āre	constit-ī	——	*consist*
Consul-ō	consul-ere	consulu-ī	consult-um	*consult*
Contemn-ō	contemn-ere	contemps-ī	contempt-um	*despise*
Coqu-ō	coqu-ere	cox-ī	coct-um	*cook*
Corrig-ō	corrig-ere	correx-ī	correct-um	*correct*
Crēd-ō	crēd-ere	crēdid-ī	crēdit-um	*believe*
Crep-ō	crep-āre	crepu-ī	crepit-um	*creak*
Cresc-ō	cresc-ere	crēv-ī	crēt-um	*grow (intrs.)*
Cub-ō	cub-āre	cubu-ī	cubit-um	*lie down*
Cūd-o	cūd-ere	cūd-ī	cūs-um	*forge*
Cupi-ō	cup-ere	cupīv-ī	cupīt-um	*desire*
Curr-ō	curr-ere	cucurr-ī	curs-um	*run*

D

Dēdic-o	dēdic-āre	dēdicāv-ī	dēdicāt-um	*dedicate*
Dēfend-ō	dēfend-ere	dēfend-ī	dēfens-um	*defend*
Dēl-eō	dēl-ēre	dēlēv-ī	dēlēt-um	*destroy*
Dēlig-ō	dēlig-ere	dēlēg-ī	dēlēct-um	*choose out*
Dēm-ō	dēm-ere	demps-ī	dempt-um	*take away*
Dēsil-iō	dēsil-īre	dēsilu-ī	dēsult-um	*leap down*
Dīc-ō	dīc-ere	dix-ī	dict-um	*say*
Dīlig-ō	dīlig-ere	dīlex-ī	dīlect-um	*love*
Dīrip-iō	dīrip-ere	dīripu-ī	dīrept-um	*plunder*
Disc-ō	disc-ere	didic-ī	——	*learn*
Dīvid-ō	dīvid-ere	dīvīs-ī	dīvīs-um	*divide*
D-ō	d-āre	ded-ī	dat-um	*give*
Doc-eō	doc-ēre	docu-ī	doct-um	*teach*
Dom-ō	dom-āre	domu-ī	domit-um	*tame, subdue*
Dūc-ō	dūc-ere	dux-ī	duct-um	*lead*

E

Ed-ō	ed-ere	ēd-ī	ēs-um	*eat*
Ed-ō	ēd-ere	ēdid-ī	ēdit-um	*give out*
Educ-ō	ēduc-āre	ēducāv-ī	ēducāt-um	*educate*
Edūc-o	edūc-ere	ēdux-ī	ēduct-um	*lead out*
Eg-eō	eg-ēre	egu-ī	——	*need (Abl. case)*
Elic-iō	ēlic-ere	ēlicu-ī	ēlicit-um	*lure out*
Em-ō	em-ere	ēm-ī	empt-um	*buy*
Evād-ō	ēvād-ere	ēvās-ī	ēvās-um	*go out*
Exc-iō	exc-īre	exciv-ī	excīt-um	*call forth*

Expergisc-or	expergisc-ī	experrect-us sum	——	*wake up (intrs.)*
Exper-ior	exper-īrī	expert-us sum	——	*try*
Exstingu-ō	exstinguere	exstinx-ī	exstinct-um	*extinguish*
Exu-ō	exu-ere	exu-ī	exūt-um	*strip off*

F

Facess-ō	facess-ere	facessīv-ī	facessīt-um	*do eagerly*
Fac-iō	fac-ere	fēc-ī	fact-um	*make*
Fall-ō	fall-ere	fefell-ī	fals-um	*deceive*
Fat-eor	fat-ērī	fass-us sum	——	*confess*
Fav-eō	fav-ēre	fāv-ī	faut-um	*be favourable*
Fer-iō	fer-īre	——	——	*strike*
Ferv-eō	ferv-ēre	ferv-ī, fervu-ī	——	*boil*
Fīd-ō	fid-ere	fīs-us sum	——	*trust*
Fīg-ō	fig-ere	fix-ī	fix-um	*fix*
Find-ō	find-ere	fid-ī	fiss-um	*split*
Fing-ō	fing-ere	finx-ī	fict-um	*form, imagine*
Flect-ō	flect-ere	flex-ī	flex-um	*bend*
Fl-eō	fl-ēre	flēv-ī	flēt-um	*weep*
Flōr-eō	flōr-ēre	flōru-ī	——	*flourish*
Flu-ō	flu-ere	flux-ī	flux-um	*flow*
Fod-iō	fod-ere	fōd-ī	foss-um	*dig*
Fov-eō	fov-ēre	fōv-ī	fōt-um	*cherish*
Frang-ō	frang-ere	frēg-ī	fract-um	*break*
Frem-ō	frem-ere	fremu-ī	fremit-um	*growl*
Frīg-eō	frīg-ēre	frix-ī	——	*be cold*
Fru-or	fru-ī	fruct-us *or* fruit-us sum	——	*enjoy*
Fug-iō	fug-ere	fūg-ī	fugit-um	*flee*
Fulc-iō	fulc-īre	fuls-ī	fult-um	*prop up*
Fulg-eō	fulg-ēre	fuls-ī	——	*glitter*
Fund-ō	fund-ere	fūd-ī	fūs-um	*rout*
Fung-or	fung-ī	funct-us sum	——	*discharge*

G

Gaud-eō	gaud-ēre	gāvīs-us sum	——	*rejoice*
Gem-ō	gem-ere	gemu-ī	gemit-um	*sigh, groan*
Ger-ō	ger-ere	ges-sī	gest-um	*carry, wear*
Gign-ō	gign-ere	genu-ī	genit-um	*beget*
Grad-ior	grad-ī	gress-us sum	——	*step*

H

Haer-eō	haer-ēre	haes-ī	haes-um	*stick*
Haur-iō	haur-īre	haus-ī	haust-um	*drain*
Horr-eō	horr-ēre	horru-ī	——	*shudder*

I

Iac-eō	iac-ēre	iacu-ī	iacit-um	*to lie down*
Iac-iō [1]	iac-ere	iēc-ī	iact-um	*throw*
Ic-ō	īc-ere	īc-ī	ict-um	*strike*
Imbu-ō	imbu-ere	imbu-ī	imbūt-um	*wet slightly*
Inclūd-ō	inclūd-ere	inclūs-ī	inclūs-um	*shut in*
Incumb-ō	incumb-ere	incubu-ī	incubit-um	*lie upon*
Indic-ō	indic-āre	indicāv-ī	indicāt-um	*indicate*
Indīc-ō	indīc-ere	indix-ī	indict-um	*announce*
Ind-ō	ind-ere	indid-ī	indit-um	*put upon*
Indulg-eō	indulg-ēre	induls-ī	indult-um	*be indul-gent*
Indu-ō	indu-ere	indu-ī	indūt-um	*put on*
Intelleg-ō	intelleg-ere	intellex-ī	intellect-um	*understand*
Irasc-or	īrasc-ī	——	——	*become angry*
Iub-eō	iub-ēre	iuss-ī	iuss-um	*command*
Iung-ō	iung-ere	iunx-ī	iunct-um	*join*
Iuv-ō	iuv-āre	iūv-ī	iūtum	*aid*

L

Lāb-or	lāb-ī	laps-us sum	——	*glide*
Lacess-ō	lacess-ere	lacessiv-ī	lacessit-um	*provoke*
Laed-ō	laed-ere	laes-ī	laes-um	*wound*
Lat-eō	lat-ēre	latu-ī	——	*lie hidden*
Lav-ō	lav-āre	lāv-ī	laut-um, lōt-um, lavāt-um	*wash*
Leg-ō	leg-ere	lēg-ī	lect-um	*read, choose*
Lin-ō	lin-ere	lēv-ī	lit-um	*smear*
Loqu-or	loqu-ī	locūt-us sum	——	*speak*
Lūce-ō	lūc-ēre	lux-ī	——	*shine*
Lūd-ō	lūd-ere	lūs-ī	lūs-um	*play*
Lūge-ō	lūg-ēre	lux-ī	——	*mourn*

M

Mand-ō	mand-ere	mand-ī	mans-um	*chew*
Man-eō	man-ēre	mans-ī	mans-um	*remain*
Merg-ō	merg-ere	mers-ī	mers-um	*dip*
Mēt-ior	mēt-īrī	mens-us sum	——	*measure*
Met-ō	met-ere	——	mess-um	*reap*
Metu-ō	metu-ere	metu-ī	——	*fear*
Mic-ō	mic-āre	micu-ī	——	*glitter*
Minu-ō	minu-ere	minu-ī	minūt-um	*lessen*

---

[1] Compounds either *conjicio, disjicio, injicio,*
or *conicio, disicio, inicio.*

Misc-eō	misc-ēre	miscu-ī	mixt-um	*mix*
Mitt-ō	mitt-ere	mīs-ī	miss-um	*send*
Mord-eō	mord-ēre	momord-ī	mors-um	*bite*
Mor-ior	mor-ī	mortu-us sum	——	*die*
Mov-eō	mov-ēre	mōv-ī	mōt-um	*move*
Mulc-eō	mulc-ēre	muls-ī	muls-um	*soothe*

N

Nancisc-or	nancisc-ī	nact-us *or* nanct-us sum	——	*obtain*
Nasc-or	nasc-ī	nāt-us sum	——	*be born*
Nect-ō	nect-ere	nex-ī, nexu-ī	nex-um	*bind*
Negleg-ō	negleg-ere	neglex-ī	neglect-um	*neglect*
Ning-ō	ning-ere	ninx-ī	——	*snow*
Nit-eō	nit-ēre	nitu-ī	——	*shine*
Nīt-or	nīt-ī	nīsus *or* nix-us sum	——	*lean*
Nosc-ō	nosc-ere	nōv-ī	nōt-um	*get to know*
Nūb-ō	nūb-ere	nups-ī	nupt-um	*marry*

O

Oblīvisc-or	oblīvisc-ī	oblīt-us sum	——	*forget*
Obsid-eō	obsid-ēre	obsēd-ī	obsess-um	*besiege*
Obst-ō	obst-āre	obstit-ī	——	*oppose*
Occid-ō	occid-ere	occid-ī	occās-um	*fall, set (of the sun)*
Occīd-ō	occīd-ere	occīd-ī	occīs-um	*slay*
Occul-ō	occul-ere	occulu-ī	occult-um	*hide*
Ol-eō	ol-ēre	olu-ī	——	*smell*
Oper-iō	oper-īre	operu-ī	opert-um	*cover*
Opprim-ō	opprim-ere	oppress-ī	oppress-um	*surprise, overwhelm*
Ord-ior	ord-īrī	ors-us sum	——	*commence*
Ori-or	or-īrī	ort-us sum	——	*rise*

P

Pacisc-or	pacisc-ī	pact-us sum	——	*bargain for*
Pall-eō	pall-ēre	pallu-ī	——	*be pale*
Pand-ō	pand-ere	pand-ī	pass-um	*spread out*
Pang-ō	pang-ere	panx-ī	panct-um	*fix*
Pang-ō	pang-ere	pepig-ī	pact-um	*fix, settle*
Parc-ō	parc-ere	peperc-ī	——	*spare (dat.)*
Par-iō	par-ere	peper-ī	part-um	*bring forth*
Pasc-ō	pasc-ere	pāv-ī	past-um	*feed (trans.)*
Pasc-or	pasc-ī	past-us sum	——	*feed (intrans.)*
Pat-eō	pat-ēre	patu-ī	——	*lie open*

Pat-ior	pat-ī	pass-us sum	——	*suffer*
Pav-eō	pav-ēre	pāv-ī	——	*fear*
Pect-ō	pect-ere	pex-ī	pex-um	*comb*
Pell-ō	pell-ere	pepul-ī	puls-um	*push*
Pend-eō	pend-ēre	pepend-ī	pens-um	*hang (intrans.)*
Pend-ō	pend-ere	pepend-ī	pens-um	*weigh, hang (trans.)*
Percell-ō	percell-ere	percul-ī	perculs-um	*cast down*
Perd-ō	perd-ere	perdid-ī	perdit-um	*destroy, lose*
Perg-ō	perg-ere	perrex-ī	perrect-um	*go on, proceed*
Pet-ō	pet-ere	petīv-ī	petīt-um	*ask, seek*
Ping-ō	ping-ere	pinx-ī	pict-um	*paint*
Plaud-ō	plaud-ere	plaus-ī	plaus-um	*clap, applaud*
Plect-ō	plect-ere	plex-ī, plexu-ī	plex-um	*plait*
Plu-it	plu-ere	plu-it	——	*it rains*
Pōn-ō	pōn-ere	posu-ī	posit-um	*place, put*
Posc-ō	posc-ere	poposc-ī	——	*demand*
Possid-eō	possid-ēre	possēd-ī	possess-um	*possess*
Pōt-ō	pōt-āre	pōtāv-ī	pōt-um (potātum)	*drink*
Prand-eō	prand-ēre	prand-ī	prans-um	*breakfast*
Prehend-ō	prehend-ere	prehend-ī	prehens-um	*seize*
Prem-ō	prem-ere	press-ī	press-um	*press*
Prōd-ō	prōd-ere	prōdid-ī	prōdit-um	*betray*
Proficisc-or	proficisc-ī	profect-us sum	——	*set out*
Prōflīg-ō	prōflīg-āre	prōflīgāv-ī	prōflīgāt-um	*dash down*
Prōm-ō	prōm-ere	promps-ī	prompt-um	*bring forth*

Q

Quaer-ō	quaer-ere	quaesīv-ī	quaesīt-um	*ask (a question), seek*
Quat-iō	quat-ere	(quass-ī)	quass-um	*shake*
Quer-or	quer-ī	quest-us sum	——	*complain*
Quiesc-ō	quiesc-ere	quiēv-ī	quiēt-um	*rest*

R

Rād-ō	rād-ere	rās-ī	rās-um	*scrape*
Rap-iō	rap-ere	rapu-ī	rapt-um	*snatch*
Recip-iō	recip-ere	recēp-ī	recept-um	*recover, receive*
Redd-ō	redd-ere	reddid-ī	reddit-um	*give back*
Refer-ō	refer-re	rettul-ī	relāt-um	*bring back*
Relinqu-ō	relinqu-ere	relīqu-ī	relict-um	*leave*
Reminisc-or	reminisc-ī	——	——	*remember*
Re-eor	r-ērī	rat-us sum	——	*think*

Repell-ō	reppell-ere	reppul-ī	repuls-um	*thrust back*
Reper-iō	reper-īre	repper-ī	repert-um	*find*
Rēp-ō	rēp-ere	reps-ī	rept-um	*crawl*
Requīr-ō	requīr-ere	requīsīv-ī	requīsīt-um	*be in want of*
Respond-eō	respond-ēre	respond-ī	respons-um	*answer*
Retin-eō	retin-ēre	retinu-ī	retent-um	*hold back*
Rīd-eō	rīd-ēre	rīs-ī	rīs-um	*laugh*
Rig-eō	rig-ēre	rigu-ī	——	*be stiff*
Rōd-ō	rōd-ere	rōs-ī	rōs-um	*gnaw*
Rub-eō	rub-ēre	rubu-ī	——	*blush*
Rump-ō	rump-ere	rūp-ī	rupt-um	*burst*
Ru-ō	ru-ere	ru-ī	rut-um	*fall*

S

Saep-iō	saep-īre	saeps-ī	saept-um	*fence round*
Sal-iō	sal-īre	salu-ī	salt-um	*leap*
Sanc-iō	sanc-īre	sanx-ī	sanct-um	*ratify*
Sap-iō	sap-ere	sapīv-ī	——	*be wise*
Sarc-iō	sarc-īre	sars-ī	sart-um	*patch*
Scand-ō	scand-ere	scand-ī	scans-um	*climb*
Scind-ō	scind-ere	scid-ī	sciss-um	*tear*
Scrīb-ō	scrīb-ere	scrips-ī	script-um	*write*
Sculp-ō	sculp-ere	sculps-ī	sculpt-um	*engrave*
Sec-ō	sec-āre	secu-ī	sect-um	*cut*
Sed-eō	sed-ēre	sēd-ī	sess-um	*sit*
Sent-iō	sent-īre	sens-ī	sens-um	*feel*
Sepel-iō	sepel-īre	sepelīv-ī	sepult-um	*bury*
Sequ-or	sequ-ī	secūt-us sum	——	*follow*
Ser-ō	ser-ere	sēv-ī	sat-um	*sow*
Ser-ō	ser-ere	seru-ī	sert-um	*knit, plait, join*
Serp-ō	serp-ere	serps-ī	serpt-um	*crawl*
Sil-eō	sil-ēre	silu-ī	——	*be silent*
Sin-ō	sin-ere	sīv-ī	sit-um	*permit*
Sol-eō	sol-ēre	solit-us sum	——	*be wont*
Solv-ō	solv-ere	solv-ī	solūt-um	*loosen*
Son-ō	son-āre	sonu-ī	sonit-um	*sound*
Sparg-ō	sparg-ere	spars-ī	spars-um	*scatter*
Spern-ō	spern-ere	sprēv-ī	sprēt-um	*spurn*
Spond-eō	spond-ēre	spopond-ī	spons-um	*pledge, promise*
Statu-ō	statu-ere	statu-ī	statūt-um	*set up, resolve*
Stern-ō	stern-ere	strāv-ī	strāt-um	*strew*
St-ō	st-āre	stet-ī	stat-um	*stand*
Strep-ō	strep-ere	strepu-ī	strepit-um	*make a noise*

Strīd-eō	strīd-ēre	strid-ī	——	*hiss, creak*
String-ō	string-ere	strinx-ī	strict-um	*strip*
Stru-ō	stru-ere	strux-ī	struct-um	*build*
Stud-eō	stud-ēre	studu-ī	——	*be zealous*
Stup-eō	stup-ēre	stupud-ī	——	*be stunned, dazed*
Suād-eō	suād-ēre	suās-ī	suās-um	*advise*
Subd-ō	subd-ere	subdid-ī	subdit-um	*put beneath*
Suesc-ō	suesc-ere	suēv-ī	suēt-um	*be accustomed*
Sūm-ō	sūm-ere	sumps-ī	sumpt-um	*take up*
Surg-ō	surg-ere	surrex-ī	surrect-um	*rise up*

T

Tang-ō	tang-ere	tetig-ī	tact-um	*touch*
Teg-ō	teg-ere	tex-ī	tect-um	*cover*
Tend-ō	tend-ere	tetend-ī	tent-um, tens-um	*stretch*
Ten-eō	ten-ēre	tenui	tent-um	*hold*
Terg-eō	terg-ēre	ters-ī	ters-um	*wipe*
Ter-ō	ter-ere	trīv-ī	trit-um	*rub*
Tex-ō	tex-ere	texu-ī	text-um	*weave*
Tim-eō	tim-ēre	timu-ī	——	*fear*
Ting-ō	ting-ere	tinx-ī	tinct-um	*dip, dye*
Toll-ō	toll-ere	sustul-ī	sublāt-um	*lift, take away*
Tond-eō	tond-ēre	totond-ī	tons-um	*shear*
Ton-ō	ton-āre	tonu-ī	——	*thunder*
Torqu-eō	torqu-ēre	tors-ī	tort-um	*twist*
Torr-eō	torr-ēre	torru-ī	tost-um	*roast*
Trād-ō	trad-ere	trādid-ī	trādit-um	*hand down*
Trah-ō	trah-ere	trax-ī	tract-um	*drag*
Trem-ō	trem-ere	tremu-ī	——	*tremble*
Tribu-ō	tribu-ere	tribu-ī	tribūt-um	*assign*
Trūd-o	trūd-ere	trūs-ī	trūs-um	*thrust*
Tund-ō	tund-ere	tutud-ī	tuns-um, tūs-um	*thump*
Turg-eō	turg-ēre	turs-ī	——	*swell*

U

Ulcisc-or	ulcisc-ī	ult-us sum	——	*avenge*
Ung-ō	ung-ere	unx-ī	unct-um	*anoint*
Urg-eō	urg-ēre	urs-ī	——	*urge*
Ur-ō	ūr-ere	uss-ī	ust-um	*burn (trans.)*
Ut-or	ūt-ī	ūs-us sum	——	*use*

V

Veh-ō	veh-ere	vex-ī	vect-um	*carry*
Vell-ō	vell-ere	vell-ī	vuls-um	*pluck*
Vend-ō	vend-ere	vendid-ī	vendit-um	*sell*
Ven-iō	ven-īre	vēn-ī	vent-um	*come*
Verr-ō	verr-ere	verr-ī	vers-um	*sweep*
Vert-ō	vert-ere	vert-ī	vers-um	*turn*
Vesc-or	vesc-ī	———		*feed*
Vet-ō	vet-āre	vetu-ī	vetit-um	*forbid*
Vid-eō	vid-ēre	vīd-ī	vīs-um	*see*
Vig-eō	vig-ēre	vigu-ī	———	*thrive*
Vinc-iō	vinc-īre	vinx-ī	vinct-um	*bind*
Vinc-ō	vinc-ere	vīc-ī	vict-um	*conquer*
Vīs-ō	vīs-ere	vīs-ī	(vīs-um)	*visit*
Vīv-ō	vīv-ere	vix-ī	vict-um	*live*
Volv-ō	volv-ere	volv-ī	volūt-um	*roll*
Vom-ō	vom-ere	vomu-ī	vomit-um	*vomit*
Vov-eō	vov-ēre	vōv-ī	vōt-um	*vow*

VOCABULARY

You will probably find the verbs more quickly in the Tables, but they are not all there. The Compound verbs are not given at all in the Tables. Further, the Vocabulary as a rule gives the meaning most useful in this book.

A

A, ab (prep., with Abl. case)...by, from
Abaliēn-ō, -āvī, -ātum, -āre...to estrange, to alienate
Abiciō, -iēci, -iectum, -icere...to cast away (or *ab-jicio, -jeci,* etc.)
Absens, -sentis...absent
Absum, āfuī, abesse...to be absent, to be away from
Ac, atque (conj., *āc* used before consonants only)...and
Accēdō, -cessī, -cessum, -cēdere...to approach (to go to)
Accidō, -cidī, -cidere...to happen
Accipiō, -cēpī, -ceptum, -cipere...to receive, accept
Acer, ācris, ācre (adj.)...sharp, keen. *Acrius* (adv.)...more keenly.
    Acriter (adv.)...keenly, fiercely
Acerbus, -a, -um (adj.)...bitter
Aciēs, -ēī, f....line of battle, battle
Acquiescō, -quiēvī, -quiētum, -quiescere...to rest, to die
Acutus, -a, -um (adj.)...sharp
Ad (prep., with Accus.)...to, towards
Addūcō, -duxī, -ductum, -dūcere...to lead to, bring to
Adeō, -iī, -itum, -īre...to go to, to approach
Adeo (adv.)...so
Adficiō. See *Afficiō*
Adhuc (adv.)...up till now, hitherto
Adjungō, -junxī, -junctum, -jungere...to join to, to unite
Admodum (adv.)...quite, very
Adorior, -ortus sum, -orīri (deponent verb)...to attack
Adoro, -avi, -atum, -are...to worship
Adstō, -stitī, ——, -stāre...to stand by. *Adstantēs*...bystanders

---

NOTE.—Quantity is marked only where serious mistakes are likely to be made.

Adsum, -fui, -esse...to be present
Advenio, -vēni, -ventum, -venire...to arrive, to come to
Adventus, -ūs, m....arrival
Adversārius, -a, -um (adj.)...opposed, hostile; (noun) enemy, opponent
Adversus (prep., with Accus.)...against
Adversus, -a, -um (adj.)...unfavourable
Aedificium, -iī, n....building
Aedificō, -āvī, -ātum, -āre...to build
Aegātēs, -um, f....the Aegates Islands
Aemilius, -iī, m....Aemilius (name of a famous Roman family)
Aeque (adv.)...equally
Aequor, -oris, n....sea
Aerārium, -iī, n....treasury
Aestimō, -āvī, -ātum, -āre...to value
Aetās, aetātis, f....age, time of life, time
Afferō, attulī, allātum, afferre...to bring to
Afficiō, -fēcī, -fectum, -ficere...to affect. *Morbō afficere,* to afflict with disease
Affirmō, -āvī, -ātum, -āre...to assert
Africa, -ae, f....Africa
Ager, agrī, m....field; territory
Agger, -eris, m....rampart
Agitō, -āvī, -ātum, -āre...to keep moving. *Mente agitare,* to ponder
Agō, ēgī, actum, agere...to do, to drive
Albus, -a, -um (adj.)...white
Aliās (adv.)...at another time. *Saepe alias*...on many other occasions
Aliēnus, -a, -um (adj.)...belonging to another
Aliquī, aliqua, aliquod (adj.)...some. Declined like *quī, quae, quod;* neut. plur. *aliqua*
Aliquis, m. and f., *aliquid,* n....someone, something
Aliquot (adj., indeclinable)...several
Aliter (adv.)...otherwise
Alius, -a, -ud...other. *Aliī . . . aliī*...some . . . others
Alpēs, -ium, f....the Alps
Alpicus, -a, -um (adj.)...Alpine. *Alpicī, -ōrum,* m....the inhabitants of the Alps
Alter, -a, -um...one of two; second. *Alter . . . alter,* the one . . . the other
Altus, -a, -um...lofty, deep
Ambulo, -avi, -atum, -are...to walk
Amīcē (adv.)...in friendly manner
Amīcitia, -ae, f....friendship
Amīcus, -i, m....friend
Amittō, -mīsī, -missum, -mittere...to lose
Amor, -ōris, m....love
Amphora, -ae, f....jar
Amplius (adv.)...more

An. See Chapter on Questions
Angulus, -i, m....corner
Angustiae, -arum, f....straits, narrowness
Anima, -ae, f....the soul, life
Animus, -i, m....the mind (as the seat of the emotions; *mens, mentis,* f....more the intellect)
Annus, -i, m....year
Ante (prep., with Accus.)...before
Antea (adv.)...before that, before
Antecedo, -cessi, -cessum, -cedere...to go before
Antiochus, -i, m....Antiochus
Anus, -us, f....old woman
Apello, -avi, -atum, -are...to call
Appareo, -parui, -paritum, -parēre...to come in sight, to be plain
Apparo, -avi, -atum, -are...to prepare
Appono, -posui, -positum, -ponere...to place near, add to.
Appropero, -avi, -atum, -are...to hasten
Apud (prep., with Accus.)...near, at (of places); in the presence of (of persons)
Apulia, -ae, f....Apulia, a district of Italy
Aqua, -ae, f....water
Ara, -ae, f....altar
Arbitrium, -ii, n....judgment, bidding, decision
Arbitror, -atus sum, -ari...to think, to believe
Arduus, -a, -um (adj.)...high
Argentum, -i, n....silver
Arma, -orum, n. pl....arms
Armo, -avi, -atum, -are...to arm, to equip. *Armati,* armed men
Ars, artis, f....art
Ascendo, -scendi, -scensum, -scendere...to climb. *Ascendere navem,* to take ship, to embark
Asper, -era, -erum (adj.)...harsh
Aspergo, -inis, f....spray
Aspicio, -spexi, -spectum, -spicere...to look at, behold
Assiduus, -a, -um (adj.)...continuous, perpetual
Astrum, -i, n....star
At (conj.)...but, but yet
Athenae, -arum, f. pl....Athens, the capital of Greece
Athenienses, -ium, pl....the Athenians
Atheniensis, -is, -e (adj.)...Athenian
Atque (conj.)...and
Auctumnus, -i, m....autumn
Audeo, ausus sum, audere...to dare, to venture
Audio, -ivi, -itum, -ire...to hear
Aula, -ae, f....palace
Aura, -ae, f....breeze
Aurelius, ii, m....Aurelius (name of a Roman family)
Aureus, -a, -um (adj.)...golden
Auris, -is, f....ear

Aurum, -i, n....gold
Aut (conj.), or. *Aut . . . aut,* either . . . **or**
Autem (conj.)...but, however
Auxilium, -ii, n....aid
Avaritia, -ae, f....avarice, greed
Ave, avete (imperative)...hail !
Avia, -ae, f....grandmother
Avunculus, -i, m....maternal uncle
Avus, -i, m....grandfather

B

Barba, -ae, f....beard
Barbarus, -a, -um (adj.)...barbarian; (as noun) a Barbarian
Balneum, -i, n....bath
Barca, -ae, m....Barca, the surname of Hamilcar
Basium, -i, n....kiss
Bellicosus, -a, -um (adj.)...warlike; *bellicosissimus* (superl.), very
    warlike
Bello, -avi, -atum, -are...to wage war
Bellum, -i, n....war
Bene (adv.)...well
Beneficium, -i, n....kindness
Biduum, -i, n....a space of two days; *biduo* (abl.), within two
    days
Bini, -ae, -a (distrib. adj.)...two each
Bis (adv.)...twice
Bonus, -a, -um (adj.)...good. *Bona, -orum,* n. pl....goods
Brevis, -is, -e (adj.)...short. *Brevi* (adv.)...in a short time
Britanni, -orum, m. pl....Britons

C

Caduceus, -i, m....herald's wand
Caecus, -a, -um (adj.)...blind
Caelum, -i, n....sky
Caeruleus, -a, -um (adj.)...dark blue, grey
Caesar, -is, m....Caesar, a famous Roman
Caius, -i, m....Caius, a Roman name
Calamitas, -tatis, f....disaster
Callidus, -a, -um (adj.)...skilful, cunning
Campus, -i, m....plain
Candidus, -a, -um (adj.)...white
Canis, -is, m....dog. Gen. pl. *canum*
Canities, -ei, f....old age
Cannensis, is, -e (adj.)...of Cannae
Canus, -a, -um (adj.)...white
Canto, -avis, -atum, -are...to sing
Caper, -ri, m....goat
Capio, cēpi, captum, capĕre...to take

Capitolium, -ii, n....the Capitol (a famous building in Rome)
Captīvus, -i, m....a captive
Capua, -ae, f....Capua, a town in Italy
Caro, carnis, f....flesh
Carthaginiensis, -is, -e (adj.)...Carthaginian
Carthāgo, -inis, f....Carthage
Carus, -a, -um (adj.)...dear
Castellum, -i, n....fort
Castrum, -i, n....fort. *Castra, -orum,* n. pl....a camp
*Casu...*by chance
Casus, -us, m....chance, accident, calamity
Cato, -onis, m....Cato, a Roman name
Catulus, -i, m....Catulus, a Roman name
Causa, -ae, f....cause, reason
*Causa...*for the sake of (prep. with Gen.)
Cedo, cessi, cessum, cedere...(1) to yield (with Dative); (2) to go
    from (with Abl.)
Celeriter (adv.)...quickly
*Celo, -avi, -atum, -are...*to conceal
Cena, -ae, f....dinner
*Ceno, -avi, -atum, -are...*to dine
Centenius, -ii, m....Centenius, a Roman name
Centum (adj., indeclinable)...one hundred
Ceteri, -ae, -a (adj.)...the rest, the others. (The singular is rare)
*Circumdo, -dědi, -dătum, -dăre...*to surround
*Circumeo, -ivi, -itum, -ire...*to go round (*circum* and *eo*)
*Circumsilio, -ire...*to hop around
*Circumspicio, -spexi, -spectum, -spicere...*to look around
*Circumvenio, -věni, -ventum, -venire...*to surround
Cito (adv.)...quickly
Civis, -is, m....citizen
Civitas, -tatis, f....state
Clam (adv.)...secretly
Clamor, -oris, m....shout
Clandestinus, -a, -um (adj.)...secret
Classiarius, -ii, m....a marine
Classis, -is, f....fleet
Clastidium, -ii, n....Clastidium, a town near the Po
*Claudo, clausi, clausum, claudĕre...*to shut
Cnaeus, -i, m....Cnaeus, a Roman name
Coelum, -i, n....the sky
*Coepi, -isse...*to begin. (Perfect form with present meaning, found
    only in perfect and tenses derived from it)
*Cogito, -avi, -atum, -are...*to think
Cognomen, -inis, n....surname
*Cognosco, -novi, -nitum, -noscere...*to discover, to learn, to know
*Cogo, coēgi, coactum, cogere...*to compel
Cohortatio, -ōnis, f....exhortation
Collēga, -ae, m....colleague

Colligo, -lēgi, -lectum, -ligĕre...to collect, to gather
Colloco, -avi, -atum, -are...to place, to station
Colloquium, -ii, n....conversation, parley
Color, -oris, m....colour
Coma, -ae, f....hair
Comes, -itis, m. or f....companion
Commemoro, -avi, -atum, -are...to recount, to tell
Committo, -mīsi, -missum, -mittere proelium...to join battle
Comparo, -avi, -atum, -are...to prepare, to get ready
Compello, -puli, -pulsum, -pellere...to drive, to force, to compel
Comperio, -peri, -pertum, -perire...to ascertain, to find out
Compleo, -evi, -etum, -ēre...to fill
Complures, -ia (and *complura*), gen. *-ium*...several
Compono, -posui, -positum, -ponere...to settle, to conclude (*bellum*, a war), arrange
Comprehendo, -di, -sum, -dere...to seize
Comprobo, -avi, -atum, -are...to approve of, to sanction
Concĭdo, -cīdi, -cīsum, -cīdĕre...to destroy
Concilio, -avi, -atum, -are...to win over. *Conciliare pacem*, to make peace
Concito, -avi, -atum, -are...to stir up, to rouse
Concordo, -avi, -atum, -are...to agree
Concurro, -curri, -cursum, -currĕre...to run together, to meet
Concursus, -us, m....meeting, attack
Condicio, -ōnis, f....condition; (pl.) terms
Conficio, -fēci, -fectum, -ficĕre...to finish
Confirmo, -avi, -atum, -are...to ratify, to make strong
Confligo, -flixi, -flictum, -fligĕre...to engage in battle, to contend
Congredior, -gressus, -gredi...to come together, to engage in battle
Conicio, -ieci, -iectum, -icĕre...to throw, to hurl
Conor, -atus, -ari...to attempt
Consentio, consensi, -sensum, consentire...to agree
Consequor, -secutus, -sequi...to obtain, to get
Consero, -serui, -sertum, -serere...to knit together. *Manum conserere*, to join battle
Conservo, -avi, -atum, -are...to preserve
Considero, -avi, -atum, -are...to consider, to deliberate
Consilium, -ii, n....plan, advice, counsel
Conspicio, -spexi, -spectum, -spicĕre...to behold
Constituo, -ui, -utum, -uĕre...to construct, to establish, to resolve (with Infinitive)
Consuesco, -suēvi, -suetum, -suescere...to become accustomed; (perf.) to be wont
Consuetudo, -inis, f....custom
Consul, -is, m....consul (chief magistrate of Rome)
Consulāris, -is, m....ex-consul
consultum, Senatus-, a decree of the Senate
Contentus, -a, -um (adj.)...contented
Contineo, tinui, -tentum, -tinere...to keep together

Contra (adv.)...on the contrary; (prep., with Accus.) against

Contraho, -traxi, -tractum, -trahere...to draw together, to gather

contrario, E (adverbial phrase)...on the contrary

Convenio, -veni, -ventum, -venire...to come together. *Condiciones non convenerunt*, terms were not agreed on

Conviva, -ae, m. or f....guest

Convoco, -avi, -atum, -are...to summon, to call together

Copia, -ae, f....abundance. *Copiae, -arum,* pl....supplies, forces

Cor, cordis, n....heart

Cornelius, -ii, m....Cornelius, a Roman name

Cornu, -us, n....horn; (of an army) wing

Corōna, -ae, f....garland, crown

Corpus, -ōris, n....the body

Corrumpo, -rūpi, -ruptum, -rumpere...to destroy, to bribe

Corruptio, -onis, f....corruption

Cras (adv.)...to-morrow

Crastinus, -a, -um (adj.)...belonging to to-morrow

Credo, credidi, creditum, credĕre...to believe (with Dative of person), trust

Creo, -avi, -atum, -are...to appoint, create

Creta, -ae, f....Crete, an island in the Mediterranean

Cretensis, -is, -e (adj.)...belonging to Crete; (m. pl.) Cretans

Crux, crucis, f....cross

Cum (prep., with Abl.)...along with; (conj.) when; since

Cumae, -arum, f. pl....Cumae, town near Naples

Cunctus, -a, -um (adj.)...all

Cupiditas, -tatis, f....greed, desire

Cupidus, -a, -um (adj.)...eager

Cupio, -ivi, -itum, -ĕre...to desire

Cupressus, -i, f....cypress

Cur (adv.)...why; why?

Cura, -ae, f....care, anxiety

Curo, -avi, -atum, -are...to take care of

Custodio, -ire...to guard, watch

Cyrenaei, -orum, m. pl. Cyrenaeans, inhabitants of Cyrene, town in North of Africa

D

De (prep., with Abl.)...from, concerning

Debeo, -ui, -itum, -ēre...to owe; (with Infin.) ought: *Debet facere*, he ought to do

Debilito, -avi, -atum, -are...to weaken

Decedo, -cessi, -cessum, -cedere...to go from, to depart, to leave

Decem (num. adj.)...ten

Decerno, -crēvi, crētum, -cernere...to contend in battle

Declaro, -avi, -atum, -are...to make plain

Decorus, -a, -um (adj.)...fitting

Dedecus, -ōris, n....disgrace, dishonour

Dedo, dedidi, deditum, dedere...to surrender
Deduco, -duxi, -ductum, -ducere...to lead, to conduct
Defendo, -fendi, -fensum, -fendere...to defend
Defero, -tuli, -latum, -ferre...to bring to, to report
Deinde (adv.)...thereafter, then
Delecto, -avi, -atum, -are...to please
Delectus, -us, m....levy (of troops)
Deleo, -evi, -etum, -ēre...to destroy, to blot out
Deliciae, -arum, f. pl....delight, darling
Deligo, -legi, -lectum, -ligĕre...to choose out
Demonstro, -avi, -atum, -are...to show
Dens, -tis, m....tooth
Depono, -posui, -positum, -ponere...to lay down, to surrender
Deproelians, -tis (adj.)...warring violently
Deproma, -prompsi, -promptum, -promere...to produce, bring forth
Deripio, -ripui, -reptum, -ripere...to tear away
Descensus, -ūs, m....descent
Descisco, -scīvi, -scītum, -sciscere...to revolt
Desero, -serui, -sertum, -serere...to desert
Desilio, -ui, -sultum, desilire...to leap down
Desisto, -stiti, -stitum, -sistere...to cease, to desist from
Desperatio, -onis, f....despair
Despero, -avi, -atum, -are...to despair
Detrimentum, -i, n....loss
Deus -i, m....a god or God.   Voc. sing. *deus*, Nom. pl. *dei, dii, di*,
     Gen. pl. *deum, deorum*, Dat. and Abl. pl. *deis, diis, dis*, Acc. pl.
     deos
Devinco, -vici, -victum, vincere...to utterly conquer
Dexter, -a, -um (adj.)...right (that is on the right)
Diāna, -ae, f....Diana, Roman goddess of hunting and of the Moon,
     etc.
Dico, dixi, dictum, dicere...to say
Dictator, -oris, m....dictator, a single magistrate appointed at Rome
     in times of danger with almost absolute power
Dies, -ei, m. or f. in sing., m. in pl....a day
Difficilis, -e (adj.)...difficult
Difficultas, -tatis, f....difficulty
Digitus, -i, m....finger
Dignitas, -atis, f....dignity
Dilectus, -us, m....levy (of troops).   See *Delectus*
Diligentia, -ae, f....diligence
Dimicō, -avi, -atum, -are...to fight
Dimidium, -ii, n....half
Dimitto, -mīsi, -missum, -mittere...to let go, to send away, to give up,
     abandon
Discedo, -cessi, -cessum, -cedere...to depart
Disertus, -a, -um (adj.)...eloquent
Disicio, -ieci, -iectum, -icere...to throw down
Dispalor, -atus, -ari (vb. deponent)...to wander about

Disputo, -avi, -atum, -are...to argue
Dissideo, -sēdi, -sessum, -sidēre...to differ, to disagree
Dissimilis, -e (adj.)...unlike, dissimilar
Dissolvo, -solvi, -solutum, -solvere...to melt
Diu (adv.)...long; comparative *diutius*, longer; superlative *diutissime*, longest
Diuturnitas, -tatis, f....length (of time)
Divinus, -a, -um (adj.)...divine, inspired
Divus, -i, m....god
Do, dedi, datum, dare...to give
Doceo, -ui, doctum, docēre...to teach
Dolus, -i, m....craft, trick
Domesticus, -a, -um (adj.)...internal, civil (lit., belonging to the house)
Domina, -ae, f....mistress
Dominus, -i, m....master, lord
Domus, -us, f....house. *Domum*, homeward. *Domi*, at home, *Domo*, from home
Dōnec (conj.)...until
Dōno, -avi, -atum, -are...to present, to gift, to give
Dōnum, -i, n....gift
Dormio, -ivi, -itum, -ire...to sleep
dubie, Haud (adv.)...doubtless, without doubt
Dubito, -avi, -atum, -are...to doubt, to hesitate
Dubium, -ii, n....doubt (really neuter of following word)
Dubius, -a, -um (adj.)...doubtful
Duco, duxi, ductum, ducere...to lead
Dum (conj.)...while; until
Duplex, -icis (adj.)...double, twofold
Dūrus, -a, -um (adj.)...hard
Dux, ducis, m. or f....leader, chief, general

E

E, ex (prep., with Abl.)...out of
Ea (adv.)...by that way (Abl. of *is, ea, id*)
Ecce !...behold !
Efficio, effēci, effectum, efficēre...to bring to pass, to cause
Effugio, effugi, effugitum, effugere...to flee, to escape
Egenus, -a, -um (adj.)...needy
Ego (pronoun)...I
Egredior, egressus, egredi...to go out
Elephantus, -i, m....elephant
Emptor, -oris, m....buyer
Emptus, -a, -um...bought (past participle of *emo*)
Enim (conj.)...for (never first in the sentence)
Enumero, -avi, -atum, -are...to number
Eo (adv.)...thither
Eo, ivi, itum, ire...to go

Eodem (adv.)...to the same place. *Eodem unde*, to the same place whence

Epistola, -ae, f....letter

Eques, -itis, m....horseman; (pl.) cavalry

Equitatus, -us, m....cavalry

Equus, -i, m....horse

Erant (3rd plur., Imperf. Indic. of *sum, fui, esse*, to be)...they were

Erat (3rd sing., Imperf. Indic. of *sum, fui, esse*, to be)...he was

Erga (prep., with Accus.)...towards

Erro, -avi, -atum, -are...to wander

Error, -ōris, m....mistake, error

Eryx, -ycis, m....Eryx, mountain in Sicily

Esse (Pres. Infin. of *sum, fui, esse*)...to be

Et (conj.)...and. *Et . . . et*, both . . . and

Etiam (adv.)...also, even. *Etiamtum* (adv.)...even then

Etruria, -ae, f....Etruria, district of Italy north of Rome

Etsi (conj.)...although

Eumenes, -is, m ...Eumenes

Exardesco, -arsi, -arsum, -ardescĕre...to blaze out

Excedo, -cessi, cessum, -cedere...to leave, to depart

Excelsus, -a, -um (adj.)...lofty

Excieo or *-cio, -civi* or *-cii, -citum, -cīre*...to stir up, to rouse; to summon

Exerceo, -ui, -itum, -ere...to exercise, to stir up

Exercitus, -us, m....army

Exhaurio, -hausi, -haustum, -haurire...to empty, to exhaust

Exigo, -egi, -actum, exigere...to demand

Existimo, -avi, -atum, -are...to think, to consider

Exitus, -us, m....departure; death

Expedio, -ivi, -itum, -ire...to release, to set free

Expello, -puli, -pulsum, -pellere...to drive out

Experior, -pertus, -periri (vb. deponent)...to try, to attempt, to make trial of

Exploro, -avi, -atum, -are...to inquire, to find out

Exposco, -poposci, ——, -poscere...to ask earnestly, to implore

Expugno, -avi, -atum, -are...to take by storm, to storm

Extra (prep., with Accus.)...outside

Extrēmo (adv.)...at last

Extrēmus, -a, -um (adj.)...last, farthest

Exul, -is, m. or f....exile

F

Fabius, -ii, m....Fabius, a Roman name

Facies, -ei, f....appearance

Facile (adv.)...easily

Facilis, -is, -e (adj.)...easy

Facio, fēci, factum, facere...to do, to make

Factum, -i, n....deed

Facultas, -tatis, f....power; (pl.) resources
Falernus, -a, -um (adj.)...Falernian
Falsus, -a, -um (adj.)...false
Fama, -ae, f....report, reputation, glory
Fames, -is, f....hunger, famine
Femina, -ae, f....woman
Fera, -ae, f....wild beast
Fere (adj.)...almost, nearly
Fero, tuli, latum, ferre...to carry, to bring
Ferocia, -ae, f....boldness, ferocity
Ferociter (adv.)...boldly
Ferox, -cis (adj.)...bold, fierce
Ferrum, -i, n....iron
Ferus, -a, -um (adj.)...fierce
Fervidus, -a, -um (adj.)...boiling hot
Fessus, -a, -um (adj.)...tired
Festino, -avi, -atum, -are...to hasten
Fictilis, -is, -e (adj.)...made of earthenware
Fidelis, -e (adj.)...faithful
Fidens, -tis (adj.)...confident. (Really Pres. Partic. of *fido, fisus, fidere,* to trust)
Fides, -ei, f....trust, good faith
Fiducia, -ae, f....confidence
Filia, -ae, f....daughter
Filius, -ii, m....son
Finis, -is, m....the end
Fio, factus sum, fieri...to be made, to become
Flagitium, -ii, n....disgraceful act, shame, disgrace
Flagro, -avi, -atum, -are...to blaze, to burn
Flamininus, -i, m....Flamininus, a Roman name
Flaminius, -ii, m....Flaminius, a Roman name
Fleo. -evi, -etum, -ere...to weep
Flos, floris, m....flower
Fluctus, -us, m....wave
Flumen, -inis, n....river
Focus, -i, m....hearth
Foederatus, -a, -um (Partic. of *foedero*)...leagued together, allied
Foedus, -eris, n....a treaty
Foedus, -a, -um (adj.)...filthy
Folium, -ii, n....a leaf
Foris, -is, f. (usually in plural)...door, entrance
Formosus, -a, -um (adj.)...beautiful
Fors, fortis, f....chance.   *Forte* (adv.)...by chance
Fortasse (adv.)...perhaps
Fortis, -is, -e (adj.)...brave
Fortidudo, -inis, f....bravery
Fortuito (adv.)...by chance
Fortūna, -ae, f....fortune
Frater, -ris, m....brother

Fregellae, -arum, f....Fregellae, town in Italy
Frequens, -tis (adj.)...frequent
Frigus, -oris, n ...cold
Frustror, -atus, -ari...to baffle, to hoodwink
Fuga, -ae, f....flight
Fugo, -avi, -atum, -are...to put to flight
Fundamentum, -i, n....foundation
Furius, -ii, m....Furius, a Roman name

G

Gallia, -ae, f....Gaul, roughly what is now France
Gallus, -i, n....a Gaul
Gaudium, -i, n....joy
Gelu, -us, n....frost
Geminus, -i, m....Geminus, a Roman name
Gens, gentis, f....race, family; nation, people
Genus, -eris, n....race, kind
Gero, gessi, gestum, gerĕre...to carry on, to wage (*bellum,* war)
Gloria, -ae, f....gloria
Gortynii, -orum, m. pl....Gortynii, inhabitants of Gortyna in Crete
Gradus, -us, m....step
Graecia, -ae, f....Greece
Graius, -a, -um (adj.)...Graian
Gratia, -ae, f....favour, popularity.   *Gratiae, -arum,* pl....thanks
Gratia...for the sake of
Gravis, -is, -e (adj.)...heavy, severe
Gremium, -i, n....lap
Grex, gregis, m....flock
Guberno, -avi, -atum, -are...to govern
Gustus, -us, m....taste

H

Habeo, -ui, -itum, -ēre...to have, to hold; to consider
Habito, -avi, -atum, -are...to dwell, to inhabit
Hac (adv.)...by this way (Abl. fem. sing. of *hic,* with *via* understood)
Hadrumetum, -i, n....Hadrumetum, town on north coast of Africa
Hamilcar, -aris, m....Hamilcar
Hannibal, -is, m....Hannibal, son of the former
Hasdrubal, -is, m....Hasdrubal, son-in-law of Hamilcar
Haud (adv.)...not.   *Haud dubie,* doubtlessly
Hereditas, -tatis, f....inheritance
Hic (adv.)...here
Hic, haec, hoc (demons. pronoun)...this
Hiems, -ĕmis, f....winter
Hinc (adv.)...hence
Hippo, -onis, m....Hippo, a town in Africa
Hispania, -ae, f....Spain

Hispanus, -a, -um (adj.)...Spanish
Hoc, Acc. neut. sing. of *Hic, haec, hoc,* this
Hodie (adv.)...to-day
Hŏmo, -inis, m....man
Honor, -oris, m....honour
Hora, -ae, f....hour
Horribilis, -e (adj.)...horrible
Hortus, -i, m....garden
Hospes, -itis, m....guest
Hospitium, -ii, n....friendship
Hostia, -ae, f....victim for sacrifice
Hostis, -is, m....enemy
Huc (adv.)...hither
Hujus, Gen. sing. of *Hic, haec, hoc,* this
Humilis, -e (adj.)...humble
Humus, -i, f....ground
Hunc, Acc. masc. sing. of *Hic, haec, hoc,* this

I—J

[The most modern texts do not employ the letter " J " at all.
" J " may be written for " I ", however, before a vowel. In this
vocabulary " I " is always used for " J ".]

Iam (adv.)...now, already
Iānua, -ae, f....door
Ibi (adv.)...there
Idem, eadem, idem (pron.)...the same
Ideo (adv.)...for that reason
Igitur (conj.)...therefore
Ignoro, -avi, -atum, -are...to be ignorant
Ille, -a, -ud (pron.)...that
Illic (adv.)...there
Illuc (adv.)...thither
Illudo, -si, -sum, -děre...to mock
Illustris, -is, -e (adj.)...famous
Imber, -bris, m....rain
Immitto, -misi, -missum, -mittere...to let loose at, to discharge against
Immolo, -avi, -atum, -are...to offer up, to sacrifice
Impedio, -ivi, -itum, -ire...to hinder
Imperātor, -ōris, m....commander-in-chief
Imperium, -ii, n....command, order; absolute authority
Impero, -avi, -atum, -are...to give orders, to order
Impetro, -avi, -atum, -are...to obtain a request
Imprudenter (adv.)...imprudently
In (prep.)...(with Abl.) in; (with Acc.) into, against
Inanis, -e (adj.)...empty
Incendo, -cendi, -censum, -cendere...to set on fire, to kindle
Incertus, -a, -um (adj.)...uncertain

Incipio, -cepi, -ceptum, -ere...begin

Incola, -ae, m. or f....an inhabitant

Inde (adv.)...thence; (of time) then

Indigeo, -ui, ——, -ēre...to have need of, to be in want of (with Gen. or Abl.)

Induco, -duxi, -ductum, -ducere...to lead into

Ineo, -ii, -itum, -ire...to enter, to go into, begin

Infans, -tis, m. or f....infant

Infero, intuli, illatum, inferre...to carry into

Infestus, -a, -um (adj.)...hostile

Infitior, -atus, -ari...to deny

Infra (prep., with Acc.)...beneath

Ingens, -gentis (adj.)...huge

Inicio, -ieci, -iectum, -icěre...to throw into or upon

Inimĭcus, -a, -um (adj.)...unfriendly, hostile

Initium, -ii, n....beginning

Innocens, -tis (adj.)...innocent

Insciens, -tis (adj.)...unknowing, ignorant

Inscribo, -scripsi, -scriptum, -scribere...to write on

Insidior, -atus, -ari...to waylay, to set an ambush (dat.)

Inspicio, -spexi, -spectum, -spicěre...to look into, to examine

Instituo, -ui, -utum, -uěre...(with Inf.) to resolve, to determine, to begin

Insula, -ae, f....island

Integratio, -onis, f....renewing

Intellego, -exi, -ectum, -egěre...to understand. (Sometimes given *intelligo*)

Intentus, -a, -um (adj.)...eager, intent

Inter (prep., with Acc.)...between, among

Interea (adv.)...meanwhile

Intereo, -ii, -itum, -ire...to die, to perish (*inter* and *eo*)

Interficio, -feci, -fectum, -ficere...to slay, to kill

Interim (adv.)...meanwhile

Interior, -us (adj., compar. degree)...inner

Intestinus, -a, -um (adj.)...internal

Intimus, -a, -um (adj.)...inmost

Intra (prep., with Acc.)...inside, within

Inutilis, -is, -e (adj.)...useless

Invenio, -vēni, -ventum, -venire...to come upon, to find

Invictus, -a, -um (adj.)...unconquered

Invidia, -ae, f....envy, jealousy

Invideo, -vidi, -visum, -videre...to envy

Involvo, -volvi, -volutum, -volvere...to wrap up

Ira, -ae, f....anger

Ionius, -a, -um (adj.)...Ionian

Irreparabilis, -e (adj.)...irretrievable

Irrideo, -risi, -risum, -ridere...to laugh at, to mock

Is, ea, id (pron.)...that, he

Ita (adv.)...so

Italia, -ae, f....Italy
Itaque (conj.)...and so, accordingly
Itemque (*item,* adv., also, and *-que,* and)...and also
Iter, itineris, n....way, road, journey
Iterum (adv.)...a second time, again
Iubeo, iussi, iussum, iubere...to order
Iudico, -avi, -atum, -are...to judge
Iungo, iunxi, iunctum, iungere...to join
Iupiter, Iovis (*Iovi, Iovem, Iove*)...Jupiter, chief Roman god
Iuro, -avi, -atum, -are...to swear
Ius, iuris, n....right, law, justice
Iusiurandum, iurisiurandi, n....an oath.   (*Ius* and *iurandum,* each
     declined separately)
Iussum, -i, n....order
Iustitia, -ae, n....justice
Iuvencus, -i, m....young bullock, steer

K

[This letter is occasionally used for C.]

Karthaginiensis, -is, -e (adj.)...Carthaginian; (pl.) the Carthagi-
     nians
Karthago, -inis, f....Carthage

L

Labor, -oris, m....toil, work, labour
Laboro, -are, -avi, -atum...to work, labour
Lacertus, -i, m....arm
Lacesso, -ivi, -itum, -ĕre...to provoke, to challenge
Lacrima, -ae, f....tear
Lacus, -us, m....lake
Laetus, -a, -um (adj.)...happy
Largitio, -onis, f....bribery, largesses (gifts of money)
Large (adv.)...abundantly
Late (adv.)...far and wide
Laudo, -avi, -atum, -are...to praise
Lectica, -ae, f....litter
Legātus, -i, m....ambassador; subordinate officer, lieutenant
Legio, -onis, f....legion
Lenis, -e (adj.)...soft
Leniter (adv.)...quietly
Lente (adv.)...slowly
Leviter (adv.)...softly
Lex, legis, f....law
Libellus, -i, m....book
Libenter (adv.)...readily
Libero, -avi, -atum, -are...to liberate
Libertas, -atis, f....liberty

VOCABULARY

Lignum, -i, n....wood
Ligures, -um, m....Ligurians, tribe in North of Italy
Littera, -ae, f....letter
Litus, -oris, n....the shore
Locupleto, -avi, -atum, -are...to enrich
Locus, -i, m....a place, position. *Loca, -orum*, n. pl.
Longus, -a, -um (adj.)...long
Longus, -i, m....Longus, a Roman name
Lucanus, -a, -un...Lucanian, belonging to Lucania, a district of Italy
Lumen, -inis, n....light
Luna, -ae, f....moon
Lutatius, -ii, m....Lutatius, a Roman name
Lux, lucis, f....light

M

Maestitia, -ae, f....sadness
Maestus, -a, -um (adj.)...sorrowful
Magis (adv.)...more
Magister, -ri, m....master
Magistratus, -us, m....an officer of state (magistracy)
Magnopere (adv.)...greatly
Magnus, -a, -um (adj.)...great, large
Mago, -onis, m....Mago, a Carthaginian
Male (adv.)...badly
Malignus, -a, -um (adj.)...malignant, spiteful
Malo, malui, malle...to prefer
Malus, -a, -um (adj.)...bad. *Mala, -orum*, n. pl....ills
Mane (adv.)...in the morning
Maneo, mansi, mansum, manēre...to remain
Manus, -us, f....hand; also a band (of men). *Manus dare*, to yield, to surrender. *Manus conserere*, to join battle
Marcellus, -i, m....Marcellus, a Roman name
Marcus, -i, m....Marcus, a Roman name
Mare, -is, n....the sea
Mater, matris, f....mother
Matrimonium, -ii, n....marriage
Maximus, -a, -um (superl., of *magnus*)...greatest
Meditor, -atus, -ari...to ponder, to consider
Mĕlita, -ae, f....Malta
Mellitus, -a, -um (adj.)...sweet as honey
Memor, -is (adj.)...mindful
Memoria, -ae, f....memory
Memoro, -avi, -atum, -are...to remind
Mens, mentis, f....the mind, the intellect, as opposed to *animus*, the mind as the seat of the feelings. *Mente agitare*, to ponder (to drive about in mind)
Mensis, -is, m....month

Mentio, -onis, f....mention
Mercenarius, -a, -um (adj.)...hired, mercenary
Meridies, -ei, f....mid-day
Merum, -i, n....unmixed wine
Miles, -itis, m....soldier
Milia, -ium (Dat. and Abl. *milibus*)...thousands. *Mille,* a thousand
Minor, (adj., compar. of *parvus*)...less. *Natu minor,* younger (lit., less by birth)
Minucius, -ii, m....Minucius
Mirabilis, -e (adj.)...wonderful
Mirifice (adv.)...wonderfully
Miror, -atus, -ari...to wonder at, to admire
Miser, -a, -um (adj.)...wretched, miserable
Mitto, misi, missum, mittere...to send
Modo (adv.)...only, now
Modus, -i, m....measure, limit, manner
Mons, montis, m....mountain
Monstro, -avi, -atum, -are...to show
Morbus, -i, m....disease
Moror, -atus, -ari...to delay
Morosus, -a, -um (adj.)...fretful, morose
Mors, mortis, f....death
Mortuus, -a, -um (adj.)...dead
Mos, moris, m....custom; (pl.) manners, character
Moveo, movi, motum, movēre...to move
Mox (adv.)...soon
Mulier, -is, f....a woman
Multitudo, -inis, f....crowd, multitude, great number
Multo (adv.)...by much. *Multo post,* long after (lit., after by much)
Multus, -a, -um (adj.)...much, many
Munio, -ivi, -itum, -ire...to fortify. *Munire viam,* to make a road
Munus, -eris, n....a gift; an office
Murus, -i, m....a wall
Mus, muris, m. or f....mouse
Muto, -avi, -atum, -are...to change.

N

Nam (conj.)...for
Namque (conj.)...for
Nascor, natus, nasci...to be born
Nasus, -i, m....nose
Natio, -onis, f....nation, race
Nato, -avi, -atum, -are...to swim
Natus, -i, m....son
Naufragium, -ii, n....shipwreck
Nauta, -ae, m....sailor
Nauticus, -a, -um (adj.)...naval
Navalis, -e (adj.)...nautical, maritime

Navigatio, -onis, f....a sailing, a voyage

Navigo, -avi, -atum, -are...to sail, to make a voyage

Navis, -is, f....ship

-ně, interrogative particle, attached to first word in questions (see Lesson XXVIII.)

Ně...In order that . . . not; lest.   *Ne . . . quidem*...not even

Nebula, -ae, f....cloud

Nego, -avi, -atum, -are...to deny, to say . . . not

Nemo, nullius (neminen, nemini, nullo)...no one

Nepos, -otis, m....descendant

Neque...and not.   *Neque . . . neque*...neither . . . nor

Nescio, -scivi, -scitum, -scire...not to know, to be ignorant

Neuter, -ra, -rum (adj.)...neither.   (Gen. *neutrius,* etc.)

Niger, -gra, -grum (adj.)...black

Nihil (neut. pron. indecl.)...nothing; (used as adv.) in no wise. *Nihilo secius,* no otherwise

Nil...to be added to.   *Nihil*

Nimis (adv.)...too much

Nimius, -a, -um (adj.)...too much

Nisi (conj.)...unless.   *Nisi cum,* save when

Niveus, -a, -um (adj.)...snowy, white

Nix, nivis, f....snow

Noceo, -ui, -itum, -ere...to injure (governs Dative case)

Noctu (adv.)...by night

Nomen, -inis, n....name

Non (adv.)...not

Non solum . . . sed etiam...not only . . . but also

Nonus, -a, -um (adj.)...ninth

Noto, -avi, -atum, -are...to mark

Novem (numeral adj.)...nine

Novus, -a, -um (adj.)...new

Nox, noctis, f....night

Nullus, -a, -um (adj.)...no, no one.   (Gen. *nullius,* etc.)

Nudus, -a, -um...bare

Num (particle introducing an indirect question)...whether.   (See Lesson XXVIII.)

Numerus, -i, m....number

Numida, -ae, m....a Numidian

Nunc (adv.)...now

Nunc tandem (adv.)...now at length

Nunquam (adv.)...never

Nuntio, -avi, -atum, -are...to announce, to bring a message

Nuntius, -ii, m....a messenger, a message

O

Ob (prep., with Acc.)...on account of, for the sake of

Obduco, -duxi, -ductum, -ducěre...to draw over.   *Obducta nocte,* night having been drawn over, that is, when night came on

Obicio, -ieci, -iectum, -icěre...to throw in the way of (Dat. of person)
Obitus, -us, m....death
Oblecto, -avi, -atum, -are...to amuse
Obscurus, -a, -um (adj.)...dark
Obses, -idis, m....hostage
Obsideo, -sedi, -sessum, -siděre...to besiege, to blockade, to beset
Obtestatio, -onis, f....request, strong entreaty
Obtrectatio, -onis, f....envious detraction, disparagement
Obviam (adv.)...against (lit., in the way (to)).   *Obviam ire,* to go in
     the way to a person, that is, to meet him
Occasio, -onis, f....chance, opportunity
Occido, -cidi, -cisum, -cidĕre...to kill, to slay
Occupo, -avi, -atum, -are...to seize, to get possession of
Oculus, -i, m....the eye
Odium, -ii, n....hatred
Omen, -inis, n....omen, forboding
Omitto, -misi, -missum, -mittere...to let go.   *Ut omittam,* to pass
     over (lit., that I may pass over)
Omnis, -is, -e (adj.)...all, every
Onus, -eris, n....burden
Opera, -ae, f....work, labour, care
Operio, -ui, -tum, -ire...to cover
Opes, -um, f. pl....resources, wealth
Oppidum, -i, n....town
Oppleo, -evi, -etum, -ere...to fill up
Opprimo, -pressi, -pressum, -primĕre...to overwhelm, to suppress
Oppugno, -avi, -atum, -are...to attack
Optimus, -a, -um (adj., superl. of *bonus,* good)...best
Opus, operis, n....work
Orno, -avi, -atum, -are...to adorn, to equip
Oro, -avi, -atum, -are...to pray
Ostendo, -di, -tum, -děre...to show, to make clear
Otium, -ii, n....ease, peace, repose, leisure

P

Padus, -i, m....Po, large river in the North of Italy
Paene (adv.)...almost, nearly
Palam (adv.)...openly.   *Palam facere,* to disclose
Par, păris (adj.)...equal, like
Parco, peperci, parsum, parcěre...to spare (governs Dative)
Pareo, -ui, -itum, -ere...to obey (governs Dative)
Parens, -tis, m. or f....parent
Parturio, -ire...to bring forth
Paro, -avi, -atum, -are...to prepare, to make ready, to obtain
Parvus, -a, -um (adj.)...little
Passer, -eris, m....pet bird
Passus, -us, m....a pace (five Roman feet)
Pastor, -oris, m....shepherd

Patefacio, -feci, -factum, -facěre...to disclose, to open, to make clear
Pater, -ris, m....father
Paternus, -a, -um (adj.)...paternal, belonging to one's father
Patria, -ae, f....fatherland
Patronus, -i, m....patron
Patruus, -i, m....paternal uncle
Pauci, -ae (adj.)...a few, some
Paulatim (adv.)...little by little
Paulum (adv.)...a little.   *Paulo*...by a little.   *Paulo ante,* a little before
Paulus, -ii, m....Paulus, a Roman name
Pax, pācis, f....peace
Pecūnia, -ae, f....money
Pecus, -udis, f....cattle
Pedester, -ris, -re (adj.)...on foot.   *Pedestres copiae,* infantry
Pello, pepuli, pulsum, pellere...to drive, to expel, to banish, to defeat
Pendo, pependi, pensum, penděre...to weigh out, to pay
Penes (prep., with Acc.)...in the power of
Per (prep., with Acc. of place)...through; also by means of
Perago, -ēgi, -actum, -agěre...to carry out, to complete
Perdūco, -duxi, -ductum, -ducěre...to lead through
Pereo, -ii, -itum, -ire...to perish, to die
Perfungor, -functus, -fungi...to discharge
Pergamenus, -a, -um (adj.)...of or belonging to Pergamum, town of Mysia in Asia
Periculum, -i, n....danger
Peritus, -a, -um (adj.)...skilled in (with Gen.)
Permitto, -misi, -missum, -mittere...to permit, to entrust (something to somebody, Acc. and Dat.), give up, leave
Perpetuus, -a, -um (adj.)...perpetual
Persequor, -secūtus, -sequi...to chase, to attack, to follow up
Persuadeo, -suasi, -suasum, -suadere...to persuade
Perterreo, -ui, -itum, -ere...to terrify thoroughly, to frighten
Pertinacia, -ae, f....persistence, obstinacy, stubbornness
Pertinax, -acis, (adj.)...obstinate
Pertineo, -ui, ——, -ere...to tend towards.   *Quae ad irridendum pertinebant,* what tended towards jeering
Pervenio, -veni, -ventum, -venire...to arrive at, to reach
Perverto, -verti, -versum, -vertěre...to corrupt, to ruin
Pes, pedis, m....foot
Peto, -ivi, -itum, -ere...to ask (Acc. and Abl.); to make for, to attack
Philippus, -i, m....Philip
Pictus, -a, -um (adj.)...painted, coloured
Pignus, -oris, n....pledge
Pipilo, -avi, -atum, -are...to chirp
Placidus, -a, -um (adj.)...peaceful
Plenus, -a, -um (adj.)...full
Plumbum, -i, n....lead

Plurimus, -a, -um (adj., superl. of *multus*)...most; (pl.) very many
Plus, pluris (adj., pl. *plures, plura, plurium, pluribus*)...more
Poena, -ae, f....penalty, punishment
Poenicus, -a, -um (adj.)...Punic, Carthaginian
Poenus, -a, -um (adj.)...Carthaginian
Poëta, -ae, m....poet
Polliceor, -itus, -eri...to promise
Pompeius, -i, m....Pompey, a Roman name
Pono, posui, positum, ponere...to place
Pontus, -i, m....the Black Sea
Populus, -i, m....the people
Porto, -avi, -atum, -are...to carry
Possum, potui, posse...to be able
Post (prep., with Acc.)...after
Postea (adv.)...afterwards, after that
Posteaquam (conj.)...after that, after
Posterus, -a, -um (adj.)...following, next.   *Postremo* (adv.)...at last
Postilla (adv.)...afterwards
Postquam (conj.)...after that, after
Postridie (adv.)...on the day after, on the next day
Postulo, -avi, -atum, -are...to demand
Potens, -tis (adj.)...powerful
Potestas, -tatis, f....power
Potissimum (superl. adv.)...especially, chiefly
Potius (adv.)...rather
Praebeo, -ui, -itum, -ere...to furnish, to supply, offer
Praeceptum, -i, n....precept, advice, warning, command
Praecipio, -cepi, -ceptum, -cipěre...to enjoin upon, to command
Praefectus, -i, m....commander, governor
Praemium, -ii, n....reward
Praenomen, -inis, n....the first name of a Roman (like our Christian name)
Praesens, -tis (adj.)...present
Praesidium, -ii, n....defence, help, garrison; (pl.) forces
Praesto, -stiti, -stitum or *-statum, -stare*...to excel
Praesum, -fui, -esse...to be at the head of, to be in command
Praeter (prep., with Acc.)...besides
Praeterea (adv.)...besides
Praetor, -oris, m....Praetor (*see* Note on Passage No. 13)
Prātum, -i, n....meadow
Premo, pressi, pressum, preměre...to press, to press hard
Prima luce (adv.)...at dawn
Primo (adv.)...at first
Primus, -a, -um (adj.)...first
Princeps, -ipis (adj. or noun)...chief; first
Pristinus, -a, -um (adj.)...former, early
Priusquam (conj.)...before that, before
Probo, -avi, -atum, -are...to approve
Probus, -a, -um (adj.)...honest

Prōditor, -oris, m....betrayer

*Prodo, -didi, -ditum, -děre...*to hand down; to betray

*Prōdūco, -duxi, -ductum, -ducěre...*to bring forward, to lead forth

Proelium, -ii, n....battle

Profecto (adv.)...assuredly

Proficiscor, -fectus, -ficisci (depon. verb)...to set out, to depart

*Profiteor, -fessus, -fiteri...*to confess, to profess

*Profligo, -avi, -atum, -are...*to overthrow, to conquer

*Profugio, -fugi, -fugitum, -fugěre...*to flee

*Prohibeo, -ui, -itum, -ere...*to prevent, to hinder

*Promitto, -misi, -missum, promittere...*to promise

*Propago, -avi, -atum, -are...*to extend

Propatulum, -i, n....an open place before the house, outer court

Prope (adv.)...almost, near

Propere (adv.)...hastily

*Propero, -avi, -atum, -are...*to hurry

Propinquus, -a, -um (adj.)...neighbouring, near

Propius (adv., with Dat.)...nearer. *Propius Tiberi,* nearer the Tiber

Propter (prep., with Acc.)...on account of

*Prospicio, -spexi, -spectum, -spicere...*to spy, to look out and see

*Provideo, -vidi, -visum, -videre...*to provide, to take thought before-hand

Providus, -a, -um (adj.)...foreseeing, prudent

Provincia, -ae, f....province

Proximus, -a, -um (adj.)...nearest, next

Prudentia, -ae, f....prudence, forethought, skill

Prusia, -ae, m....Prusia (Nominative sometimes *Prusias*)

Publice (adv.)...in the name of the State

*Publico, -avi, -atum, -are...*to confiscate, to make public property

Publicus, -a, -um (adj.)...belonging to the State, public

Publius, -ii, m....Publius, a Roman name

Puella, -ae, f....girl

Puerulus, -i, m....little boy

Pugio, -onis, m....dagger

Pugna, -ae, f....battle, fight

*Pugno, -avi, -atum, -are...*to fight

Pulcher, -ra, -rum (adj.)...beautiful

*Pulso, -avi, -atum, -are...*to strike

Punicus, -a, -um (adj.)...Carthaginian. (Same as *Poenicus*)

Puppis, -is, f....stern (of a ship)

*Puto, -avi, -atum, -are...*to think, to suppose (but " thinking " = *ratus,* not *putans*)

Q

Qua (adv.)...where, by which way

Quacunque (adv.)...wheresoever

*Quaero, quaesivi, quaesitum, quaerěre...*to ask (a question)

Quam, Acc. fem. sing. of *Qui, quae, quod*, which
Quam (adv. with adj.)...how. *Tam . . . quam*, so . . . as; (with superl.) as . . . as possible. *Quam plurimi*, as many as possible
Quamdiu (adv.)...how long, as long as
Quando (adv.)...when
Quantus, -a, -um (adj.)...how great
Quare (conj.)...wherefore, why, for which reason
-que...and
Qui, quae, quod (rel. pron.)...who, which, etc. *Qua* is used for *quae* = any
Quia (conj.)...because
Quidam, quaedam, quoddam (subs. *quiddam*) (pron.)...a certain person or thing
Quidem (adv.)...indeed, even
Quin (conj.)...but that. (See Lesson XXVII.)
Quinquies (numeral adverb)...five times
Quintius, -ii, m....Quintius, a Roman name
Quintus, -i, m....Quintus, a Roman name
Quis, m., f., *quid*, n. (inter. pron.)...who? which? also, after *si, ne* = anyone, anything. (In other cases this is like *qui*)
Quisquam, quicquam (pron.)...anyone, anything
Quisque, quaeque, quodque (subs. *quidque*) (pron.)...each, every
Quisquis (pron.)...whoever
Quisnam, quidnam...who in the world. (*Quis* and *nam*)
Quod (conj.)...because
Quod (rel. pron., neut.)...which. *Quod nisi*, but unless (as to which if not)
Quoque (adv.)...also
Quot (indeclinable pron.)...how many
Quotannis (adv.)...every year
Quotienscumque (adv.)...as often as ever
Quum (conj.)...when, since. (Also written *cum*)

R

Ratio, -onis, f....reason, plan, method
Recipio, -cepi, -ceptum, -cipěre...to recover, to receive back. *See recipere*, to retreat
Recupero, -avi, -atum, -are...to recover
Recuso, -avi, -atum, -are...to refuse
Reddo, reddidi, redditum, reddere...to give back, to restore
Redeo, -ii, -itum, -ire...to return
Reficio, -feci, -fectum, -ficěre...to repair, to restore, to refresh
Regio, -onis, f....region, district
Regnum, -i, n....kingdom
Regulus, -i, m....Regulus, a famous Roman
Religio, -onis, f....religion, superstition
Relinquo, -liqui, -lictum, -linquěre...to leave behind, to forsake.
Reliquus, -a, -um (adj.)...left, remaining

Remitto, -misi, -missum, -mittere...to send back

Removeo, -movi, -motum, -movere...to remove, to keep away (trans.)

Renovo, -avi, -atum, -are...to renew

Renuntio, -avi, -atum, -are...to bring back word

Reor, ratus, reri (deponent vb.)...to think. *Ratus*, thinking

Repente (adv.)...suddenly

Repentinus, -a, -um (adj.)...sudden

Reperio, reppĕri (rĕperi), repertum, reperire...to find, to discover

Repo, repsi, reptum, repere...to creep, to crawl

Repōno, -posui, -positum, -pŏnere...to put back, to lay up for safety

Requiesco, -quievi, -quietum, -quiescere...to rest

Requiro, -ere...to require

Res, rei, f....a thing, affair, matter

Rescisco, -scivi, -scitum, -sciscere...to get to know, to ascertain

Resisto, -stiti, -stitum, -sistere...to resist (with Dat. case)

Respondeo, -spondi, -sponsum, -spondere...to reply

Responsum, -i, n....a reply

Respublica, reipublicae, f....the State. (*Res* and *publica*)

Restituo, -ui, -utum, -ĕre...to restore, to give back

Retineo, -inui, -entum, -inere...to hold back; to retain, to preserve

Revertor, -versus, -vérti...to return

Revoco, -avi, -atum, -are...to recall

Rex, regis, m....king

Rhodănus, -i, m....the river Rhône, in France

Risus, -us, m....laughter

Robustus, -a, -um (adj.)...strong, vigorous

Rogo, -avi, -atum, -are...to ask

Roma, -ae, f....Rome, capital of Italy and of Roman Empire

Romănus, -a, -um (adj.)...Roman

Ruber, -ra, -rum (adj.)...red

Rufus, -i, m....Rufus, a Roman name

Rumor, -oris, m....rumour

Rursus (adv.)...again

Rus, ruris, n....country, country estate

S

Sacrifico, -avi, -atum, -are...to sacrifice, (trans. and intrans.) to offer up

Saepe (adv.)...often

Saevus, -a, -um (adj.)...savage, fierce

Saltus, -us, m....defile, pass

Salus, -ūtis, f....safety

Saluto, -avi, -atum, -are...to greet

Sanitas, -atis, f....health

Sanus, -a, -um (adj.)...healthy

Sapiens, -tis (adj.)...wise

Sapientia, -ae, f....wisdom

Sarmenta, -orum, n. pl....twigs, brushwood

Satis (adv.)...enough, sufficient

Saucius, -a, -um (adj.)...wounded

Scapha, -ae, f....a light rowing boat

Sceleratus, -a, -um (adj.)...wicked

Scilicet (adv.)...doubtless, of course. (*Scire licet*, it is permitted to know, you may know)

Scio, scivi, scitum, scire...to know

Scipio, -onis, m....Scipio, a famous Roman

Scribo, scripsi, scriptum, scribĕre...to write

Se, sese (Acc. of the reflexive pronoun)...himself, etc. (See Lesson XIV.)

Secundus, -a, -um (adj.)...second; favourable

Sed (conj.)...but. *Sed etiam*, but also

Segrego, -avi, -atum, -are...to separate

Seiungo, -iunxi, -iunctum, -iungĕre...to separate

Semel (adv.)...once

Semper (adv.)...always

Senatus, -us, m....senate (the supreme council of nobles at Rome). *Senatum dare*, to give audience of the senate. *Senatusconsultum*, a decree of the senate

Senectus, -utis, f....old age

Sententia, -ae, f....opinion, vote, decision

Septem...seven

Septuagesimus, -a, -um (ordinal numeral adj.)...seventieth

Serpens, -tis, f....serpent

Serus, -a, -um (adj.)...late

Servator, -oris, m....saviour

Servilius, -ii, m....Servilius, a Roman name

Servio, -ivi, -itum, -ire...to serve

Servulus, -i, m....a little slave

Servus, -i, m....a slave

Severus, -a, -um (adj.)...severe, stern

Si (conj.)...if

Sic (adv.)...so

Sicilia, -ae, f....Sicily

Sidus, -eris, n....star

Signum, -i, n....signal; standard

Silens, silentis (adj.)...silent

Silva, -ae, f....wood

Simul (adv.)...at the same time. *Simul atque*, as soon as

Simulo, -avi, -atum, -are...to pretend

Sine (prep., with Abl. case)...without

Sinus, -s, m....fold, bosom

Societas, -atis, f....alliance

Sol, solis, m....sun

Solatium, -ie, n....solace

Solitudo, -inis, f....solitude

Solitus, -a, -um (adj.)...usual, customary

Solum (adv.)...only

Solus, -a, -um (adj.)...alone
Solvo, solvi, solutum, solvĕre...to loosen, solve
Somnus, -i, m....sleep
Specto, -avi, -atum, -are...to look at, to behold
Spero, -avi, -atum, -are...to hope, to hope for
Spes, spei, f....hope
Splendor, -oris, m....splendour
Stella, -ae, f....star
Statim (adv.)...at once
Statua, -ae, f....statue
Statuo, -ui, -utum, -ĕre...to resolve, to determine; to establish
Sto, stĕti, stătum, stāre...to stand
Studium, -ii, n....zeal, desire, eagerness, study
Stulte (adv.)...foolishly
Stultus, -a, -um (adj.)...stupid
Subigo, -egi, -actum, -igĕre...to subdue
Subito (adv.)...suddenly
Successus, -us, m....success
Succumbo, -cubui, -cubitum, -cumbĕre...to lie prostrate
Sufficio, -feci, -fectum, -fcere...to choose in the place of any one
Sulpicius, -ii, m....Sulpicius, a Roman name
Sum, fui, esse...to be
Summa, -ae, f....the sum, the whole amount. *Summa imperii,* the supreme authority
Summus, -a, -um (adj., superl. degree of *superus*)...highest, greatest
Sumo, sumpsi, sumptum, sumere...to take
Sumptus, -us, m....expense
Sunt (third pers. plur. Pres. Indic. of *sum*)...they are
Superior, -us (compar. of *superus*)...(1) higher; (2) victorious; (3) former
Supero, -avi, -atum, -are...to overcome, to defeat
Superus, -a, -um (adj.)...upper
Supra (adv.)...above. Also Prep., with Acc. case
Suscipio, -cepi, -ceptum, -cipĕre...to undertake
Suscito, -avi, -atum, -are...to arouse
Suspicio, -spexi, -spectum, -spicĕre...to look up at, to admire
Sustineo, -inui, -entum, -inere...to endure, to sustain
Susurrus, -i, m....whispering
Suus, -a, -um...his own, her own, its own, etc. (referring to subject of sentence)
Syracusae, -arum, f. pl....Syracuse, largest town in Sicily
Syria, -ae, f....Syria, region of Asia Minor

T

Tabellarius, -ii, m....letter-carrier, messenger
Taceo, -iu, -itum, -ere...to be silent
Talis, -e (adj.)...such, of such a kind

Tam (adv.)...so, to such a degree
Tamdiu (adv.)...so long
Tamen (adv.)...nevertheless, however
Tandem (adv.)...at length. *Nunc tandem*, now at length
Tanquam (adv.)...as if
Tantum (adv.)...only (*see* Modo)
Tantus, -a, -um (adj.)...so great
Tellus, -uris, f....earth
Templum, -i, n....temple
Tempus, -oris, n....time
Tenebricosus, -a, -um (adj.)...dark, gloomy
Teneo, tenui, tentum, tenere...to hold
Ter (numeral adverb)...thrice
Terentius, -ii, m....Terentius, Roman name
Terra, -ae, f....land. *Terra marique*, by sea and land. (Note the Latin order)
Terror, -oris, m....terror, fear, panic
Tertio (adv.)...thirdly, for the third time
Tertius, -a, -um (ordinal numeral adj.)...third
Thermopylae, -arum, f. pl....Thermopylae, a pass in Greece
Tiber, -eris, m....Tiber
Tiberius, -ii, m....Tiberius, a Roman name
Tibi (dat. of *Tu*, thou)...to you
Timeo, -ui, ——, -ere...to fear, to be afraid of
Tollo, sustuli, sublatum, tollere...to take away, to remove, to destroy
Tot (indecl. pronoun)...so many
Tōtus, -a, -um (adj.)...whole
Trādo, tradidi, traditum, tradĕre...to hand over, to surrender
Trāduco, -duxi, -ductum, -ducĕre...to lead across
Transeo, -ii, -itum, -ire...to cross
Transitus, -us, m....passage across
Trasumenus, -i, m....Lake Trasumenus, in Etruria
Trebia, -ae, f....Trebia, tributary of the Po
Trecenti, -ae, -a (numeral adj.)...three hundred
Tres, tria (numeral adj.)...three
Triennium, -ii, n....period of three years
Triumphans, -tis (adj.)...triumphant
Tum (adv.)...then, at that time. *Tum quidem* (adv.)...then indeed, just then
Tumulus, -i, m....tomb
Turba, -ae, f....crowd
Turgidus, -a, -um (adj.)...swollen
Tuus, -a, -um...thy or thine, your

U

Ubi (conj.)...where; when
Ullus, -a, -um (Gen. *ullius*)...any (after a negative)
Umbra, -ae, f....shade

Umbrosus, -a, -um (adj.)...shady
Unde (conj.)...whence
Undique (adv.)...from every side, on every side
Universus, -a, -um (adj.)...whole, entire; (pl.) all together
Unquam (adv.)...ever. (When " ever " equals " always " use *semper*)
Unus, -a, -um (numeral adj.)...one
Urbs, urbis, f....city
Usque (adv.)...ever, right on. *Usque ad,* right up to (the time of)
Usus, -us, m....use, experience. *Usu venire,* to actually happen
Ut (adv.)...as; (conj.) when; so that, in order that; that
Uter, utra, utrum...which of two?
Uterque, utraque, utrumque...each of two
Utica, -ae, f....Utica, town in Africa
Utor, usus, uti...to use (with Ablative case)
Utpote (adv.)...namely, as being
Utrobīque (adv.)...on both sides, on both elements (sea and land)
Uvidus, -a, -um (adj.)...damp
Uxor, -oris, f....wife

V

Vacuus, -a, -um...empty
Vado, -ere...to go
Vae ! (exclam.)...alas !
Valens, -tis (partic. pres. of *valeo*)...strong. *Valentissimus* (superl.) strongest
Valeo, -ui, ——, -ere...to be strong. *Vale, valete* (imperative)...farewell !
Valetudo, -inis, f....health; bad health, illness
Vallis, -is, f....valley
Vallum, -i, n....rampart
Varius, -a, -um (adj.)...manifold, various
Vas, vasis, n....vessel, dish. (Plur., *vasa, -orum, -is,* irregular)
Vectigal, -alis, n....tax, tribute
Veho, vexi, vectum, vehere...to carry
Vel . . . vel...either . . . or. *Vel*...even
Velo, -avi, -atum, -are...to cover, veil
Velociter (adv.)...swiftly
Velum, -i, n....sail
Velut (adv.)...even as, as
Vendo, vendidi, venditum, vendere...to sell
Venenatus, -a, -um (partic. of *veneno*)...poisoned
Veneno, -avi, -atum, -are...to poison
Venenum, -i, n....poison
Venio, veni, ventum, venire...to come
Ventus, -i, m....the wind
Venus, -eris, f....goddess of love, love
Venusia, -ae, f....Venusia, town in Italy

Verbum, -i, n....word
Vereor, -itus, -eri...to fear; to reverence
Veritas, -atis, f....truth
Verto, verti, versum, vertĕre...to turn
Verus, -a, -um (adj.)...true
Vester, -ra, -rum (adj.)...your own, your (referring to more than one)
Veto, -avi, -atum, -are...to forbid
Vetus, -eris (adj.)...old
Vetustus, -a, -um (adj.)...old
Vexo, -avi, -atum, -are...to harass
Vicesimus, -a, -um (ordinal numeral adj.)...twentieth
Victor, -oris, m....conqueror
Victoria, -ae, f....victory
Video, vidi, visum, videre...to see. *Videtur*, it seems
Vinco, vici, victum, vincere...to conquer
Vinum, -i, n....wine
Violo, -avi, -atum, -are...to break, to violate. *Violare legem*, to break
   a law
Vir, -i, m....a man
Virco, -ere...to be green, vigorous
Virgo, -inis, f....virgin
Virtus, -utis, f....bravery, manliness, virtue
Vis (Acc. *vim*, Abl. *vi*; Plur., *vires, virium, viribus*), f....strength
Visus, -us, m....sight, appearance
Vita, -ae, f....life. (Do not use plural in this sense; *vitae* means
   " biographies ")
Vito, -avi, -atum, -are...to avoid
Vivo, vixi, victum, vivere...to live
Vivus, -a, -um (adj.)...living, alive
Vix (adv.)...scarcely
Volo, volui, velle...to be willing, to wish
Volucris, -s, f....bird
Voluntas, -atis, f....will, wish, desire

Z

Zama, -ae, f....Zama, a town in Africa, near Carthage

INDEX

A

Ablative, Absolute, 78, 148 (5), 179 (5)
  agent, 101
  comparison, 119
  description, 49, 184 (3), 223
  means, 223
  prepositions governing, 36
  of Present Participle, 61
  separation, 138
  time within which, 42, 146, 223
  time when, 42
  verbs governing, 182 (3)
Abstract Nouns, 74
Accent, 18
Accusative, and Infinitive, 86
  Prepositions governing, 36
  time how long, 42
Adjectives, 1st and 2nd Declension, 40–42
  in -er (rules), 42
  3rd Declension, 59, 60
  comparison of, 118–121
  Genitive in -ius, Dative in -i, 88, 89, 94, 95
  as nouns, 43, 44
Adverbs, comparison of, 191
  formation of, 190
After, 46, 47
Age, 138 (2)
  Aliter ac, 123
  Alius, 94, 95
  Alter . . . alter, 257
Although, 111, 170
  Amplius, 221
  Antequam, 173, 174, 185
Apposition, 31, 32
Article, Definite and Indefinite, 25
Ask (two Accusatives), 71 (1)
At, with verb of motion, 55

B

Before, 173, 174
Bottom of, 121

C

Cardinal numerals, 177, 286, 287
Cases, translation of, 21–23
  Causa (with Gerund and Gerundive), 114, 115
Commands, direct, 129
  indirect, 124, 125
  negative, 130
Comparative, adjectives, 118, 119
  adverbs, 191
  in final clauses, 126 (2), 151 (3)
  irregular, 120, 191
  of six adjectives in -is, 119
Conditions, construction of, 131, 132, 136, 140
  future, 46
  in Oratio Obliqua, 172 (2), 182, 183
  negative, 132
Conjugation, 28
Conjunctions, 185
Consecutive clauses, 91, 92
  negatives in, 92
  with Qui, 170, 176 (1)
  Cum (Conjunction), although, 111
  since, 70, 139 (6)
  when, 70, 173
  whenever, 175 (4)
  Cum (Preposition), 36
  with pronoun, 44, 223

D

Dactyl, 154
Dative, of Agent, 113

341

TEACH YOURSELF BOOKS

LATIN DICTIONARY

A. Wilson

A concise practical dictionary for the student of Latin, containing extensive Latin–English and English–Latin vocabularies.

Specially compiled for use with *Teach Yourself Latin* and for the student of Roman literature, this dictionary also includes an extensive section covering the basic points of Latin grammar.

Another compact working dictionary from *Teach Yourself Books*.

TEACH YOURSELF BOOKS

ITALIAN

K. Speight

A working knowledge of Italian is not difficult to acquire, and the pronunciation of the language is relatively simple and consistent.

This book offers a complete course in modern conversational Italian for beginners studying at home. Pronunciation, grammar and syntax are fully explained in easy stages illustrated by examples, and a basic grounding in the everyday vocabulary is provided.

TEACH YOURSELF BOOKS

SPANISH

N. Scarlyn Wilson

As a language of world importance, Spanish rivals French and German. There are over 115 million speakers of the language in the world, both in South America and Spain, and obviously a knowledge of Spanish is useful — not only to the student but also to the tourist and the businessman.

Because of its phonetic simplicity and the basic regularity of its grammatical forms, Spanish is a relatively easy language to learn. This book takes the reader through a series of graded lessons which have been designed both for use in the classroom and for study at home. Each lesson comes complete with exercises and translation pieces and the aim is that the reader, on working his way through the course, should have a sound command of Spanish.

Anyone who works through this volume intelligently should be able to read and speak Spanish. No student should fail to obtain this excellent course.

Journal of the Incorporated Association of
Assistant Masters

TEACH YOURSELF BOOKS

SPANISH DICTIONARY

M. H. Raventos

This book offers an invaluable aid for students, tourists, businessmen and all who wish to become proficient in modern Spanish.

Full Spanish–English and English–Spanish sections, each with some 25,000 entries, provide clear definitions for a wide range of words and phrases in convenient form; in addition there are special sections on proper names and abbreviations in each language, and on weights, measures and currency.

'One of the best, if not the best, class dictionaries available.'

Higher Education Journal

TEACH YOURSELF BOOKS

FRENCH DICTIONARY

N. Scarlyn Wilson

This dictionary provides the user with a comprehensive vocabulary for working French. With over 35,000 words in both sections, special care has been taken to include current usage including some slang. A complete list of Irregular Verbs, a selection of French Idioms and Phrases, lists of Christian Names and Geographical Places are all included. For the student of French, an extensive and workmanlike dictionary which will prove to be invaluable.

TEACH YOURSELF BOOKS

FRENCH PHRASE BOOK

Sarah Boas and Shirley Mungall

This phrase book, in a handy pocket size, will help you
to be readily understood on all everyday occasions; to
get you quickly and easily, *where* you want and *what*
you want; and to enable you to cope with those minor
problems and emergencies that always seem to arise on
holiday. A pronunciation guide accompanies each
phrase, the topic of which can quickly be found by
reference to the contents list or index. Subjects include:
On Arrival at the Hotel – Medical Treatment – Shopping
– Sightseeing – Restaurants, cafés and bars.

TEACH YOURSELF BOOKS

ARABIC

A. S. Tritton

Arabic is not an easy language to learn; both the script and the structure are quite unlike that of any European language. The aim of this book is to reduce to a minimum the difficulties the student will encounter in learning Arabic.

The script and grammar of the language are clearly explained in a series of carefully graded lessons, each of which contains many examples and exercises. The result is a detailed and practical course in the classical language of Arab civilisation and culture.

The author, A. S. Tritton, is a distinguished Oriental scholar with many years experience of teaching Arabic. He has written a book invaluable both to the student of Arabic and to the absolute beginner.

ALSO AVAILABLE IN
TEACH YOURSELF BOOKS

☐ 05498 0	**LATIN DICTIONARY** A. Wilson	£1.25
☐ 05798 X	**ITALIAN** K. Speight	75p
☐ 05819 6	**SPANISH** N. Scarlyn Wilson	75p
☐ 05820 X	**SPANISH DICTIONARY** M. H. Raventos	£3.50
☐ 05784 X	**FRENCH DICTIONARY**	£1.50
☐ 05579 0	**FRENCH, EVERYDAY** N. Scarlyn Wilson	95p
☐ 18260 1	**FRENCH PHRASE BOOK** Sarah Boas & Shirley Mungall	75p
☐ 05771 8	**ARABIC** A. S. Tritton	£1.25
☐ 05774 2	**ARABIC, COLLOQUIAL** T. F. Mitchell	95p

All these books are available at your local bookshop or newsagent, or can be ordered direct from the publisher. Just tick the titles you want and fill in the form below.

Prices and availability subject to change without notice.

TEACH YOURSELF BOOKS, P.O. Box 11, Falmouth, Cornwall.

Please send cheque or postal order, and allow the following for postage and packing:

U.K. – One book 25p plus 10p per copy for each additional book ordered, up to a maximum of £1.05.

B.F.P.O. and EIRE – 25p for the first book plus 10p per copy for the next 8 books, thereafter 5p per book.

OTHER OVERSEAS CUSTOMERS – 40p for the first book and 12p per copy for each additional book.

Name ....

Address ....

....